READING ADS SOCIALLY

This book argues that advertisements are an ideal site for observing how the logic of the commodity form expresses itself culturally and socially. The aim is to produce a study of visual ideology which will move students to consider the deep ideological structure of ads. Though our media pundits blather endlessly about ads, the fixation on whether ads are deceptive or subliminal diverts us from the real material and ideological impact of ads in modern society. The material impact of ads lies in producing and reproducing a currency of sign values that can be joined to commodities; ideologically the sheer number of ads that we process numbs us into an acceptance of the social logic imposed by the framework of the commodity form. It is here that mystification takes place, it is here that we are encouraged to embrace reified social logic as if it were natural.

The author examines how advertisements frame meanings, and how these frames help to organize the ways we see the world. By dissecting and decomposing these frames, advertisements can be made to locate the meaning of hegemony in relation to commodity culture. The book shows how ads commodify meaning. It also tracks the cultural contradictions of commodifying meaning in consumer advertising and examines ad campaigns which attempt to distance themselves from the rhetoric of the commodity self, pseudo-individuality and commodity fetishism. Original, powerfully argued and full of illuminating examples, this book will fast become a benchmark in the study of advertising culture.

Robert Goldman is Associate Professor of Sociology at Lewis and Clark College, Portland, Oregon.

READING ADS SOCIALLY

Robert Goldman

London and New York

First published in 1992
by Routledge
11 New Fetter Lane, London EC4P 4EE

Simultaneously published in the USA and Canada
by Routledge
a division of Routledge, Chapman and Hall Inc.
29 West 35th Street, New York, NY 10001

Typeset in 10/12pt Baskerville by LaserScript, Mitcham, Surrey
Printed and bound in Great Britain by
Biddles Ltd, Guildford and King's Lynn

British Library Cataloguing in Publication Data

A catalogue record for this book is available from the British Library.

Library of Congress Cataloging in Publication Data

Goldman, Robert, 1949–
Reading ads socially/Robert Goldman.
p. cm.
Includes bibliographical references and index.
1. Advertising – Social aspects. 2. Advertising – Social aspects –
United States. I. Title.
HF5821.G58   1992
659.1′042′0973 – dc20   CIP

ISBN 0–415–05399–4 (hbk)
ISBN 0–415–05400–1 (pbk)

CONTENTS

v

ILLUSTRATIONS

ACKNOWLEDGEMENTS

Reading ads is an intrinsically social process, even when the reading process is performed alone. For me, it has also been a social activity done in the company of students, colleagues and friends. The readings included in this volume have sometimes been collaborative endeavors. Four of these chapters were co-authored in their original versions – chapter one with John Wilson; chapter six with Sharon Smith and Deborah Heath; and chapters eight and nine with Steve Papson. My collaborators, however, should not be held responsible for the revisions and shifts which I have subsequently made in the theoretical arguments and the textual readings. Over the years, many students have joined me in dialogues about the critical analysis of ads and these studies are enriched by their observations. It is hard to single out a few from the many, but I thank Mindy Faber, Adam Weisberg, Sarah Jones, Noreen Nakagawa and Mark Viehe. I am grateful to Sharon Smith, Jane Atkinson, Doug Kellner, Mike Montagne, Adam Weisberg, Julia Watson, Rika Goldman and Joe Goldman for their thoughtful criticism of various portions of this manuscript as they took shape. David Reeck assisted in getting the ads reproduced. Finally, I owe a significant intellectual debt to John Wilson and Steve Papson, each of whom has endured more than their share of theoretical talk about advertising and commodities and signs.

Those chapters based on prior versions originally appeared as:

Robert Goldman & John Wilson, 'Appearance & Essence: The Commodity Form Revealed in Perfume Advertisements,' *Current Perspectives in Social Theory*, 1983, 4: 119–42. Greenwich, Conn.: JAI Press.

Robert Goldman, 'Marketing Fragrances: Advertising & the Production of Commodity Signs,' *Theory, Culture & Society*, 1987, 4, 4 (November): 691–726.

Robert Goldman, 'Legitimation Ads, Part I: The Story of the Family, in Which the Family Saves Capitalism from Itself,' *Knowledge & Society: Studies in the Sociology of Culture*, 1984, 5: 243–67. Greenwich, Conn.: JAI Press.

Robert Goldman, Deborah Heath & Sharon L. Smith, 'Commodity Feminism,' *Critical Studies in Mass Communication*, 1991, 8, 3 (September): 333–51.

Robert Goldman & Steven Papson, 'Levi's & the Knowing Wink: Commodity Bricolage,' *Current Perspectives in Social Theory*, 1991, 11: 69–95. Greenwich, Conn.: JAI Press.

Robert Goldman & Steven Papson, 'The Postmodernism that Failed,' in David Dickens & Andrea Fontana (eds), *Postmodernism & Social Inquiry*. Chicago: University of Chicago Press (forthcoming).

INTRODUCTION

Ads have become the trivia of daily life. They are a favorite topic of the commercial soft-news media which good-naturedly present wry or clever stories about the hot advertising spot of the moment – Spuds McKenzie, the little old lady from Wendy's, Joe Isuzu or Bo Jackson. With a wink and a grin, reporters remind us of absurd advertising excesses such as hundreds of thousands of dollars per half minute of Super Bowl ad time. Since advertisements are treated as part of the entertainment complex, it is easy to consider them immune from the world of ideology. Presiding over a world where images reign supreme, the mass media in the 1980s drifted toward professing to be 'wise' about advertising – aware that ads promote a hazy realm of image management and simulation. In a society that extols the freedom of personal choice, the freedom to be an individual, there is some dissonance to resolve with respect to advertising. Though advertising is widely acknowledged as having an impact on 'society,' most people claim to have acquired personal immunity from its 'effects.' Cries of 'manipulation' offer a comforting resolution of the contradiction between individuality and the conformist 'effect' ads have on us. Notions like subliminal seduction have gained popular appeal because they glamorously rationalize the power of ads: the self cannot be held to be weak or gullible if tricks were used. Unfortunately, such glitzy and spectacular criticism diverts attention from the far more mundane structural role advertising plays in reproducing social domination.

Advertisements saturate our social lives. We participate, daily, in deciphering advertising images and messages. Our ability to recognize and decipher the advertising images that confront us depends on our photographic literacy and our familiarity with the social logic of advertising and consumerism. Yet, because ads are so pervasive and our reading of them so routine, we tend to take for granted the deep social assumptions embedded in advertisements. We do not ordinarily recognize advertising as a sphere of ideology.

1

But there is a great deal more at stake in reading ads than simply whether or not to buy. Advertisements have sociocultural consequences and repercussions that go beyond the corporate bottom-line, even though it is that bottom-line which motivates and shapes the ads. This critical reading of ads seeks to excavate the social assumptions that are conventionally made (and glossed over) in the split seconds that it takes us to decipher an ad and move on to the next. Reading ads in terms of the social knowledge necessary to their interpretation enables us to isolate and detail the ideological codes that animate the ads. Suspending the taken-for-granted attitude that accompanies the reading process can turn the reading of ads from depoliticized diversion into a political act.

Advertising is a key social and economic institution in producing and reproducing the material and ideological supremacy of commodity relations. Cultural hegemony refers to those socially constructed ways of seeing and making sense of the world around us that predominate in a given time and place. In the latter twentieth-century US the supremacy of commodity relations has exercised a disproportionate influence over the ways we conceive our lives. Every day that we routinely participate in the social grammar of advertisements, we engage in a process of replicating the domain assumptions of commodity hegemony. These domain assumptions are important because they condition and delimit the field of discourse within which our public and private conversations take place.

The premise of this book is that ads can be flipped over and critically reread to map the cultural reproduction of commodity hegemony. In a society that is fundamentally structured by commodity relations – by the relations of private property and wage labor – ads offer a unique window for observing how commodity interests conceptualize social relations. By peeling back the layers of linguistic and social assumptions made in advertisements we can specify the conditions for taking meaning from ads. This search for the underlying social grammar of meaning in ads is an essential step toward grasping the deeper ideological significance of ads in our cultural and political lives. Yet, because ideological meanings 'do not reside in images . . . [but] are circulated between representation, spectators and social formation' (Kuhn, 1985: 6), the social grammar of hegemony is never static, but subject to its own dialectical contradictions. This point is so important it bears repeating. The frames and codes of advertisements are the starting point of interpretation, not the outcome: 'meaning is always negotiated in the semiotic process, never simply imposed inexorably from above by an omnipotent author through an absolute code' (Hodge & Kress, 1988: 12).

This study of advertisements covers the period from 1977 to 1990 in the United States. Watching ads for over a decade has made it possible to track how a dialectic of interpretive contestation and ideological reincorporation unfolds in a commodity culture – a dialectic of hegemony, alienation

2

and resistance played out in the mass media. And let's not forget that treating culture as a sphere of market competition introduces yet another dimension of cultural contradiction. When I began studying them in the late 1970s, advertisements were structured around strict framing formulas to ensure the most efficient mass-mediated semiotic process possible. They seemed totally one-dimensional. But the long arm of the dialectic is ever with us: efficient production of competitive product images also occasions surplus meanings and subversive readings. Though the vast majority of ads continue to rely on standard framing formulas, since 1984 a new stage of advertising has developed in response to viewer alienation, prompted by the endless barrage of predictable advertising narratives. Whereas advertisers in the late 1970s tried to make the reading process as transparent as possible, by 1989 opaque and ambiguous ads had the virtue of getting viewers to pause and look at ads rather than skipping past them. To counter viewer alienation and ensure brand name differentiation, advertisers incorporated criticism of advertising into their ads and brought into the foreground the tacit background rules which premise the routine reading of ads. Advertising reflexivity has thus been directed at re-motivating spectators to participate in the assumptions of consumption.

The many contradictions of commodity culture are evident in the 1984 Association of American Advertising Agencies ad campaign designed to shore up the sagging public legitimacy of advertising. Using the tagline 'Advertising. Another word for freedom of choice,' one ad (Figure 1) asked 'Is society a reflection of advertising or is advertising a reflection of society?' In trying to debunk the view that advertising promotes mindless conformism, this ad deviates from the basic logic or code that premises nearly all advertisements. Advertisements usually position viewers to participate in an interpretive process based on 'false assumptions' (Williamson, 1978), positioning viewers to presume a line of equivalence between the product and the glamorized traits of the model. Ads tend to invite us to step into the 'space' of the ad to try on the social self we might become if we wore the product image. But here, the advertising industry denies this symbolic equivalence exchange by caricaturing the logic of identity between the viewer and the commodity ideal, positioning viewers to dis-identify with such a foolish and mimetic consumer. Even though we are daily inundated by ads urging us to express our individual identity through our style and image – e.g., 'the look that gets the looks' or 'wear the look that's right for you' – the 4-A's ad photographically stacks the deck against the proposition that 'society is a reflection of advertising' by ridiculing the consuming viewer's exaggerated imitation of the TV glamour image. Ironically, our ability to recognize this as a caricature is predicated on our acceptance of orthodox advertising narratives about pleasure, popularity and self-worth which conceptualize the self as a desirable appearance whose value can be maximized by adhering to the codes of consumer style. At the same time

Figure 1 4-A's

Source: Time, 1984

that the 4-A's ad tries to mislead us about the nature of the mirror relationship in the advertising text, it accurately articulates one of advertising's fundamental ideological principles. Notice how the ad sets up the question about the relationship between society and advertising by conflating society (America) and the individual (you). Although this is an obvious case of mistaken identity, collapsing the category of society into the category of the individual is an ideological maneuver made necessary by institutions based on commodity relations.

FRAMING MEANINGS INTO A CURRENCY OF SIGNS

When we recognize an advertisement as such, we recognize a framework or a context within which meanings are rearranged so that exchanges of meaning can take place. The motive of the advertisement becomes part of the unspoken framework within which we attempt to interpret particular combinations of meaning. Without such an understanding we would be baffled by the arbitrary photographic juxtapositions of antidepressant tablets and a rose or high heel shoes and a Michelangelo painting. Below the surface of any particular ad, every ad works with meaning systems that have been abstracted from context and then reframed in terms of the assumptions and interpretive rules of the advertising framework. Before we know what an ad says, we must have a general sense of how its reading rules work.

Throughout this study, I have theorized advertising as a political economy of sign values, and advertisements as vehicles for producing commodity-signs. As a system of signification, advertisements compose connections between the meanings of products and images. The organization of meanings in ads is governed by *frames*. To study ads is to study the framing of meaning. All meanings and activities exist in a social context – meaning is always relational and contextual. Remove an activity from its context and its meaning changes. Advertisements photographically isolate meaningful moments, remove them from their lived context and place them in the ad framework where their meaning is recontextualized and thus changed. Every image that appears in advertisements has been framed. It could not be otherwise.

As part of the culture industry, advertising constitutes an apparatus for *reframing meanings* in order to add value to products. Ads arrange, organize and steer *meanings* into *signs* that can be inscribed on products – always geared to transferring the value of one meaning system to another. In this way, advertising comprises a system of commodity-sign production designed to enhance the exchange value of commodities, by differentiating the meanings associated with each commodity. A commodity-sign is the image that attaches to a product – e.g., the functional utility of a *Rolex* watch is supplemented by its image of affluent status. The *Rolex* watch has not only

5

become *a sign* of affluence, its sign value now socially eclipses its utility as a timepiece. When signs are defined as real, they are real in their consequences. 'If I wear *Calvin Klein* jeans, my experience of the product is qualitatively different than if I wear *Levi's* jeans – because of the difference in image' (Houghton, 1987: 18). Because we are aware of the meanings given off by the objects we consume and wear, commodity-signs have become every bit as socially real as the products they ride on. Witness how *Nike* has taken the meanings of superstar athletes like Michael Jordan and funneled them into a sign value that has become one of the most visible emblems in the lives of inner-city youth.

As an institutionally rationalized process of fitting meanings to commodities, advertising breaks meanings down into their most fundamental units – into signifiers and signifieds – for the purpose of creating differentiated commodity-signs. The internal structure of the sign is made to operate as a political economy in which the process of joining signifiers to signifieds is driven by the logic of the commodity form – the goal of profit. Born in the 1920s, sculpted and streamlined between 1950 and 1985, a dominant advertising form has become the standard vehicle for producing signs. As exercises in framing exchanges of meaning, advertisements commodify semiotics for the purpose of building a currency of sign values. A currency is 'a system of values emanating from exchange relations' that permits the value of one thing to be expressed in terms of another (Williamson, 1978: 42). Hence, when an ad campaign for a pharmaceutical antidepressant correlates the image of a lunar eclipse with the illness of depression, it reduces this symbolization of depression and its transcendence to a visual sign which becomes equated with the meaning of the product name. The semiotic reductionism necessary for producing a currency of commodity-signs involves transforming complex meaningful relations into visual signifiers. It then turns the relationship between signifier and signified into one of equivalence, so that the visual signifier can be substituted for the signified of the product. A remarkably explicit advertising text for *Silver* cologne (Figure 2) articulates the message of commodity fetishism contained in the interpretive structure of all ads: '*Silver*. It makes every man a valuable commodity.' *Silver* cologne is represented as currency – a means of increasing the value of the self in the marketplace of desire.

Advertisers *compete* to have the hottest sign – the one that can command the greatest market advantage. But this approach to constructing signs that have market value exacts a societal cost, because when meaning systems are systematically abstracted and plundered as a resource for producing commodity-signs, the penetration of the commodity form has a 'dissolving' influence on culture. Paraphrasing Marx's analysis of an earlier stage of capitalist development, the continuous recirculation of commodity-signs must endlessly draw 'new continents' of meaning into the 'metabolism of

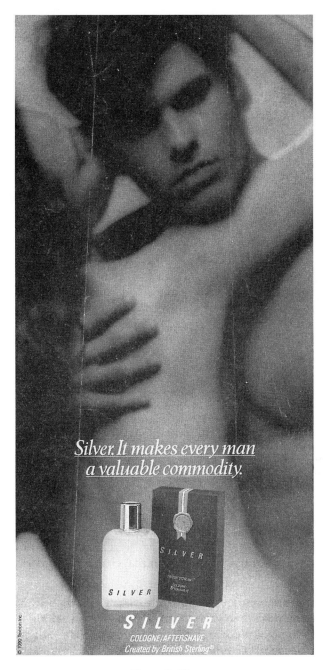

Figure 2 Silver

Source: *People*, 1991

circulation' (Marx, 1973: 224–5). Advertising has become a form of internal cultural colonialism that mercilessly hunts out and appropriates those meaningful elements of our cultural lives that have value. Whether or not advertising screws us up as individual personalities, its 'dissolving' influence on culture may be advertising's most significant and haunting historical consequence.

ADVERTISING, IDEOLOGY AND THE COMMODITY FORM

From the start, this has been a project aimed at bringing critical theory down to earth by grounding it in the relations and texts of daily life. It did not begin as a study of advertisements, but as a theoretical analysis of the relationship between the commodity form (a concept used by Marx to grasp the institutional framework necessary to a capitalist society) and processes of ideological reproduction. One day, by chance, I picked up a fashion magazine and turned to a perfume advertisement. In a sudden flash of recognition I thought I saw revealed in that perfume ad the structural inner workings of the commodity form. Here was the ideal social text for charting the relationship between the commodity form and ideology. Chapter one represents the sometimes laborious effort to read ads as an exercise in unraveling the commodity form – literally mapping out how a dominant advertising form, and the interpretive moves it makes necessary, replicated the deep structural logic of the commodity form.

Chapter one is not about semiotics, but about deconstructing commodity logic. When these studies began, I knew 'semiotics' as little more than a dictionary definition. In fact, chapter one is all but silent about the nature of visual signification in ads. Still, this initial inquiry into what Georg Lukács once called the 'riddle of the commodity structure' seemed to press theoretically in the direction of a commodity semiotics. As I reread advertisements over and over through the theoretical prism of the commodity form, I slowly realized that my rudimentary practice of semiotics was also conditioned by my status as a native viewer. From here on I began to work off the hypothesis that commodity culture encourages the development of a commodity semiotics as a practical methodology for producing and reading commodity texts. While the initial reading of ads as cultural texts and as ideology drew on Karl Marx's theory of the commodity form (mediated by the interpretations of Henri Lefebvre and Theodor Adorno) and a general immersion in Frankfurt school critical theory, my subsequent studies were indebted to John Berger's analysis of photographic meanings and Judith Williamson's methodological analyses of how ads mean.

Because my students were so familiar with advertising texts, using ads in the classroom permitted me to raise critical theory questions that they otherwise refused to tune into. Decoding ads allowed us to broach the question of what it meant to talk about ideological hegemony. Working with ads permitted us to explore how ideological assumptions were present in the ordinary discourses of daily life and, most importantly, that ideology was not merely the product of conspiracy or a ministry of propaganda – that, in fact, ideology is something we enter into and participate in. Grounding the theory in our reading of ads not only made the theory more accessible, it also made it relatively easy for students to evaluate the fit of the theory with the data of how they saw the ads.

Despite their apparently free-floating character, advertisements are social texts motivated by competition for market shares. Using Dallas Smythe's concept of the 'audience as commodity' to contextualize the commodification of meaning in ads, chapter two analytically dismantles *how we read ads* (decoding) in relation to how the perfume industry's marketing and advertising practices shape an encoding process designed to prompt the most efficient articulation of commodity-signs by viewers. Setting up the question in this way made it obvious that turning an advertiser's *preferred* interpretation into a commodity-sign requires that viewers participate in completing the transfer of meanings in the advertisement. Chapter two treats the articulation of ideology in ads and the construction of commodity-signs as two sides of the same coin. By locating the construction of commodity-signs at the intersection between the commodity form and the advertising form, ads can be investigated as material, social sites for the production and reproduction of both sign values and ideology. Whereas chapter one is a reading of ads in the context of the commodity form, the second inquiry reads ads as a sign form for the construction of commodity-signs. This stage of the inquiry suggested three theoretical propositions that have guided my subsequent studies. First, because this construction process works with, and on, *meaning*, the process of producing and circulating commodity-sign values is literally inseparable from processes of ideological reproduction. Second, though ads appear to be merely about consumption, the act of reading and interpreting ads comprises a form of *value-producing labor*. Third, motivating readers to perform the labor of assembling commodity-sign values can never be taken as a given by advertisers.

I was now convinced that decoding ads offered a method of uncovering the deeper relationship between our culturally predominant 'ways of seeing' and the structure of the commodity form. For me, deciphering ads became the task of methodically decomposing the political economy of commodity-sign production, while the task of understanding the political economy of commodity-signs became a matter of disassembling the conditions of joining and differentiating meanings in ads. Chapter three, 'The Mortise and the Frame,' seeks to disentangle the deep structural mechanics of how ads operate as encoding practices. How do we make sense of ads? Could disassembling ads permit us to recover the social understandings

9

that premise our making sense of ads? The goal of linking how we decipher ads to the production of commodity-signs motivated me to identify conceptually the primary framing mechanism in ads as the *mortise*. What was it about the product box that led students to look for a connection between it and the primary image on the page? Woodworkers know the mortise and tenon as a basic assembly technique that permits two parts to be joined by cutting a cavity in one piece so that it can receive the end of another piece. It looked like the same practice was at work in ads, only in the context of ads the mortise cavity box carried semiotic directions about constructing relationships of identity and difference between meaning systems. This stage of the inquiry concludes with the thesis that the metastructure of advertisements reproduces the ideological hegemony of the commodity form. Dissecting the advertising form and the tacit interpretive conventions required to make sense of it suggests that reification, as an interpretive stance, literally becomes a material tool for producing sign values and exchange values in our society. In its internal structure, this advertising form reproduces and replicates the commodity form – or more precisely, its constituent moments of abstraction, equivalency and reification – as a constant circuitry of semiotic interpretation.

Chapter four puts this methodology to work on a style of television advertising called 'Legitimation ads' – corporate ads that represent their presence in our lives in explicitly social terms. Legitimation ads for consumer goods are akin to public relations and what Edward Bernays once called the 'engineering of consent.' Ads for *McDonald's, Hallmark, Kodak* and *General Electric* in the 1980s produced complex commodity-signs out of carefully simulated scenic reproductions of treasured experiences in our lives. These scenes draw on our most cherished relations and desires – needs for family, community and acceptance – so that these memories can be returned to us, attached to the products and services of supposedly benevolent corporate sponsors. Our relations and our values become their corporate signs, and in so doing offer ideological cover for the exercise of vast corporate power.

Chapters five and six explore the cultural contradictions embedded in gender representations targeted at women in ads for pantyhose, cosmetics and weight-control items. These ads present narratives about women's increased social power as a function of voluntary self-fetishization. While these ads continue to position women as commodity selves posed for an absent male spectator-owner, they hail female subjects with the flattering ideological rhetoric that appropriately outfitted women can be confidently in charge of their lives and their relations with men. Representative ads from 1980 to 1984 can be read as commodity narratives about the relationship between envy, desire and power. These ads translate the capitalist male narrative of possessive individualism into a scenario for women that hinges on owning one's Look: ads thus transmute the 'male gaze' into a 'mirrored gaze' in which female readers become simultaneously the spectator and owner of the desired appearance.

By 1987 advertisers were trying to incorporate feminist critiques into new commodity-signs by changing how their ads addressed and positioned female subjects. Improved marketing tools for pinpointing and identifying audience (market) segments gave advertisers the ability to target their consumer profiles more specifically. As market segments proliferated, advertisers competed at translating feminist sensibilities into differentiated brand signs. Fashion magazines now revealed a multiplicity of gender representations. Was this evidence of a new cultural pluralism, or did there remain an underlying unity to all of these ideological constructs – a unity built on commodity logic? Chapter six explores the ways in which advertisers sought to cool out discontent by departing from stereotypical representations of women and managing the ideological contradictions between femininity and feminism. This chapter builds on the premise that the many faces of feminism in women's ads and the shifting modes of photographic signification used to represent them are an example of an ongoing dialectic between dominant and oppositional discourses organized by the pragmatic agenda of gaining market share. The analysis of commodified feminism points to a general question which must concern critical theorists. Reframing feminism through the commodity form turns the political discourse of feminism into the discourse of style. What happens to the arena of democratic public discourse when *any* ideological position can be reduced to a stylized signifier that is displayed and then tossed out to make way for the renewal of the commodity cycle?

As the decade passed, accumulating advertising clutter and viewer alienation made the advertising goal of establishing differentiated sign values problematic. As the old formulas began to exhaust themselves, some ads left out the familiar framing devices such as the mortise, forcing viewers to wonder 'why the frames are absent' and 'how do I interpret this without the usual cues?' Chapter seven explores strategies developed in the late 1980s to disguise the agenda and the mode of address of ads. Where advertisers had previously sought to repress social contradictions, now a few entertained ambivalence and a relish for uncertainty. After decades of advertising that sold glamorized desire, ads like those for *Obsession* in the late 1980s hailed us with scenes of neurotically self-indulgent narcissists tortured by their own desire. Though ads in the late 1980s continued to instruct us 'to live by the code' of the look, it was now ironically a consumer code articulated by breaking the codes of advertising. Notice how the *Code West* ad (Figure 3) violates the pictorial codes of advertising in order to preserve the code of glamorous consumption. In the semiotics of advertising, the torn and burnt edges of the frames and the mud on the boots are signifiers of imperfection – they are neither immaculate nor flawless. Their significance lies in how they address alienated, self-absorbed commodity

Figure 3 Code West

Source: LA Style, 1989

souls about the dynamic of envy and desire. Glamour thus becomes restylized as the calculated estrangement of signifiers of perfection from the social construction of the code.

Chapters eight and nine examine TV ad campaigns that were constructed as responses to the semiotic formulas of ads with their standardized narratives of pseudo-individuality. The *Levi's* 501 ad campaign from 1984 to 1986 was the exemplar of 1980s' ads that confronted the gap between reality and commodity fiction in ads. The *Levi's* campaign hailed viewers with a 'knowing wink' that acknowledged the artifice of advertising appearances. In addition, the *Levi's* campaign rerouted the discourses of the Blues, the ghetto and street culture to simulate the authenticity of youth culture and personal expression. *Levi's* appropriated the cultural expressions of an oppressed black population, and turned their connotations of authenticity into a second-order signifier – a myth called *501*-style. *Levi's* debunked one set of myths in order to articulate another.

The *Levi's* campaign was a triumph, but a failed campaign can be just as educational. The last chapter uses *Reebok*'s failed 1988 'UBU' campaign to frame the messy cultural terrain of postmodernism as, at least partially, a product of advertising's constant routing and rerouting of signifiers and signifieds. The *Reebok* ad campaign pointed to a crisis in the political economy of commodity-signs, where constant product proliferation and sign saturation make sign differentiation nearly impossible. Unceasing reproduction of commodity-signs contributes to a generalized cultural crisis characterized by cynicism, nihilism and a vanishing capacity for collective memory. When culture is reduced to that which can signify and give added exchange value to products, we may anticipate a diminished capacity for collective discourse about anything but the hot sign of the moment. As the logic of Capital extends into cultural life, so too do the crisis tendencies of Capital.

Campaigns like those of *Levi's* and *Reebok* confront the cultural contradictions of advertising in order to avert viewer/consumer resistance to advertising. Even when advertising assists in reproducing the material hegemony of commodity relations, it must be stressed that advertising is not a closed cultural universe. Since viewers' interpretive labor is essential to the continued extension of commodity-sign value production (generating surplus value), it would be foolish indeed not to anticipate forms of resistance to this exploitation. Where *Levi's* winked at viewers, acknowledging that we were all hip to the fiction of commodity fetishism, the *Reebok* campaign turned its back on trying to signify reality at all, opting instead to pursue a postmodern aesthetics and appellation structure. By the end of the 1980s a chief sociocultural consequence of advertising and the commodification of culture was the ripening of cynicism and distrust.

Though mass media advertising has contributed to reproducing the ideological hegemony of the commodity form, its basic methodology of carving up and appropriating culturally valued meanings has had an ironically corrosive effect on bourgeois-capitalist ideology and morality in the last fifteen years. Though hegemonic ideology in the US has been historically synonymous with bourgeois-capitalist ideologies, since the 1960s there has been a gradual loosening of capitalist hegemony from the moorings of dominant class interests – supplanted by the purer, more structural, logic of market shares and market segments. A widening fissure between pure commodity interests and class interests marked the end of the 1980s. As the logic of targeting market niches becomes more sophisticated, viewers grow more alienated as decoders and privatized meanings proliferate. Although bourgeois homilies still punctuate our mass-mediated discourses, the climate of relativism and cynicism fostered by the practices of the culture industry cuts away from the credibility of bourgeois narratives. Class-based capitalist hegemony as a unified dominant ideology has now given way to a form of fractured hegemony grounded in the privatizing discourse of commodified desire.

1

SUBJECTIVITY IN A BOTTLE
Commodity form and advertising form

Marx organized his analysis of capitalism on the basis of a strict hierarchy of conditions of possibility, the most fundamental of which was the commodity form. The commodity form, rather than the abstract categories of orthodox economics, was to be the starting point of historical materialism. In the use value and exchange value of the commodity Marx saw 'the real relation' underlying the phenomenal forms of capitalism such as wages and prices. He anticipated that as the capitalist model of production matured the commodity form would permeate all reaches of society.

THE COMMODITY FORM

What is the commodity form? How does it function as 'the model for all objective forms in bourgeois society together with all the subjective forms corresponding to them' (Lukács, 1971: 83)? There is no shortage of commentary on 'the consumer culture' in contemporary social life, or on the escalating alienation that accompanies it. Criticism often refers to 'the fetishism of commodities' to convey a loss of freedom by human beings as they become more and more the slaves to possessions, no longer the willing agents of their own destinies. However, the precise meaning of the concept 'commodity' is rarely clear or consistent. Even less attention is devoted to elucidating the logic of the commodity form. In what sense can commodities be said to possess a logic?

This chapter maps three moments, or clusters of meaning, that comprise the commodity form. We examine the potential impact of the commodity form on consciousness by looking at advertising, a primary channel through which the commodity form is extended and reproduced. Advertising amplifies and reinforces the exchange value of existing goods and transforms into commodities those goods and services not considered commodities before. The advertising industry is located at the frontier of expanding the commodity form and thus provides a locus in which its

15

transforming power can be readily observed. In advertisements, we can see images of commodified social relations, a popular consciousness of social relations structured by the commodity form.

THE EXTENSION OF THE COMMODITY FORM

Marx was not the first to be concerned that the advent of capitalism fundamentally altered the nature of work and social relationships. Many before him expressed apprehension about the 'cash nexus.' However, for Marx, locating the problem of capitalism in the cash nexus concealed its real foundation in the commodification of labor power. It was this, rather than the use of money or the exchange of goods, that Marx designated as the essential precondition for capitalism.

With the capitalist's expropriation of the means of production and the separation of workers from ownership or control over capital, there emerged a labor market in which 'free' labor could meet with owners of capital. Forcibly removed from the land, people were compelled to sell their labor power in order to survive. Concomitantly, a self-regulating market for consumption goods emerged, transforming what had once been collective and asymmetrical exchange into 'a series of discrete dual exchanges of equivalents' as individual laborers converted their wages into food, clothing, shelter and other subsistence needs (Brenkman, 1979: 99). Capitalist development did not immediately absorb the population into fully commodified relations. The stage characterized by absolute surplus extraction demanded long hours of work and little pay; thrift and abstemiousness were enjoined on all workers in the interests of savings and investment. Consequently, levels of consumption adequate to permit subsistence could not be achieved through the marketplace and non-commodity relations survived (Davis, 1978: 264). Many reproductive activities (e.g., food preparation) and consumption activities (e.g., leisure pursuits) remained outside the cash nexus. The transition to monopoly capitalism around 1900 saw a shift of emphasis from absolute to surplus value extraction; from a strategy of prolonging the working day to a strategy of increasing the productivity of labor through mechanization and rationalization of the labor process. Higher productivity, higher pay and increased leisure time accelerated the extension of the commodity form. More and more social relations were transformed as first goods production and then services were rendered amenable to commodification. The sequel was the invention of new goods and new services by means of mass advertising. In this sales effort, corporations reorganized themselves to become marketing as well as producing units, allocating greater amounts of money to advertising, product differentiation, market research, packaging and credit schemes (Braverman, 1974).

Activities involving relations among members of households and neighborhoods were replaced by activities mediated by individuated buying and

16

selling. Thus, activities like bread baking or music making, depending on skills and routines learned and performed in the context of family members and neighbors, were replaced by activities characterized by separation and serialization, the bread purchased in an anonymous supermarket, the music purchased from packaged personalities. Commercial markets also expropriated and displaced the collective, community recreations of traditional culture (Goldman and Wilson, 1977).

The extension of the commodity form was not only the structural accompaniment of mass production technologies and mass consumer habits, but also an important legitimating mechanism of capitalist relations. Its extension must be recognized as part of Capital's struggle to reproduce its hegemony over Labor. The commodity form redefines social relations as transactions, severs personal contacts from their social context and offers back to workers, in the form of the consumption of images, what has been denied them in the wage contract, namely status, individuality, freedom and sensuality. Under mass consumerism, achievements are interpreted according to the personal allocation of money and leisure time, 'achievements which may not, in principle, be interpreted politically' (Habermas, 1970: 112). The rise of mass consumerism reproduces wage labor relations at the level of consumption, and it legitimates the bourgeois public sphere by impeding the development of a proletarian public sphere (Brenkman, 1979; Hohendahl, 1979). It does not deny the worker a public status but redefines that status in terms of consumption criteria. Individuality is now derived from the goods people consume and how they appear. Mass-produced objects that give off appearances are touted, ironically, as having been made 'especially for you' (Marcuse, 1964: 92). Individuality is expressed in the unique package of satisfied wants each person has accumulated (Lefebvre, 1971: 107).

Modern advertising emerged at roughly the same time as a series of crisis tendencies were pressing a transition from competitive to corporate capitalism. Capitalist development had encountered diminishing rates of profit, declining opportunities for capital investment in the sphere of goods production and skewed capacities for 'overproduction' and 'underconsumption' that forced significant institutional and ideological changes. Modern advertising was one response to a crisis in the reproduction of exchange value. American corporate advertising constituted an attempt to penetrate and open up the sphere of Culture (as a reservoir of personal meaning) as a new territory for producing exchange value. To fortify the commodity form, a new layer of value production – the commodity-sign – was made to ride piggyback on the commodity form. Roughly seventy-five years later, we have inherited the cultural contradictions set in motion by the institutionalized competition to transform the sphere of culture and desire into a sphere of the capitalist economy.

Early advertising concentrated principally on the use value of products.

As selling techniques became more sophisticated, and as the need for new markets became more pressing, advertisements began to stress the 'psychological utility' of their products. Commodities began to 'appear as personified expressions of human characteristics and relationships' (Kline and Leiss, 1978: 17). Today, very little space in national brand packaged-goods advertising is devoted to giving information on the use value of products. Even when factual information is given it tends to be interpreted in terms of exchange value. Thus an energy-efficient appliance is touted as appealing to the thrifty, budget-conscious consumer. One acquires not only the practical use of the good but its symbolic properties as well. Advertisers then move beyond trying to persuade you that by buying the appliance you *become* budget-conscious, to the position where they try to persuade you that because you *already* belong to the category of budget-conscious people you will 'naturally' want to buy the appliance (Williamson, 1978: 47).

Escalating emphasis on the symbolic properties or psychological utility of goods represents a qualitative change in the commodity form. No longer need commodities have fixed meanings determined largely by their use value. Nor need commodities simply be defined by that for which they can be exchanged on the market. A new layer of meaning emerges, called the *commodity-sign*. The commodity-sign is a composite of a signifying unit and signified meaning. The signifying unit or signifier could be a word, a picture, a sound or an object. The signified is a meaning (a mental image, concept of impression) suggested by a signifier. The precise relation between signifier and signified is not fixed but emerges out of social practice.

The commodity-as-sign operates when images are allied to particular products and the product images are then deployed as signifiers of particular relations or experiences. Suppose we begin with an image of 'successful mothering.' A particular mental image of being a successful mother is detached from the total context of being a mother and attached to a particular product so that the image appears realizable through the purchase and consumption of the good: it might be attached to toothpaste, mouthwash, detergent or frozen food. The signified, being a good mother, has been separated from the totality of relations within which its real accomplishment must take place and been transformed into a discrete image. This image is then arbitrarily attached to a product which has *itself* been detached from the customary relations of usage formerly associated with it. In the process, the product becomes equivalent to the discrete image (e.g., toothpaste = successful mothering) and begins to function as a sign of that image, so that when we think of the product we think of the image and when we think of the image we think of the product. The original totality of the signified slips from view. The immanent relationship between act and context is 'bracketed' (it cannot be abolished) and replaced with the appearance of immanence between product and image:

18

the product gives rise to the image. The true nature of the product is also obscured. It is disengaged from its context, stripped of its content, divorced from the labor process employed in its production and arbitrarily associated with the image.

Modern advertising thus teaches us to consume, not the product, but its sign. What the product stands for is more important than what it is. A commodity-sign is complete when we take the sign for what it signifies. For example, 'diamonds may be marketed by a likening of them to eternal love, creating a symbolism where the mineral means something not in its own terms, as a rock, but in human terms, as a sign' (Williamson, 1978: 12). The diamond is no longer a means of securing eternal love, it has become eternal love. Conversely, eternal love assumes diamond-like qualities. Finally, the act of consumption becomes as important as the thing consumed. We begin to derive pleasure from using up the symbolic properties of goods so that we might be allowed to consume again. We draw pleasure from the image-making process itself, the glorification of the product by associating it with important social qualities becoming our satisfaction too. One index of this is the interest in name brand products (rather than brand name products), the reversal of words showing the reversal of priorities (Boorstin, 1961: 198). Few women's perfumes were 'positioned' by designer name in 1970, but by 1979 14.7 per cent of women's fragrances were positioned by reference to designer name, and another 5.5 per cent were positioned according to celebrity/authority referent (Lebowitz, 1979: 10). A more general indicator of a heightened emphasis on sign values may be seen in the growing volume of imitations of designer products and the 'pirating' and counterfeiting of designer labels.

THE LOGIC OF THE COMMODITY FORM

'Commodities do not assert themselves *qua* things but rather *qua* a kind of logic' (Lefebvre, 1971: 98). A logic is a framework within which social practices are defined and enacted. The logic designates the cognitive and procedural rules which mediate exchanges between people. These rules are evident in the formally rationalized contractual and juridical codes of capitalist society but, more significantly, they comprise tacit and underlying principles which define what is 'real' about individuals and the social relations they form.

In *Capital,* Marx sought to unravel the form or logic underlying the social categories and social relations necessarily implied in a society based upon the production and exchange of commodities. This was an exercise somewhat akin to decoding a language (Balbus, 1977: 584; Lefebvre, 1971: 204) in which form is given priority over content (Buck-Morss, 1977: 37). The assumption was that disparate practices and institutions of capitalism could be connected and explained by uncovering the underlying form (D'Amico,

19

1978: 91). Thus, an institution like law could be linked to other social institutions, and its particular phenomenal forms explained by reference to the logic of commodification. Extension of the commodity form into the sphere of law meant a victory for the formal principle of freedom and equality of opportunity. Capitalist development brought about fundamental changes in the law, including

> the emergence and consolidation of private property; its universal expansion to every kind of object possible as well as to subjects; the liberation of land and soil from the relations of dominance and subservience; the transformation of all property into moveable property; the development and dominance of relations of liability; and, finally, the precipitation of a political authority as a separate power, functioning alongside the purely economic power of money, and the resulting more or less sharp differentiation between the spheres of public and private relations, public and private law.
>
> (Pashukanis, 1978: 40–1)

Capitalist legal systems do not therefore directly and overtly coerce non-bourgeois classes. The legal system perpetuates the dominance of the bourgeoisie because the logic of legal concepts corresponds to the logic of social relations of commodity exchange. 'All concrete peculiarities which distinguish one representative of the genus *Homo sapiens* from another dissolve into the abstraction of man in general, man as a legal subject' (Pashukanis, 1978: 113). It is in its logic that the force of capitalist law is to be found. Specific laws might run counter to the interests of Capital. Laws controlling the rents charged by landlords run counter to the interests of the landowning class, but the form in which these laws are written and the definition of rights under the law nevertheless reproduce capitalist social relations.

THE ELEMENTS OF THE COMMODITY FORM

Three general consequences result from the commodity form in capitalist societies. The commodity form *universalizes* social relations. Formalized standards and rules of the market are imposed upon social relations to effect a quantitative, standardized process of exchange. All human qualities are reduced to quantitative measures. The commodity form also *atomizes* social relations, dissolving traditional forms of social reciprocity. Once labor becomes a commodity, customary bonds of exchange are replaced by 'the seriality of the exchange of equivalents' (Brenkman, 1979: 100). The commodification of labor transforms the essentially social activities of producing, exchanging and consuming into a series of discrete dual exchanges of equivalents as each worker uses their wages to meet subsistence needs. Atomization is epitomized in the explosion of the mass media 'in

20

which the members are connected with one another only in so far as they are isolated from one another' (Brenkman, 1979: 100). A third consequence of commodification arises from the fact that, when labor becomes a commodity, its value appears to be a property of the commodity itself rather than a relation of which labor now forms a part. A relation between humans appears 'in the form of a property of a thing' (Rose, 1978: 47). Social relations, the outcome of human agency, thus take on the appearance of objects. Social relations are *reified*.

The logic of the commodity form consists of a shifting combination of these elements. The commodity form imparts the property of universality or *abstraction*; the property of seriality or *equivalence*; and the property of *reification*. Before proceeding to an analysis of perfume advertisements, it is necessary to elucidate the meaning of each of these properties in more detail.

Abstraction

The commodity form detaches human characteristics from people and treats them as exchangeable entities. Entities are made to appear independent of any subjectivity or purpose 'or to refer to a subject or purpose that appears independent of any objective condition of existence' (Bologh, 1979: 21). Abstracted social relations are taken out of their actual organic context.

Abstraction has its roots in the separation of use value and exchange value brought about by the extension of the commodity form. As a social object is metamorphosed into a commodity it 'splits into quality and quantity, matter and form, use value and exchange value' (Lefebvre, 1971: 95). As a result, 'qualitatively different objects become what they are not: equal' (Balbus, 1977: 573). This means that, when labor is commodified, abstract labor is separated from concrete labor because, in order to facilitate the buying and selling of labor power, the fiction that all kinds of labor have an axis of commensurability must be established. Qualitatively different kinds of labor are treated as if they were identical. Labor is abstracted from the natural and social context within which it actually exists and is treated as 'labor in general.'

Although abstraction has its roots in the commodification of labor, it is not confined to the sphere of production. It is present wherever social relations have been split into quality and quantity, form and content. It is present wherever social relations are detached from the personal biographies of those who constitute them (Bologh, 1979: 130). It is present wherever we are encouraged to refer exclusively to the abstract quality of things and people 'to a neglect of relating oneself to their concreteness and uniqueness' (Fromm, 1955: 106). And it is present wherever individuals relate to each other as private proprietors of the multiple expressions of

21

value that accrue to the 'owners' of rationalized selves. Abstraction, insofar as it treats the appearance of things, their exchange value, as their prime reality, is both ahistorical and non-dialectical.

Equivalence

When an object becomes a commodity its use value is subordinated to its exchange value. An object's exchange value is the rate at which it can be exchanged for other objects. A commodity must enter into formal relations of equivalence with other commodities. Money facilitates commodification because it serves as a universal economic equivalent to express the value of all other commodities. In this sense alone, money becomes the measure of all things. Equivalence thus means that the quantitative value of things becomes dominant, to the neglect of that which is individual, personal and specific.

The principle of equivalence makes it necessary to construct standardized units to facilitate the comparison of items which would otherwise be incommensurate. The extension of the commodity form reduces objects to their comparable characteristics. In the process, individuals and their social relations are removed from their specific contexts and placed within a universalized, standardized framework. Thus reduced to numbers, human beings become treated as objects, impersonal entities, only serially related to other people.

Impersonalism does not mean the submergence of individuality so much as its redefinition. Individuals come to 'relate with indifference without recognizing their history of mutual dependence' (Bologh, 1979: 132).

> The reciprocal and all-sided independence of individuals who are indifferent to one another forms their social connection. The social bond is expressed in *exchange value*, by means of which alone each individual's own activity or his product becomes an activity and a product for him; he must produce a general product – exchange value, or the latter isolated from itself and individualized-money. The individual carries his social power, as well as his bond with society, in his pocket.
>
> (Marx, 1973: 157)

As social beings, commodified individuals find their individuality in the mass-produced goods they make. They find their uniqueness in how much they resemble others rather than in how different they are from them. They are promised individuality through the consumption of mass-produced commodities and in the practice of collectively organized labor. Theirs is a pseudo-individuality, the kind of specious individuality contained in the message conveyed by Madison Avenue, that 'the market thinks of you personally, it prepares for you personally specially personalized items' (Lefebvre, 1971: 107).

Reification

Marx (1967: 72) described the commodity as 'a mysterious thing, simply because in it the social character of men's labor appears to them as an objective character stamped upon the product of that labor . . . a definite social relation between men . . . assumes, in their eyes, the fantastic form of a relation between things.' Labor's commodification means that a laborer's skills and aptitudes are no longer considered an organic part of his/her personality. 'Individuals treat their own bodies as objects made up of component units, each having its own demands' (Leiss, 1976: 18). The individual, as both producer and consumer, is decomposed and a new unity is created consisting of a unique package of saleable parts. Images of abstracted body parts such as hands, legs, lips and hair are *styled* and endowed with a life of their own, so that desirable social relations tend to appear mediated by purchased objects.

Reification refers to the tendency for human beings and social relations to be transformed into things, while those nonhuman objects seem to assume human powers. Things produced by human activity take on the appearance of being active agents. Witness the tendency to attribute human qualities to goods for sale and the tendency to endow certain marketed goods with the power to create a social situation like an enjoyable weekend. Fetishism and totemism go hand in hand here.

THE COMMODITY FORM IN ADS

The manner in which the commodity form structures popular consciousness is most evident in the world of advertising where the aim is, after all, to commodify more and more goods and services. Modern selling makes extensive use of mass advertising as a technique of persuasion. But advertising is not solely a form of consciousness. It can safely be assumed that advertising campaigns are effective only if they resonate with lived practice. Not all campaigns are successful, of course, and the fact that much advertising becomes the object of ridicule testifies to people's ability to distance themselves from its appeal. However, since our goal here is to make clearer the meaning of the commodity form, it is expedient to choose a subject in which that form is clearly revealed.

Perfumes are packaged fragrances. Yet, advertisements for perfume rarely attempt to describe either the scent or the material properties of the perfume. Rather, they concentrate on the product's sign value. Purchasing the right perfume means that a woman will not only acquire a particular odor at a particular price but 'a gorgeous, sexy, young, fragrance.' A customer will, in consuming the product, acquire the qualities of being gorgeous, sexy and young? No, she acquires a sign of being gorgeous, sexy and young. It is the *look* we have come to desire; and, the look we desire is the *object of desire*. People thus become a kind of *tabula rasa*, a slate filled with desired attributes by the objects they consume; the object becomes an active agent capable of doing all the things that a gorgeous, sexy and young person can do. The act of consumption establishes a relationship between the product (the signifier) and what the product means in terms of social relations (the signified). A perfume (the signifier) has been connected to sensual beauty and confidence (the signified), and, just that quickly, the roles of signifier and signified reverse. Let us now turn to the meaning and significance of this relationship, using the elements of the commodity form.

Abstraction

Abstraction means empty of content, unsituated, without human purpose or aim, a separation of means and ends. Abstracted individuals and relationships are those in which means (consumption) and ends (whatever consumption yields) have no relation other than that provided by the commodity. Commodified relations have no clear end, no specific aim: why a person would want to acquire the quality 'sexy' is not the point. Sexiness is separated from the total social situation of which it is really a part and situated within a new context provided by the commodity. The commodity creates a new, but fabricated, context in which its own consumption makes sense. Perfumes thus create their own most suitable setting. In this new setting social relations are brought about by, and judged in terms of, the commodity. Sociability is pictured not as a natural outgrowth of the individual's capabilities but as an outgrowth of access to commodities. Social skills become purchasing skills.

Since abstracted relations have been separated from any genuine personal affectivity, their subjectivity is imparted by the commodity. Consciousness, or spirit, emanates not from an individual subject but from the product consumed. Perfume ads locate spirit in named commodities, and suggest that subjectivity can be expressed and celebrated by possessing the commodity. The inversion between subject and object is explicit in an advertising narrative for *Jovan Sport Scents* that describes their fragrances as being as 'active and alive as the people who wear them . . . . Wear them . . . . And let their spirit move you.' This is truly subjectivity in a bottle. *Shalimar* poetically captures the ideology of commodified subjectivity:

> Like every woman, every great perfume has both an outer expression and a deeper, inner mood . . . . Outwardly, *Shalimar* expresses elegance, calm . . . a serene femininity. But stay with the magnificent

24

scent long enough and you will discover its inner mood . . . a clipper ship slicing through the seas, the power of a storm about to break, a deep sensuality waiting to be released.

Shalimar expresses feelings and possesses an inner mood which it will release upon its purchase and consumption. Other perfumes, if they do not claim to possess spirit, profess to have the power to awaken spirit in the purchaser. A named perfume supposedly supplies the motive force for subjectivity in the '*Masumi* Experience.'

> You touch *Masumi. Masumi* touches you. Tranquil. Serene. As *Masumi* lingers your inner beauty emerges. You feel renewed. Experience *Masumi.*

The consumer may experience 'inner beauty' as a consequence of *Masumi*'s 'touch.' The world of experience is embodied in the form of the commodity and can be transmitted to an individual in the act of consumption. Where Masumi stimulated experience, Partage merely claims that the commodity permits the expression of true subjectivity.

> *Partage* heralds you, the newest woman. Confident enough to show your vulnerability. Secure enough to share your secret self. *Partage* is your sensuous, sensitive new window to the world.

Partage is not only a window, it represents your sensuality, your desire. Ads like those for *Shalimar* and *Masumi* and *Partage* portray the human capacity for experiencing subjectivity as an empty slate, a condition remedied by application of the appropriate commodity that carries the appropriate feeling state.

Partage heralds you. It hails you, naming you, ensnaring you in this system of meaning exchange. Do these descriptions fit you – are you confident, do you want a secure ego-identity? Does this perfume contain feelings of self-confidence? Can buying it impart such feelings? Detaching the signified from its relational contexts in daily life and reconstituting it within a context of commodities, the question of personal identity gets severed from its socio-temporal context as the unification of past, present and future. Divorced from biography, personal identity becomes located in a perpetual future of consumption self-images. In these ads identity is truly timeless, unified in the ahistorical appearances of commodities. Hence, *Cabriole* assures that a woman's 'delicious contradictions' – unresolvable in daily life – can be harmoniously united by the syllogistic commodity presence. An infamous *Enjoli* campaign promised too much and invited media ridicule: 'You can bring home the bacon. Fry it up in the pan. And never let him forget he's a man.'

Fantasies sell commodities and commodities sell fantasies. A *Chanel* ad campaign took this logic even further into the colonization of fantasies. In a television commercial for *Chanel Nº5*, surrealistic cinematography guides viewers through a mysteriously alluring woman's fantasy as she sunbathes by a luxurious swimming pool. The phallic shadow of a jet plane glides over, a man dives into the pool opposite her, swims toward her and appears to rise from the pool between her legs as he evaporates. The ad concludes with a local voiceover: 'Find your fantasy at Sanger-Harris.' The fantasy weaves together the imagery of opulence, a spiritual unity with nature and sensualism ('I am made of blue sky'). Even fantasies can be packaged. Produced by someone else, 'your fantasy' is available in a store awaiting its acquisition.

From the merchandiser's point of view, the association of fragrance with fantasy is simply a means of expanding sales and profits.

> A customer doesn't buy a fragrance because she needs it. She buys it because it is part of a fantasy – a fantasy that tonight or tomorrow is going to be exciting; a fantasy that she is going to be as beautiful (or he as handsome) as she always dreamed .... We have capitalized on this everyday fantasizing.
>
> (Nichols, 1979)

The most rational approach to selling perfume is to sell moods and fantasies. For every mood, for every imagined experience, there is an appropriate fragrance. Revlon merchandised *Charlie* to communicate and address 'a joyous genre of exciting, adventuresome, rule-breaking, world-shaking young women who shape their own lives and carve out their own careers with style and class' (Boiko, 1977: 26). Subsequently, Revlon introduced *Jontue* to appeal to the sensuous, romantic, more traditional side of women and, later still, *Scoundrel*, which emphasized the night-time elegance of mature women who seek both a man and a career (Sloan, 1980: 59). Still other perfumes tout themselves as being flexible enough to accommodate many moods and experiences, e.g., *Cie* is 'For Every Mood, Every Moment.'

The theme of abstraction is strikingly revealed in an advertisement for *Givenchy* men's cologne that visually renders 'The Evolution of the Art of Being a Gentleman.' The ad is divided into four frames portraying different historical stages in the evolution of gentility. In the first quadrant, Sir Walter Raleigh's 'acts of chivalry' mark him as a gentleman. In the second, Casanova achieves gentility through his 'devilish charm and savoir-faire.' Beau Brummell's sartorial splendor earns him the status of a gentleman in quadrant three, and the fourth quadrant is occupied by a picture of *Givenchy Gentleman* cologne. Beneath this frame the caption reads:

> These days, being a gentleman takes a different kind of style and finesse. So now the man of today can be a gentleman just by wearing *Givenchy Gentleman*.

In the first two frames the criteria for being a gentleman have to do with relations with other people. Beau Brummell represents a more individuated sense of gentlemanliness, more oriented to outward appearances. The fourth frame also suggests a relation, but it is a relation between the man (the reader/consumer) and the bottle of cologne. The product now defines gentlemanliness, and it can be had just for the wearing. In the process, the mode of social relationships has been decontextualized, abstracted from the social relations of the times.

Equivalence

Equivalent objects have a common measure of value. They are comparable. Equivalence thus connotes interchangeability. And equivalent objects, having lost their uniqueness, can be reproduced and repeated without loss of identity. In selling perfume, smell is sundered from its natural context. It is no longer a sign but a second-order signifier. It thus becomes available for attachment to a variety of things or for use in exchange for a variety of experiences. Experiences such as joy, wonder, peace, sexual pleasure and fulfillment are in turn treated as equivalent in that they, too, are reproducible and interchangeable. An advertisement for *My de Myurgia* toilet water shows a man wearing a black tuxedo embracing a woman dressed in a red, flowing evening gown. The caption beneath the picture reads, 'MY choice to share with you . . . because we have so much in common.' Framed beneath this caption is a picture of interlocking bottles of toilet water, one labelled 'Red for her' and the other labelled 'Black for him.' The ad thus equates the interlocking of things with the embrace of a man and a woman. The equivalence expressed in the commodity is transferred to the relationship between man and woman.

Print ads for *Charlie* (Figure 1.1) employ framing devices to create the impression that model and named perfume are interchangeable equivalents. Each can be read as currency for the other insofar as written across both model and perfume is the identical inscription, 'Charlie.' This encourages readers to see the model's perceived attributes (the signified) embodied in the bottle, so that she might hope to appropriate, upon purchase, the promise of the sign inscribed on the bottle. The reader 'is meant to imagine herself transformed by the product into an object of envy for others,' just as in reading the ad she envies the commodity-mediated attributes of the model (Berger, 1972: 134). The advertising *form* itself functions as a transformational field within which this currency is established and begins to circulate.

Equivalence does not destroy but redefines individuality. Adorno (1941: 207) saw 'pseudo-individualization' the other side of the standardization brought about by mass-production and mass-consumption. Mass-produced objects are offered as a means of establishing one's individuality. Thus *Cachet* is 'As Individual as You Are.' It is capable of being a mass-produced

Figure 1.1 Charlie

Source: Vogue, November 1979

object and being unique at the same time. The woman who wears it, who thus joins the crowd, is contradictorily capable of thereby asserting her individuality.

> *Cachet* is different on every woman who wears it. You see, the moment it touches your body, *Cachet* blends with your own special chemistry. And suddenly, it's you. Other women may wear *Cachet*, but you make it yours alone.

Cachet's special chemistry will counteract uniformity, but only by virtue of its uniformly individuating effect. Even the active language expressing the equation between self and perfume is designed to deny the formulaic fashion in which individuality can be acquired by the consumer: 'you make it yours alone.'

Appeals to pseudo-individuality in perfume advertisements rest on the unstated premise that each consumer represents a standardized unit of consumption. Qualities of individuality, playfulness and spontaneity seem to emanate from the product:

> *CIE* is me. And maybe it's you too. Imaginative. Soft. Unpredictable ... *CIE* ... here to dazzle the free-world of women.

The repeated premise is that such qualities are transmitted to the user of the product, who derives her individuality from them.

Pseudo-individuality is hammered home by the continuous repetition of ambiguous personal pronouns. Pronouns like 'you,' 'yours' and 'me' are employed in the text of perfume ads to refer to the product itself, to the model who appears in the photograph *and* to the reader. Ads for *Me!*, *Babe* and *Ritz* claim

> There's nobody else exactly like *Me!*

> There's a new *Babe* in town. And it's you.

> You're hard to keep up with. Sometimes you're restless and reckless and couldn't be sassier ... *Ritz.* The fragrance that's filled with spirit. And expresses yours. Because you'd rather be yourself than anyone else.

Ambiguity as to the precise referent of the personal pronoun in these ads is a structuring device which assists in generating the illusion of equivalence (identity) and then individuality. Ads suggest a relationship between the desired 'you' that is the model and the actual 'you' that is the reader. 'So advertisements appellate us as unique; although this uniqueness is a universal one, since the advertisement speaks to an imaginary individual which then becomes us' (Williamson, 1978: 53). This form of advertising creates a condition in which people are related to one another only insofar as they are isolated from one another, a condition Sartre called 'seriality.' People are first separated by denying their traditional bonds and then reconnected through the consumption of a commodity that is somehow tailored to each and yet can provide a common bond between them.

The meaning of equivalence is revealed when something thought of as unique is rendered reproducible. Benjamin (1969) described how works of art lose their 'aura' when copies can be easily made and sold. They lose their quality of inimitable uniqueness, a singularity in time and space which is the hallmark of their authenticity. When produced *en masse*, the originality or singularity of a work of art becomes a matter of indifference, insofar as every work is now replaceable. This is truly the triumph of equivalence. 'To pry an object from its shell, to destroy its aura, is the mark of a perception whose "sense of the universal equality of things" has increased to such a degree that it extracts it even from a unique object by means of reproduction' (Benjamin, 1969: 223). The work of art is alienated from its primary and traditional status as a use value, an object of aesthetic experience, and becomes an exchange value, an object whose character is determined first and foremost by its relation to the market.

Advertising so frequently lays claim to the territory of art that we often cease to notice. Wrapped in the rhetoric of 'hand-crafted perfection' or 'original artworks' to set themselves off from 'mass-produced,' upscale products offer consumers status by representing themselves as works of art, while others are presented as a means of turning self into a work of art. When individuality depends on how one presents oneself as a work of art then the circuit of freezing and packaging experience as 'commodity aesthetics' is complete. Lifestyle has come to refer to experiences defined by consumption of aesthetically coded sets of commodified appearances. When the Look, personal identity and lifestyle become culturally synonymous, a *Code West Boots* ad can bluntly command 'Live by the Code' because it presumes that we already accept the general formula of equivalence between commodity-sign and lifestyle image. As they say at *Sebastian Artistic Centers,* 'We're much more than a haircut. We're a lifestyle.'

Benjamin's reflections are no less pertinent to the portrayal of *experiences* which, like works of art, are fetishized if they are no longer sought for their intrinsic merit but are prized for their commercial sign value. Advertising works best where it effectively freezes the meaning of an experience in a photographic image, and then offers us packaged bundles of abstracted experience. *Chaps* cologne, for example, brings you the romantic West. Ads joined the meaning systems of *Chaps* and the West via a series of equations.

> The West . . . . It's an image of men who are real and proud. Of the freedom and independence we all would like to feel. Now Ralph Lauren has expressed those feelings in *Chaps*, his new men's cologne. *Chaps is* a cologne a man can put on as naturally as a worn leather jacket or a pair of jeans. *Chaps*. It's the West. The West you would like to feel inside yourself.

The *Chaps* ad reveals the assumptions made necessary for expressing subjectivity in commodity format. Freedom must be completely abstracted from any set of relationships. To do this, we must convert the condition of freedom and independence into an image. Impoverished subjectivity may be supplemented by wearing a commodity-sign endowed with the meaningful feelings of freedom and independence. *Chaps* is positioned as possessing spirit and as the conduit to desirable experiences of authenticity. The product is thus connected to, and eventually becomes, the lifestyle to which it is an accessory. 'So the product and the "real" or human world become linked in the advertisement, apparently naturally, and the product may and does "take over" the reality on which it was, at first, dependent for its meaning' (Williamson, 1978: 35).

Reification

Horkheimer and Adorno wrote that 'all reification is forgetting,' a process in which people forget the part their own activity has played in producing the social world. The characteristics of acting subjects are attributed to objects, while relations between subjects appear as the relation between objects. Reified social relations assume 'the fantastic form of a relation between things' (Marx, 1973: 75). The language of reification is prosaic in perfume advertisements that assign human, social qualities to packaged fragrance products. *Chanel N° 19* is 'The Outspoken Chanel,' of course, it is 'witty, confident, devastatingly feminine.' *Givenchy III* is 'the "contemporary." She's today . . . . Vital, versatile, alive and alert to change.' *The Female Factor* has a 'foxy and flirtatious personality' while *The Male Factor* is 'macho and mischievous.' *Ambush* is 'vibrant, alive, high-spirited.' Relationships thus appear mediated through the structure of the commodity and its sign. Indeed, situated next to the model's face in the *Charlie* ad is the caption 'Let's dance.' The dance of commodities begins as commodity self encounters commodity self. Marx's metaphor for commodity fetishism was never more appropriate than here: objects apparently possess human characteristics ('gorgeous, sexy-young'), while humans only appear to possess the qualities of living, active beings when they possess (wear) the appropriate corporately made object-signs (*Charlie* 'By Revlon.').

Advertisers often invest perfumes with the features essential to being human. Fragrances are said to embody the essence of femininity or masculinity. *Caleche* is 'the essence of femininity.' *Woman* is

a dynamic blend of total femininity and magnetic new stimuli . . . . It doesn't just say who you are. It says what you are.

Advertisements thus separate the intrinsic qualities of being human from actual living humans. The link can be restored only by the purchase of the commodity. Human qualities must be bought back, re-appropriated by means of consuming the commodity-sign. Reification imparts a time-lessness to the manufactured product, e.g., *'Diana* is forever.' At the same time, human qualities become time-bound, contingent on possessing the product's properties. The essential becomes only the appearance; the appearance is made to seem essential.

Reification is also evident in the way ads obscure the fact that social relations, traits and experiences are made by humans, suggesting that they come to us ready-made, as part of the goods we purchase. Social relations are no longer seen as the means to the production and consumption of goods. Instead, the acquisition of goods is presented as the means of forming social relationships. The goods acquire a life history, while humans lose theirs. Commodities become active, the consumer becomes passive. This inversion is evident in perfume ads such as 'Your *Windsong* stays on my mind,' where the socio-biographical construction of the implied relationship is forgotten, conveniently obscured from view. What is remembered is the commodity's presence in creating and giving meaning to the relationship.

This approach is taken one step further in an advertising campaign where the introduction of dialogue creates the impression of a more concrete, less anonymous relationship, thereby strengthening the association between the commodity and the relationship depicted. A *Paco Rabanne* ad for men's cologne sets the scene in a darkened photographer's studio. A virile young man stands in a lit doorway, shirtless, with a towel around his neck as he speaks on the telephone. In the column next to this scene the narrative is given in dialogue form between the man (Marc) and an unseen woman (Biffy). The dialogue frames the scene as an example of how 'hip' people negotiate social relationships. Beneath the text is a picture of a cameo brooch (employed to indicate female cleavage and signify the promise of more) situated adjacent to an appellated bottle of cologne, which has been used to imply the possibility of male sexuality. The relation of the objects has been made to stand for the sexy relationship between Marc and Biffy as alluded to in the dialogue. Indeed, the greater significance of the product is signalled by Marc's misremembering Biffy's name (he calls her Buffy) and by the slogan beneath the portrait of the cologne:

Paco Rabanne
A cologne for men
What is remembered is up to you.

The ad appears to particularize the relationship by introducing personal, even intimate conversation. This is again pseudo-individualization. Construction of the advertisement and the text instructs readers to interpret the message simultaneously as a particular instance of the way in which a relationship is enhanced by the presence of a cologne (this is a story about one particular man who uses it) and as a paradigm for readers' own relationships. The reader is guided toward performing a two-fold abstraction, from the implied relationship between the model 'Marc' and the absent 'Biffy' to the reader's own possible relations and from the relations between objects to a particular style of social relationship, a relationship which is glamorous, anonymous, fleeting and easily reproducible. Axes of interchangeability are thus established. One runs between the model and the product. Another runs between the product and the relation desired. And a third runs between the reader and the model. Both the man and his behavior are cast as representative of the cologne's powers but the cologne has also come to stand for the man's actions.

A complex logic thus links consumer with commodity-sign and, through the sign, to the material product. Ads for fragrances, watches, jewelry, stockings, shoes, hair products, liquor, cigarettes and cars in magazines such as *Cosmopolitan, Esquire, Glamour, SELF* and *Vogue* make clear that fashionable, attractive, popular, interesting people must be skilled and accomplished consumers. Individuals are portrayed as displayers of a collection of commodified surfaces, consisting of fetishized body parts – lips, eyes, hair, legs, nails – each serviced by appropriate commodities. Ads equate the abstracted body part and its commodified representation with self-identity. Over the years the severity of abstraction has become both more extreme and more routine. For example, *Max Factor* lipstick ads are so extreme in their visual abstraction that mouth and nose are separated from soul and body. Though they no longer bear an identity, they are invested with the capacity to compose identity. When framed by slogans such as 'Don't You Love Being a Woman?' lips that have been visually coded 'female' by lip sculpturing commodities are turned into the universal existential essence of female desire.

ADVERTISING AS SOCIAL PRACTICE

Our focus on themes found in ads does not mean that advertising is merely a medium for transmitting messages, simply a set of ideas and impressions we have about the world of material goods and real social relations that surround us. An advertisement is more than a 'tag' attached to a commodity announcing its availability. Advertising is a stage in the production process itself, part of the material object rather than simply a sign pointing to its location. This is especially true of 'image' products like perfumes where 'consumers want not only the physical thing but its "image," the "statement" the product makes about the user' (Schudson, 1981: 5–6). At this level, an advertisement is a material object, as material as the goods we handle in the shop.

Advertising is a form of lived practice, has a materiality, at another level. Besides helping produce commodities, advertising is itself a commodity, produced to be consumed by the purchaser of advertising ideas and objects. The advertising industry has its own practices and routines for producing and distributing commodity-signs. Indeed, the advertising industry can be viewed as a system for the production and exchange of commodity-signs. The extent to which this industry has been rationalized is marked by the creation of organizations like the *Image Bank*, where photographers can deposit their photographs and advertisers can search the inventory for that specific image which corresponds to a particular positioning concept for their commodity. For example, a beer campaign might want an image of a snow-covered mountain to suggest purity and sharpness of taste. The *Image Bank* is a clearing house or market for commodity-signs.

Advertising is part of the production process insofar as the media in which ads appear are themselves commodities. Newspapers, magazines, television programs and other vehicles for advertising guide the production of, and are themselves shaped by, the commodification of advertisements. These media help create the clientele for commodities, actively lending a hand in constructing consumers' sense of themselves as composed by particular kinds of product-images – providing the materials for 'Reinventing your looks, your self.' Magazines

> establish and reproduce hierarchies of value in their fields. They tell their readers who is a good skier, what is good stereo equipment, what constitutes a good garden, and in the process help confirm their part-time identities as skiers, listeners, gardeners.
>
> (Gitlin, 1981b: 68)

In this sense, the 'audience' for advertisements has itself been produced as part of the marketing process.

Advertising is also a form of social practice insofar as corporate profitability and control over markets relies on the existence of a built environment which presupposes commodified relations, such that the world depicted in advertisements comes to be thought of as the only possible world. Marketing now embraces not only direct advertising but also the expansion of administrative planning to encompass all the social arrangements surrounding mass-consumption. Lifestyles are defined and choreographed in terms of privatized consumption. Hairstyles, cars, jeans, stereos, liquor, cigarettes, pets, furniture and apartments are packaged and positioned as lifestyle ingredients. The task of assembling this ensemble of commodified meanings and the subsequent acts of exchanging and valorizing the commodity-signs each person possesses necessitate the existence of a suitable built environment. The franchising of food establishments, the selling of vitality and beauty through fitness clubs, the creation of retirement havens, the construction of instant 'communities' in apartment complexes and the manufacture of a new kind of public gathering space in sanitized shopping malls create the social spaces most appropriate for

34

privatized consumption. This level of commodification is inseparable from the world of magazine advertising we have been observing.

IDEOLOGY IN THE COMMODITY FORM

We have used advertising as a vehicle for examining the logic of the commodity form, the starting point for Marx's analysis of the capitalist model of production. The commodity form articulates three clusters of meaning which comprise its logic. This logic reproduces itself in the relationships advertisements depict. The structuring practices of abstraction, equivalence and reification constitute an ideology of commodity fetishism. In the process of producing commodity-signs, advertisements set forth a reified social logic that is culturally reproduced via the advertising *form.* This goes hand in hand with the ideological structure of appellation with its stress on individual freedom of choice. The manifest ideological content of any given advertisement may vary widely depending on the 'positioning' concept used to market a given product, but a deeper ideological residuum permeates all advertisements that share a common structure. Gender undeniably influences the ideological content of fragrance ads, but whether ads foreground patriarchal ideology or privatized narcissism, underlying every theme is a common *frame* that social relations are either derivative from, or associated with, the consumption of a named fragrance. 'Publicity is not merely an assembly of competing messages: it is a language in itself which is always being used to make the same general proposal' (Berger, 1972: 131).

Advertisements can tell us nothing directly about how social relations are actually lived. It is possible that ads portray only a fantasy world, providing vicarious satisfaction for people whose circumstances are quite remote from the lifestyles depicted. In this sense, advertising might be thought of as ideological, truly an 'opiate' to transport us from the pains of the present. However, we do not believe ads are ideological in this sense. Although no claim can be made that ads depict real life 'one can probably make a significant negative statement about them, namely, that *as pictures* they are not perceived as peculiar and unnatural' (Goffman, 1976: 25).

We do not see advertisements as mere illusions. We believe they accurately portray social relations which are illusory. These relations are merely phenomenal forms concealing the real relations which underlie them. Advertisements, which depict phenomenal forms as the real, natural foundations of social life, thus provide a foundation for living an alienated life. They serve 'to confirm the immutability of circumstances' (Horkheimer and Adorno, 1972: 149). The real truth of the commodity-sign can thus be understood only by grasping the alienation of the condition it represents as authentic. The advertisement's logic conceals this by inverting the relation between subject and object, depicting commodified relations as real (or as desirable and attainable). The advertising industry thus mystifies even the process of its own functioning by implying that the world it depicts is real. The triumph of the commodity form is that we do not recognize its presence at all.

2

ADVERTISING AND THE PRODUCTION OF COMMODITY-SIGNS

A commodity-sign joins together a named material entity (a good or service) as a signifier with a meaningful image as a signified (e.g., Michelob beer/'good friends'). Though people have invested objects with symbolic meanings for thousands of years, the production and consumption of meanings associated with objects has become institutionally organized and specialized according to the logic of Capital in the twentieth century. Commodity relations systematically penetrate and organize cultural meanings in the interest of extending the domain of exchange values. In our 'society of the spectacle' or the 'bureaucratic society of controlled (sign) consumption' the linguistic unity of signifier and signified is systematically split to fashion a commercially viable language of appearances and images (Debord, 1977; Lefebvre, 1971).

What is a political economy of sign value? 'In order to ground the "rational" circulation of values and their play of exchange in the regulated equivalence of values,' corporate capital reorganizes consumption practices to convert economic exchange value into sign value and vice versa (Baudrillard, 1981: 147, 113). Not only are commodities joined to signs, commodities get produced *as* signs and signs become produced *as* commodities.

> Because the logic of the commodity and of political economy is at the very heart of the sign, in the abstract equation of signifier and signified, in the differential combinatory of signs, signs can function as exchange value (the discourse of communication) and as use value (rational decoding and distinctive social use).
>
> (Baudrillard, 1981: 146)

Commodity-signs are organized by, and into, 'the code' which is 'determinant – the rules governing the interplay of signifiers and exchange value' (1981: 146). Alas, instead of locating the mode of production and the forms of social labor which gird the circulation and exchange of sign values,

Baudrillard's analysis of 'the code' preaches to the choir, glossing over the dynamics of competition in a political economy of signs and turning a blind eye to its internal contradictions.[1]

BUILDING SIGN VALUES

Ads conceal the nature and relations of production, and, 'gloss over the capitalist moment of exchange' (Winship, 1980: 217; Williamson, 1978). In producing commodity-signs, the origin of surplus value lies in the structure of the communicative exchange set up by ads. The advertisement's *mode* of address, not necessarily its content, invites a series of imaginative exchanges between viewers and the advertisement which positions viewers as subjects of the discourse. Viewers must supply the interpretive labor necessary to assemble sign values, and, hence, the possibility of surplus values. Producing commodity-sign values requires the reified interpretive labor of viewers. The rationalized system of producing sign values also requires raw materials, which it secures by colonizing meanings from the lifeworlds of viewers.

Advertisements are message systems that organize perceptions and 'create structures of meaning' (Williamson, 1978: 12). Consumer advertising aims to provide a new image or meaning for a product. A Coca-Cola communications research manager says,

> We nominate Pavlov as the father of modern advertising. Pavlov took a neutral object and, by associating it with a meaningful object, made it a symbol of something else; he imbued it with imagery, he gave it added value. That is what we try to do in modern advertising.
>
> (Koten, 1984: 31)

This value-added process, based on a formula of rerouting meanings, is a process of assembling commodity-signs: associating a meaningful object with a symbol of something else. Ads draw on meaning systems that already have currency with an audience. Ads do not create meanings, but rather provide an arena in which to transfer and rearrange meanings. The *form* of advertisements permits advertisers to convert the 'raw material' of already existent meaning systems into hybrid meanings that suit their particular purposes. Advertisers can do this, and viewers can decipher, because 1) there are shared meaning systems and cultural codes, and 2) rules guiding interpretation of an ad are both drawn from other ads and applicable to other ads, forming an 'interchangeable system' of rules (Williamson, 1978: 13).

For those socialized to recognize an ad as such, a taken-for-granted understanding of its agenda prefaces all subsequent interpretation of messages. This keeps us on guard and wary of claims made by ads, but also numbs us to the process of recombining meanings. David Ogilvy, a preeminent US advertiser in the post-war era, understood that advertising is a system of manufacturing commodity-signs.

> Every advertising must be considered as a contribution to the complex symbol which is the brand image . . . . The manufacturers who dedicated their advertising to building the most favorable image, the most sharply defined personality for their brands are the ones who will get the largest share of these markets at the highest profit – in the long run.
>
> (in Mayer, 1958: 36)

Advertising is a locus for production insofar as it is a site where meanings (signs) are attached to commodities. The result is the production of commodity-signs, and, hence, sign values.

Ads teach us to consume signs. The value produced by consumer-goods advertising is the image. The primary value consumed is the symbolic image of the good that can be displayed. Ads generate sign values insofar as they compose a transformational field in which a language of images is turned to accommodate a language of exchange value.

> The advertisement provides a supreme arena for this: a 'meta-structure' where meaning is not just 'decoded' within one structure, but transferred to create another. Two systems of meaning are always involved: the 'referent system' and the product's system.
>
> (Williamson, 1978: 43)

Constructing commodity-signs takes place in the social space where viewer and advertisement come together. There is nothing passive about the reception and assembly of meanings into commodity-signs in ads. Producing and realizing sign values begins with advertising as a communication form requiring the viewer's participation in the interpretation of meaning. Interpreting an ad, constructing meaning and producing sign value are inseparable and simultaneous processes. Each task is accomplished in consumer-good ads via structured interpretive practices of abstraction, equivalency and reification.[2] The logic of these decoding practices corresponds to the logic of the commodity form. When advertisers try to organize, arrange and steer interpretation of a signifying image in relation to a product by overstructuring the ad's composition, then entwined in the ad's preferred interpretation is an ideology of commodity fetishism. Through the prism of this encoding/decoding logic, ads represent social relations in terms of fetishized visual signs.

A dominant advertising form uses 'positioning' strategies to establish associative links between product meanings and selling ideas. The advertising format analyzed here is prominent in print ads for consumer goods (a similar format utilizing video cuts and edits has been adapted to TV advertising). Its main features include: 1) a photographic signifying image;

2) a *mortise*, a boxed insert containing the image of a named product. Variations abound. The box around the product image sometimes disappears, leaving only the product image in apposition to a signifying image – then the product as sign-object carries its own tacit mortise. Or, the relationship between signifying image and product image may be reversed so that the former occupies the mortise; 3) framing copy – a headline, slogan or caption defines the relationship between signifying image and product; 4) graphic framing devices (lines, color, shape) differentiate and connect the contents of the page.

Though advertisers seek to steer meanings, they cannot guarantee interpretations. Since 'only the signifier . . . exists as a material entity, the sign requires the presence of a (constituting) subject' (Wren-Lewis, 1983: 181). Readers' active interpretation of advertising texts may result in ratification of advertisers' 'preferred' meanings *or* in 'aberrant' meanings. Even readers who share tacit social knowledge *about how ads mean*, may produce disparate interpretations of *what is meant*. Readers are neither homogeneous nor passive. Interpretations vary by subculture and interpretive community, as well as by class, gender and race. How active 'readings' are also depends on how open or closed advertising texts are. 'Because in advertising the signification of the image is undoubtedly intentional . . . we can be sure . . . these signs are full, formed with a view to the optimum reading' (Barthes, 1977: 33). But, no matter how condensed and over-structured, the meanings generated by ads are never finite. Complex negotiated interactions between texts and readers actively engaged in producing interpretations tend always to generate surplus meanings. Some 1980s ad campaigns tried to capitalize on this facet of reading ads: e.g., *Pepsi* TV ads strung together oblique, ultra-close-up shots in a way that made interpretive closure impossible, a fact that did not imperil production of commodity-signs since *Pepsi*'s prime concern was that viewers associate their interpretations of the different format (or narrative structure) to the product. Elsewhere, surplus meanings may imperil corporate signs: e.g., Proctor & Gamble's decision to abandon their corporate logo due to persistent grassroots rumors linking the logo to devil worship.

De-composing ads allows us to observe how commodity-signs are assembled, and how, in the process of producing sign values, ideologies of commodity fetishism and pseudo-individuality become constituent ingredients in the articulation of sign value. Actively completing the meaning of ads according to advertisers' 'preferred interpretation' requires use of a fetishized code, reproduces reified meanings and may culminate in the assembly of commodity-signs. Since fragrance ads most nearly approximated the conditions of pure sign value circa 1980 in the United States, they provide a convenient focus.

MARKETING FRAGRANCES

A division of the cosmetics industry, the fragrance industry manufactures and markets 'hopes and dreams.' At the 1980 Cosmetics, Toiletries and Fragrance Association convention, a vice-president of Yankelovich, Skelly & White justified this as serving the 'self-defined' needs and interests of a consumer constituency: 'looking good has become increasingly equated with feeling good' and 'personal care products are perceived as stress reducers; instant, inexpensive hope-in-a-bottle for an enormous majority of consumers with too many lifestyle options' ('Ears on,' 1980: 40). Extending the metaphor, another executive proclaimed that 'Putting on a perfume is like taking a pill. It's a euphoria thing. It nullifies all the badness within' (Seeman, 1981: S18).

Intense industry competition (over 700 fragrances on the market) means that companies push products by selling moods, feelings and lifestyles. Industry analysts believe that advertising/promotion, packaging/design and space/display are the decisive factors in selling fragrance products. Conversely, only '8 cents of the cosmetics sale's dollar goes to pay for ingredients.' The additional cost of 'prestige products' is due to 'fancier packaging, splashier promotion, and the fact that the swankier cosmetics are made in limited quantity for sale through prestige stores' ('Cosmetics,' 1978: 94). In short, the fragrance industry relies on producing sign values: 'We sell an image and we will use any vehicle to emphasize it. It's all done by design' (Lauerman, 1980: B1). The merchandised product is a signifying image attached to a fragrance: a commodity-sign. Successful management practices in the industry invariably dwell on marketing and promotional techniques which contribute to the efficient production of sign values.[3]

Valorizing sign values is predicated on the view that 'people are attracted to a perfume because of the image they have of themselves – their self-concept and their relationships with others' (Levy, in Lauerman, 1980: B1). Behavioral science is thus enlisted to help appraise people's self-images so these may be reconstituted as sign values. Profitable production of sign values dictates using rationalized methods calculated to maximize 'how you get the fragrance message across!' Conventional wisdom in the industry puts fragrance sales in direct correspondence to money spent on advertising.[4] Ads in industry trade journals say the efficiency of ad spending depends on message frequency and repetition.

This year we're spending a bundle broadcasting the message of *Me!* A whopping 7-figure budget will bring 493,541,000 TV and print messages to women 18 to 49. (60% of the U.S. female population) . . . *Me! The fragrance that hits her where she lives with a message that's right on the nose. (And the big dollars to make it stick.)*

(*Product Marketing*, April 1980: 38)

Extrapolate this ratio between one advertising budget and the number of messages it generates to the total advertising expenditures for all non-durable consumer goods and the number of messages spawned becomes staggering. Exposure frequency of this magnitude ensures a *taken-for-granted familiarity with the advertising form* and the generalized decoding practices necessary to its interpretation.

Mechanisms are established to monitor the potential consumer population continuously. Survey questionnaires permit corporate decision makers to gauge more effectively how to make their fragrance 'an extension of the lifestyle of that time period's consumer' ('Men's Scents,' 1979: 48). Marketing strategies and campaigns attempt to tailor messages so they dovetail with responses gleaned from surveys. Though these surveys contribute to the impression that successful firms are proficient in reflecting and catering to popular expressions of needs and desires, the surveys are actually a crucial tool for producing audiences. The audience becomes a commodity which, like the product, must be made and remade (Smythe, 1977).

Marketing specialists insist that making a fragrance a commercial success requires 'a consumer profile bill of specifications.' These profiles are elaborated by using audience demographics, a tool employed by advertisers and marketers since the early 1950s as a 'template (or cultural map) for producing most of our culture's symbolic forms of expression' (Czitrom, 1982: 190). However, growth of sales based on simple audience demographics eventually encountered diminishing returns, and advertisers developed new research tools such as lifestyle patterns, psychographics and VALS as methods of expanding markets (Bernstein, 1979; Plummer, 1979; Atlas, 1984). Newer techniques combine demographics with the 'dimensionality of psychological characteristics,' thereby permitting advertisers to subdivide markets based on age, income and occupation into a multiplicity of markets based on moods, attitudes and composite consumption patterns.

Variations on a basic five-step approach are used to fit a fragrance product into the 'habit patterns and lifestyle of a significant group of consumers.' These steps are 1) defining a target market in terms of demographic and lifestyle attributes; 2) identifying motivations of target populations; 3) establishing 'protoconcepts,' which are translated into signifying images that tap into targeted aspirations; 4) pretesting both concepts and name; and 5) quantifying market research to refine the fit between target population and concepts, as well as assisting further market segmentation (Hyde, 1981: 70). With *Scoundrel*, Revlon spent three years of research picking a name and image with the right appeal to potential consumers.

Matching concepts and names to a fragrance product involves marketers in the making and remaking of audience segments. Concept selection generally precedes the fragrance, and the process of fitting audience to product does not stop following a 'successful launch.' Nine years after Revlon introduced their vision of the 'quintessential liberated woman' to position *Charlie*, they altered its image to accommodate new social trends. Pictured without a man and wearing pants, *Charlie* emerged in 1973 as Revlon's reflection of women's shifting lifestyles – a likeness that recast the liberation in the apolitical terms of consumer appearances. A 1982 *Charlie* campaign drew on research by Yankelovich, Skelly & White claiming renewed interest among young women in traditional relationships, marriage and families. Now 'Charlie' was seen with a man who proposed marriage – and, she was considering it. The saga continued into the mid-1980s when 'Charlie' was shown playfully squeezing the tush of her beau – as Revlon's marketers continued to abstract social values from social contexts, and then 'oversimplify and stylize the idea in order to sell products and make profits' (Abrams, 1982: 9). When marketers claim to act merely as cultural barometers of the time period, they tell but half the story: 'reflecting' the values of target markets in pursuit of profits involves marketers in continuous maneuvering to refract meanings and reposition audiences in relation to their products.

Another dimension of commodifying audiences stems from magazines' practice of selling themselves to advertisers on the basis of guarantees to deliver an audience with specified demographic characteristics. *Cosmopolitan*'s ads on the *New York Times'* back page 'try to create an image of the girl who reads our magazine' (Henkoff, 1979: 195). *Vogue*, the leader among women's magazines in advertising pages, 'offers advertisers a market with vast discretionary purchasing power.'

> Each month our beauty and health pages inspire a highly receptive audience with ideas and trends which motivate them to try new products. This environment of authority and expertise is highly recognized by the beauty industry. A lot of women buy *Vogue* as much for the ads as for the editorial product.
>
> (Shortway, in Ellenthal, 1979: 19)

Magazines actively assemble a particular currency of appearances that reinforce, and tap into, the commodity-signs set forth in the advertisements.

Claims by industry analysts that personal care products such as fragrances have become perceived by consumers as necessities take on added significance in view of these attempts to colonize audiences. Surveys of women's beauty care habits conclude that 'beauty products are part of getting dressed – whether they are slipping into business suits or jeans' ('Working Women,' 1980: S-56). Industry analysts candidly acknowledge that this transformation of perfumes from luxury items to 'unquestioned parts of life' has been carefully calculated and engineered. A vice-president at Sanger Harris department stores boasts, 'We have trained our customer that she simply cannot leave home without her fragrance' (Nichols, 1979: S-2).

Measurement of values and attitudes is then translated into product positioning. 'Consumer-oriented positioning' is 'the basic selling concept used to motivate consumers to select a given product over that of competition.' Marketers position products to differentiate them from competitive brands that share the same basic attributes. Consumer-oriented positioning concepts 1) sell 'ideas . . . based on the unique manner in which the consumer is to "perceive" the product, regardless of its physical properties or product characteristics'; 2) 'mold consumers' perception by associating its product with such issues as lifestyles and/or sex appeal'; 3) sell 'ideas to which consumers can more easily relate because of their association with a lifestyle or some other frame of reference with which consumers identify themselves' (Ennis, 1982: M43).

Positioning situates products in relation to particular signifying images, in relation to the psyches (self-images) of potential consumers. Advertisers apply positioning techniques as a method of associating a product in the consumer's mind with an already familiar referent system. Positioning offers advertisers a tool for translating survey 'trends' into distinctive product 'personalities.'[5] 'Personalities' (or signifieds) – e.g., audacious, innocent, forthright, confident, liberated – are thus linked with market segments. Positioning involves packaging and matching the product and the audience – each a separate but interrelated commodity.

Though positioning aims at differentiating one brand from others, many consumer products employ a 'me too' marketing approach that mimics the positioning concepts and advertising formats that have proven successful for competitors. Advertisers try to reflect changes in the salient values of target populations even as they crystallize these positioning concepts into standardized formulas. Romance was a predominant positioning category for perfumes in 1970, but declined sharply by 1979. By 1979, 'reference group' positioning ('celebrity, lifestyle and designer, any position in which an authority figure is meant to be emulated, capitalizing on people's desire to be told how to behave') had surfaced, and in the early 1980s fantasy/escape, lifestyle and 'ego-sense' (positive self-image) were the trend (Lebowitz, 1979: 10).

In constructing commodity-signs, the positioning concept literally becomes the sign associated with the particular commodity being advertised. Revlon associated their brand name (*Charlie*) with the positioning concept of young, independent women. Their ad campaign sought to translate that concept into a sign. Identified with her long stride, 'Charlie' signified a youthful, carefree, independent, confident and insouciant lifestyle. The 'Charlie' model represented an idealized signifier of that lifestyle and personified the powers of *Charlie* perfume – the mass-produced fragrance

44

came to embody the 'gorgeous, sexy-young' qualities made manifest by the model. The advertising technique rested on, and reproduced, a reified interpretive grammar. Any positioning concept will inflect an ideological slant, but all perfume ads that use standardized advertising formats embrace an underlying ideology of commodity fetishism rooted in the advertising form. Viewers may find the content of particular ads receding from consciousness, but not their form – not their rules.

TRANSLATING POSITIONING PRACTICES INTO INTERPRETIVE PROCEDURES

An ad's compositional form translates positioning logic into the social logic of the commodity-sign. In social practice this translation takes place via the interpretive procedures of abstraction, equivalency and reification. The *Vanderbilt* ad (Figure 2.1) is an exemplar of how positioning concepts and framing devices are used in ads to develop commodity-signs. Analyzing ads begins by *de-composing* the connections advertisers compose through their structuring of the ads. Advertisers have one overriding purpose: to convey to as many viewers as possible (given the target audience) an association between a positioning concept and the product name. The advertiser's job is to 'create structures of meaning' via the ad's composition in order to maximize this 'preferred interpretation' of an ad. Though the process is far from simple, advertisers encode meanings and viewers decode meanings. While advertisers go to great lengths to evaluate the fit between their encoding and viewers' decoding, there is virtually never an exact 'symmetry' between encoding and decoding (Hall, 1980: 131). No matter how careful an ad's construction, some portion of a mass audience will create 'non-preferred interpretations' of its meaning. However, the presence of non-preferred interpretations intensifies advertisers' efforts to 'increase the probability' that meanings of their messages 'will be decoded similarly by different receivers.' It

> imposes a discipline on the encoders which ensures that their messages are in touch with the central meaning systems of the culture, and that the codes in which the message is transmitted are widely available.
>
> (Fiske and Hartley, 1978: 63, 81)

Reading ads always involves more than simply reading the ad at hand. Readers decode in the light of their prior familiarity with ads: readers carry a repository of understandings concerning the content of 'referent systems' and the nuances of signifying images (Goffman, 1976). Most importantly, readers acquire a knowledge of the language practices embedded in the advertising form. The form is 'devoid of meaning, except insofar as meaning is constantly' passed 'through the form of its perpetual translation' (Williamson, 1978: 43).

Figure 2.1 Vanderbilt

Source: *Glamour*, 1983, photograph used by special permission from Cosmair Inc.

Five compositional elements are immediately obvious in the *Vanderbilt* ad. From top to bottom readers see the name '*Vanderbilt*' across the page; a soft-focus picture of a white swan taking flight across water; a mortise insert containing the bottled fragrance's image and name; across the bottom, the caption 'Let it release the splendor of you.' A fifth compositional element occupies all parts of the page – the lines dividing the page function as frames that provide interpretive guidelines that steer assembly of other elements on the page into a meaningful whole.

An outer frame below the title '*Vanderbilt*' encompasses most of the page and informs readers that pictorial images of the swan and perfume bottle fall under its common definition. An apparent break in the frame at the top is no break at all, but an announcement that everything within this named frame is 'by Gloria *Vanderbilt*.' Both swan and perfume bottle share the same source and appellation. Yet, this large rectangular frame is obviously composed of two frames as the bottom right-hand quadrant containing the bottle's picture clearly occupies its own separate frame. This permits the two frames to be set in opposition (differentiation) to one another even as they are joined within the larger frame.

Multiple techniques communicate that the named bottle and swan's image share an identity. The framed boxes juxtapose the two so readers might recognize a connection between them. The etching of a swan on the bottle reinforces the equivalency, and purple coloring in both frames along with the presence of water beneath each scene provides additional connective devices. Finally, the caption, 'Let it release the splendor of you,' transforms the swan's image at the moment of taking flight into a metaphor for achieving authentic female selfhood and inner beauty, at the same time linking this metaphor to the named fragrance.

The ad is set up so the preferred direction for scanning the page is from top to bottom and left to right. Studies show illustrations catch viewers' eyes first, and copy is most likely to be cognitively processed when situated below the illustration (Ogilvy, 1983: M-48). Ad composition is most effective when it 'conforms to the habitual, culturally determined reading behavior' (Kroeber-Riel and Barton, 1980: 150). But ads like this one are so redundantly overstructured they can be read from virtually any direction with the same results.

To achieve the preferred interpretation of this ad, three simultaneous conceptual maneuvers are probable. First, readers must abstract (separate) the question of inner beauty as authentic individuality from the total social situation within which it might actually develop, and resituate it within a new context provided by the commodity. When, in the extreme, positioning concepts are used without regard for the product's material characteristics, readers must abstract both the positioning concept and the particular commodity from their usual contexts to the context of the advertising form itself. That this is not perceived as peculiar or unnatural is indicative of how readers have been socialized (as a result of having 'read' thousands of ads) to accept the advertising form as a sensible and un-problematic context in and of itself. Yet another level of abstraction is performed when the reader abstracts from the swan as a representation of the emergence of inner beauty to her own possible realization of that 'presence.'

Second, readers are encouraged to view the *Vanderbilt* perfume bottle and the swan's signifying image as equivalent manifestations of the same thing. Emphasizing the signifying image as a representation of *your* (reader's) splendor, an equivalency is drawn between this metaphoric model and the reader's self. Axes of interchangeability are generated between the reader, the *Vanderbilt*-mediated metaphor of inner beauty and the commodity *Vanderbilt*.

Third, the caption cements a reified interpretation of the relationship between image, product and reader. This reified interpretation has already been facilitated by the familiar structural layout of the page. The caption not only steers interpretation of the swan's image, it also projects a relation of causality from *Vanderbilt* perfume to the feeling state represented by the imagery. The association established between image and product becomes a 'precursor to the subjective identification of causality' (Mowen, 1980: 53). The passive linguistic construction of 'Let it (*Vanderbilt*) release the splendor of you' bestows the appearance of human agency on the object *Vanderbilt*, while the human subject awaits in a state of plasticity. As used here, the verb 'release' connotes emergence of a human spirit ordinarily unrealized.

The ad represents *Vanderbilt* in terms of the meaningfulness of the swan's image. Connected with the defining slogan, the swan's image be-comes polysemic, signifying a mood of quiet, natural beauty; graceful, sleek elegance; freedom and individuality.[6] In *Vanderbilt's* TV campaign, a beauti-ful woman flows past the camera, immersed in her own introspective presence, and the video cuts back and forth between swan and woman to equate them metaphorically. Feelings of emergent inner beauty suggested by the swan are read into the product, and *Vanderbilt* is made to define the achievement of feelings of splendor. By framing the swan's image with the slogan in the context of the named product, the swan comes to stand for what one respondent called 'the freedom to let go of the individuality inside yourself.' *Vanderbilt* is not unique in using this transformational logic: virtually every consumer-good ad utilizing this basic advertising format (positioning concept, mortise and caption) reproduces this trans-formational logic. Perfume ads, because they associate moods and feelings with fragrances, are particularly prone to transforming freedom, authen-ticity and individuality into privatized subjective experiences that are sup-posedly reproducible in every consumer since every consumer is presumed to constitute an identical unit.

Figure 2.2 Blue Stratos

Source: Gentleman's Quarterly, October 1981

It is worth illustrating the point once more. A *Blue Stratos* ad (Figure 2.2) signifies freedom with a scenic image of a man hang-gliding in a clear sky over a rugged, unpopulated coastline. Across the hang-glider is an image of a white soaring bird, an image identical to that on the *Blue Stratos* bottle. The bottle has been superimposed over the foreground of the coast. The bottle top has been removed and the bottle angled so a direct line can be drawn from it to the hang-glider above. This relationship is amplified by the bottle neck's penetration into the space between 'the' and 'spirit' in the slogan 'UNLEASH THE SPIRIT!' Where the advertiser began by using an image of a hang-glider to give meaning to the product, now the relation between signifying activity and object is inverted with the statement, 'The feeling begins with Blue Stratos.' Now it becomes doubly apparent that *Blue Stratos* does the acting, for it is 'bold' and 'adventurous.' What began as merely an association culminates in a commodified formula for achieving freedom defined in terms of leisure risk-taking.

COMMODIFIED SOCIAL RELATIONS IN PERFUME ADS

The practice of using positioning concepts in combination with the formal structure of the ad culminates in a reified world-view. Since the 1920s, advertising has helped define the parameters for the 'commodity self' (Ewen, 1976: 47), which designates an ensemble of isolated and fetishized body parts – lips, eyes, hair, legs, nails, breasts and even spirit – defined by specific commodities. Selves become defined by collections of commodity-signs. Ads isolate a body part, represent it in terms of a commodity, and equate the commodified part with an imaginary type of person. A *L'Erin* cosmetics campaign epitomizes this approach with the slogan 'Let L'Erin do the talking.' One ad features fingernails 'saying' their possessor is 'captivating,' 'tempting' and 'fascinating.' Their capacity for speech stems from the *L'Erin* brand of nail polish covering them.

This is one meaning of reification: qualities of acting subjects are attributed to objects, while relations between subjects appear as a function of relations between objects (commodities). Acquiring commodities is presented as a prerequisite to forming successful social relations, as objectified nails, eyes and expressive aura are depicted conducting social relations. Perfume ads depict a social universe inhabited by commodity selves engaged in fetishized social relations. These ads apply positioning concepts to *frame* self and self–other relations in terms of signifying objects. Relations of individuality, sensuality, romance, success, happiness and prestige, to mention but a few, are defined in a language of commodity relations. Day in and day out, ads inscribe our social desires on commodities and signify their absence in non-consumers. Social interaction is shown taking place between commodity selves able to mobilize idealized social traits via their possession of commodity-signs. Ads become a kind of educational forum concerning the exchange and valorization of commodity-signs between interacting commodity selves.

Reified interpretations in no way ensure the purchase of commodities. A reader/consumer may internalize a generalized reified world-view from repeatedly interpreting ads that share a similar metastructure, and still not want to purchase a given product advertised around a given sign. Alternatively, purchase of a product cannot be taken as a measure of having internalized a reified world-view. You may purchase a given commodity because you like its use value – its smell.

The advertising form as a metastructure permits the transfer of meaning back and forth between named product and the image used to represent the positioning concept. Ads 'provide a structure which is capable of transforming the language of objects to that of people, and vice versa' (Williamson, 1978: 12). The very nature of this advertising form entails the articulation of reified meanings – objects are cast in the language of humans, and humans are simultaneously cast in the language of objects.

The advertising form encourages fetishized meanings. This is obvious in the link between fragrance names and positioning concepts. Names such as *Scoundrel, Macho, Trouble* or *Beautiful* invest the fragrance with the human qualities evoked by their positioning concept, simultaneously naming both the photographic imagery and the product. Perfume and cologne ads typically anthropomorphize their fragrance when human action and spirit are inscribed on nominated commodities. *Megara Parfum* is, for instance, 'complex, fascinating, and unpredictable (like a woman should be).' Invariably, it is the advertising form itself that makes unproblematic the use of adjectives such as 'heroic,' 'witty,' 'high-spirited' or 'adventurous' to describe objects.

Though obviously culture-bound, fragrance ads also imprint supposedly universal species traits on their commodities. *Ralph Lauren* advertising claims 'his' fragrances (produced by chemists and technicians in corporate laboratories) 'capture the essence of a certain way of living, a kind of timeless style.' Another cologne named *Kouros* claims to

> Recall an Age when Demigods walked among Men. In Ancient Greece, manhood was not simply celebrated, it was worshipped. Today, Yves Saint Laurent captures that Golden Age of Man, that pure and perfect essence, which he exalts in his new fragrance for men.

Framed in sensual and sexual terms, investing human essence in the substance of commodities implies a potential absence of essence in human subjects. These intensely narcissistic narratives detach essence, the transcendent quality of being human, from real living beings. Instead it is 'captured' and made available as a fragrance bearing a ready-made aura. Generic characteristics of human beings are no longer intrinsic features of the human condition, but may be reappropriated via the exchange of money for a mass-produced reproduction of that essence. While the historicity of shaping the human condition is obscured by reified formulas of timeless essence, human faculties are made to appear contingent on the possession of objectified signs.

COMMODITY-MEDIATED SELF–OTHER RELATIONS

Reified social relationships appear activated by commodities bestowed with 'living, human powers' (Balbus, 1977: 574). Human relationships acquire the characteristics of relationships between commodities, between objects. *Jovan* ads equate sculpturally interlocking bottles with intertwined man and woman – the female bottle, of course, receiving the man's shape. A reified representation of social relationships as commodified relations is illustrated in an ad for *Vivre* perfume.

> You'll love me. I know.
> You'll be jealous. I know.
> You'll take me to Venice. I know.
> You'll never leave me. I know.
>
> I know what Vivre means.

Poised above this stanza is a photograph of a young woman's face in a seductive, glamorous pose. Her expression is that of 'a woman responding with calculated charm to the man whom she imagines looking at her . . . . She is offering up her femininity as the surveyed' (Berger, 1972: 55). Each imperative is apparently directed to her 'true lover – the spectator-owner,' as visually she offers up her femininity to that anonymous other. But the written text makes her glamour her source of power over the unseen male lover. The pose is submissive, the utterance assertive. And what is the source of her certitude that she will maintain control over her dyadic relation? *Vivre*. *Vivre* means purchase and use of this named fragrance will produce a hypnotic attractiveness sufficient to generate social relations of love, jealousy, leisure hedonism and security. The perfume not only bears the *power* to provoke such relationships, it also comes to stand for them, since between these desired relations and the product an equivalency has been fashioned at the end of every line. Playing on a female fantasy that being overwhelmingly attractive will win any man, the ad suggests readers can resemble the model and her implied relations through use of *Vivre*.

Once labelled as possessing specific human qualities, the perfume visually appears to intervene as the decisive actor in achieving desirable male–female relationships. A *Chimere* ad depicts a male making love to an attractive woman, or is it to the packaged fragrance image inserted inside a halo hovering beside her face? The ad depicts the woman at work and in an intimate setting, because *Chimere* has both a public side and a private side.

52

Similarly a *Nuance* ad frames romantic male–female relations as a function of the fragrance's 'whisper.' A full-face photo of a young sensual-looking woman, her extended forefinger in front of her slightly pursed lips, signifies 'whisper.' The causality implied by the text is confirmed by the handsome male face nuzzling her ear. It is no coincidence that perched on her shoulder is the image of *Nuance* which 'like a whisper, is almost impossible to resist.' The 'delicate' fragrance is made equivalent to the signifying image of 'whisper' and its stimulating effect on the attentive male. As a depiction of gratifying relations between commodity selves, ads draw on already established referent systems of commodity-signs (cf. Goffman, 1976; Williamson, 1978). This ad's visual imagery is an arranged compilation of familiar commodity-signs such as the carefully polished nails, red full lips, hair, ear-rings and eyes that have already been established through advertising for products that define those features of the commodity self.

Targeted at the 'modern woman of 30 who is ambitious and upscale with more than the usual sense of style and self,'[7] *Scoundrel* ads focus on self-assured women initiating romantic interludes. Print ads position a woman in a bare-backed black evening dress standing in a half-opened doorway (presumably her presence addresses an unseen male) while suggestively (to us) holding a red mask behind her derrière. The signifying tagline, 'seize the moment,' gives us license to interpret this as a moment of sexual flirtation, while the perfume is nominated as 'a brave and a beautiful new spirit.' The woman's act and personality apparently originate with the perfume's personality, since 'seizing the moment' is obviously contingent on applying the 'spirit' of *Scoundrel* – she draws strength to take the sexual initiative from the perfume she wears.

COMMODITY-MEDIATED STATUS AND LIFESTYLE

Positioning fragrance by status or lifestyle seems doubly appropriate since ads become luminous appeals to utilize the commodity *as a sign* to communicate the user's relative social position. Long considered luxury items, the association of fragrances with prestige and high status is well established, and perfumes such as *Joy* or *Chanel N° 5* are recognized badges of feminine social respectability and freedom. Perfumes which denote status have 'positional' value. Vested with symbolic attributes of social status, they serve as emblems or badges of rank – a sign currency designating a prestige hierarchy. Though various methods are used to inscribe the appearance of high status on a fragrance, relatively few fragrances positioned as status emblems rely on the advertising format discussed thus far.[8] Instead, most ads for elite market fragrances feature an image of the bottle design along with the name and, perhaps, a framing caption. Designer fragrances concentrate on the product name along with a picture of the bottle design because 'the name carries enormous authority.' These ads merely transfer the meaning systems already associated with *Halston, Calvin Klein* or *Geoffrey Beene* to the fragrances. Other ads rely on the imagery of bottle design to signify luxury, wealth, art and aesthetic sophistication. *Miss Dior*'s bottle as work of art or *Joy de Jean Patou*'s sparkling cut-crystal bottle confirm the preciousness and exclusivity of the product. Another perfume by Jean Patou, *1000*, appeals to exclusivity by invoking the scarcity principle: 'So rare . . . and available to so few . . . each flacon is registered.' Like a signed work of art or a pedigree, this registration permits the consumer to distinguish herself from the mass of other women because the product stands apart from the mass-reproduced commodity (not art). *Lanvin* endorses the same logic: 'Hand painted in gold, fitted with velvet pouf and fringed tassel, and filled with two ounces of incomparable Arpege extract.' *Lanvin* speaks the traditional discourse of 'true luxury,' while *Gucci* ads let the rich golden hue of their bottle's contents address the reader, framed as 'Liquid Assets' or 'There can never be too much elegance in your life.' In these ads the sign currency designating status and prestige draws its force from a currency system of exchange value.

Lifestyle appeals are to the mass market what status appeals have been to elite markets. Non-existent as a product-positioning category in 1970, lifestyle has become the 'hottest' positioning category for consumer goods. It targets a consumer type labelled by industry researchers as '"outer-directed" people who buy things for their "badge value"' (Cook, 1983: D-8).

> The term *lifestyle* best captures the essence of the current version of the ideology of consumerism . . . . It reduces all life to a style, equating how one lives with what one consumes.
>
> (Czitrom, 1982: 190)

Lifestyle research describes the *ensemble* of commodity-mediated activities and appearances, encompassing clothing, hair styles, apartments, cars, furnishings, leisure interests and work activities (cf. Plummer, 1979). When translated back into the universe of advertising, lifestyle is decontextualized and reduced to a set of experiences defined and arranged by consumption of appropriate commodities. Institutionally, advertising aims to redefine collective identities in terms of aggregated individual consumption patterns. The sign-inscribed commodity becomes

> a message in itself. Considered as information it is a means by which the consumer may communicate to others his relationship to a complex set of abstract social attributes – it identifies him or her within the social structure.
>
> (Kline and Leiss, 1978: 19)

Le Sport ads feature a photo collage of a vital, vibrant young woman skiing, beating a beau at tennis and walking along a beach at dawn with her male lover. 'Play with style!' commands the headline, while the text below narrates the relationship between fragrance and a sporty, leisure lifestyle.

Le Sport is more than a fragrance.
It's a way of life. The look.
The feeling. The vitality of the
new sport lifestyle. Day and night,
you play with style.

The commodity is defined as 'a way of life' and now signifies the range of experiences associated with a consumption lifestyle. Commodities promote a way of life grounded in 'the look.' In an epoch characterized by privatism and impersonality, impression management of the *currency of appearances* may, indeed, become a way of life. Corporate organization of the built environment has established 'anonymous public spaces' where individuals display themselves as they 'move through the field of commodities on display' (Featherstone, 1983a: 19). Ads provide a field in which sign values get articulated, but the circulation and valorization of sign values takes place via the continually negotiated exchanges surrounding these displays.

APPELLATION AND PSEUDO-INDIVIDUALITY

When capitalist systems of mass production entered the cultural sphere, the fundamental characteristic of culture became standardization. With standardization, the spectre of conformity threatened the autonomous individual with eclipse (Horkheimer, 1947). Adorno (1941) observed two basic processes in the commodification of culture – part interchangeability and pseudo-individualization. Marketers soon developed an approach of attaching the promise of individuation to the same commodities contributing to standardization.

Pseudo-individuality is the indispensable capitalist complement to part interchangeability . . . . Part interchangeability results from the drive to minimize the cost of production; pseudo-individualization results from the imperative to maximize sales.

(Gendron, 1986: 21)

Pseudo-individualization stems from the market imperative to differentiate the act of consuming multiple versions of essentially the same product. Themes of pseudo-individuality are, as we have seen, blatant in perfume ads. 'All you have to be is you,' commands a *Liz Claiborne* ad that shows us how the space of the fragrance image permits the real 'you' to articulate itself. Ads repeatedly equate commodity images with 'you' to offer a new improved identity: 'It's *More* you' proclaims a More cigarette ad. So many ads address us as 'you' that we may forget we are being drawn into this process of equivalence exchange. Williamson (1978) has, however, demonstrated that the mode of address – how ads appellate or hail the reader – does not require the explicit use of personal pronouns in order to establish an identity between the named commodity, the model appearing in the adjacent photograph and the reader. Reading ads presupposes what Williamson calls 'appellation.' Consumer ads name us through their mode of address, asking us to insert ourselves when the model fits. Seeing a potential 'you' in the mirror of the ad, we are invited to perform a critical interchange of meanings.

In these examples an ideology of pseudo-individuality is overt, but it is an unspoken premise in ads using the mortise in relation to a photographic representation of human subjects. This advertising form metacommunicates two intertwined reading rules: first, the model stands for the desired self of the reader as she/he might be if 'transformed by the product' (Berger, 1972: 134; Williamson, 1978: 60); second, each reader *qua* consumer is an equivalent, homogeneous unit. This principle of *abstract consumption* presupposes an invariant (i.e., a natural) relationship between the standardized unit of the commodity and the homogeneous unit that is the consumer/reader. As a result, one message communicated through the creation of commodity-signs is that regardless of the reader's personal characteristics, consumption of the commodity-sign will exact a uniform effect. 'Pseudo-individualization is prescribed by the standardization of the framework' (Adorno, 1941: 124). Hence the formulaic logic of perfume ads. Personal history and socio-spatial context are ideologically expunged and erased by processes of producing and consuming commodity-signs. But while predicated on abstraction from the concrete consumption of real persons, the commodity-sign is ideologically depicted as the source, even the stimulus, of individuality. This promise of individuality through the consumptive exchange of commodity-signs is rooted in a fundamental deception since the commodity-sign can deliver individuality only through its denial of individuality.

The concept of pseudo-individuality challenges the premise of consumer-goods advertising that an integrated autonomous ego can be realized through commodity consumption. Individuality may be achieved in many ways, some of them, even, by reworking the meanings of commodities – but individuality is either achieved or not achieved in the context of the actual conditions of daily life. Individuality is a social relation, not an object. Commodity-signs are based on preconstituted formulas for individuality which deny the fundamental social nature of personality. To paraphrase Marx, the social character of people's consumption appears as an objective character stamped on the object of consumption.

REIFICATION IS THEIR MOST IMPORTANT PRODUCT

Three theoretical considerations emerge from the thesis that advertisements are a site for producing commodity-signs via readers' participation in completing the signs. First, though ads are ideological, their ideological content is derivative from the process of producing sign values *qua* exchange values. Second, since readers' participation is required in completing the signs, acts of interpretation become fundamentally enmeshed in a political economy of sign value. This means rigid distinctions between the material character of political economy and the ideational features of interpretation must be discarded when analyzing advanced capitalist society. Third, corporate advertisers seek to rationalize and streamline the interpretation process in their interest of maximizing exchange values – which depends on transferring currency back and forth between sign values and exchange values. Advertisers have turned the cognitive practice of reification into a tool for producing value. Given this feature of contemporary mass media, elements of a reified consciousness become embedded and taken for granted in our deepest interpretive vocabularies. And yet, the mode of producing sign values also makes the whole process particularly dependent on readers' participation and, hence, vulnerable to their withholding participation. As a result, readers' social participation in this mode of interpretation must be continually motivated. From the marketers' perspective this motivation is always problematic and must constantly be redefined *ab extra.*

To be sure, there have been a range of consumer responses to the production and valorization of sign values, from overt resistance to less conscious and unorganized patterns of coping. The 1960s' counterculture developed into a minor social movement that was easily reintegrated by the culture industry. More recently, overt resistance has come from several directions. 'Punk style' attempted to subvert the currency of appearances by turning style against itself (Hebdige, 1979). Unlike their hippie predecessors who sought to withdraw from consumerism, punk adherents turned the field of style into one of confrontation by shattering the ensemble of signs and recombining its elements to their own (dis)liking. Feminist critiques of advertising have grown more fashionable. Elsewhere, a rebirth of conservative values has been touched off, in part, by the excesses of advertising extolling the joys of hedonism and sexual permissiveness. Some parents of teenagers have grown so distressed by the sexual come-ons of jeans and toothpaste ads that they refuse to validate the sign values and threaten collectively to boycott certain sponsors.

A less overt middle-class response involves a 'consumer reports' mentality in which the edifice of sign value is subordinated to an interest in the functional quality of products and the rate of use value return per exchange value. More generally, a vague popular skepticism of ads has grown up as advertisers are forced by market imperatives continually to top both themselves and one another. The more advertisers promise in association with their products, the more they strain the credulity of increasingly 'savvy' viewers, who react with postures of indifference and cynicism. Such skepticism frequently amounts to a defensive posture meant to reassure oneself and others that one can see through advertising manipulation and not be affected by it. New media technology has made possible another form of individuated resistance. As cable TV enters a growing number of homes, remote controls make it possible to switch stations rapidly – 'zapping' – and thus bypass ads. Advertisers have expressed anger at this and even threatened to quit supporting 'free' television entertainment.

Embattled on many fronts, advertisers are most concerned about state regulation. Complaints about abuses bred by corporate advertising methods for producing sign values lead to demands that the State intervene and regulate advertising practices. The Federal Trade Commission regulates 'false advertising' and 'unfair or deceptive practices.' It struck down use of 'subliminals' as a method for completing sign values by bypassing the conscious mind, thus ensuring viewers' rights of, at least, nominal consent in completing sign values. Like wage workers who formally agree in the wage contract to the terms of their exploitation (equivalence exchange), consumers must 'freely' enter into the colonization of their 'ways of seeing.' Still, the FTC has so far adhered to narrow, legalistic definitions of deception and done little to threaten the production of sign values based on fetishized codes.

Leaders in the advertising industry were troubled by early 1980s polls showing 52 per cent of respondents felt TV ads were 'seriously misleading,' and 58 per cent found ads uninformative. The industry was stung by consumer criticism of advertising as 1) needlessly adding to the cost of consumer goods, 2) subliminally manipulative in organizing needs, 'creating desires for, and "making" people want "bad" things,' 3) 'too shrill, too pervasive, too all-encompassing and offensive to the consumer's intelligence' ('C-E's O'Connor,' 1980: 47S). These criticisms led to an industry effort to advertise on behalf of advertising as a means of counteracting the public's low opinion of advertising ('ARF's Object,' 1983: 158).

As a political economy of sign values in advanced capitalist society matures, advertisers seek more rationalized methods to increase the efficiency of the sign-value production process. Analogous to rationalizing the labor process in goods production, techniques such as voice-pitch analysis and PRIZM are developed as means of more efficiently managing readers' interpretations as value-producing activities.

Still, the interests of advertisers and marketers do not always coincide with those of their audiences. As a result, production of sign values may become politicized – witness the brief furore over sugared-cereal ads aimed at children, where parents sought legal remedies to prevent advertisers from using state-of-the-art techniques to produce what parents considered 'unhealthy' desires/sign values. Though they lost, there will doubtlessly be other consumers who mobilize in efforts to register an impact on state regulating agencies via court rulings and legislation, thus disrupting a political economy of sign value. The contradictions of a rationalized political economy of sign value based on reification as a production practice are only beginning to flower.

NOTES

1 Baudrillard's argument is 'pitched at so abstract, indeed metaphysical level, that the whole theoretical construct, despite itself, effectively replicates the historical closure that forms the "real" object of its critique' (Wernick, 1984: 20). Abstraction from historical specificity yields a reified model of 'the code.' Even simple moments of unevenness and contradiction thus become obscured: e.g., corporate advertisers *compete* against each other for market shares. They not only build on, and contribute to, an overarching grammar and vocabulary of signs and visual images, they also attempt to subvert each other's sign values.
2 The advertising page is a Gestalt of perceptual organization in which contiguity and juxtaposition establish relations of identity and differentiation within a unitary whole.
3 For example, an *Aramis* in-store promotional effort offered consumers a free umbrella carrying the sign (logo) of the cologne. Such promotions encourage consumers to participate – insofar as they now share an immediate interest in the sign's respectability – in promoting recognition of the logo as a signifier/signified of status.
4 From 1967 to 1976, cosmetic industry sales expanded at an annual rate of 9 per cent, with real unit gains between 5 and 10 per cent during the years women poured into the work-force. But between 1976 and 1984, growth flattened. Cosmetics became a 'maturing' market where profits came primarily from price increases and not unit sales increases – in 1984 unit sales were up by 2 per cent. Industry analysts saw advertising and aggressive marketing as primary vehicles for restoring growth rates. Revlon spent an ad budget in excess of $30 million in 1978 to help garner profits of $125 million on sales of $1.5 billion. The rule of thumb among the industry's corporate giants is spend up to 25 per cent of sales on advertising. 'Yet national advertising is only the tip of the media iceberg. Much more money is poured into stores to push the products. Training the woman behind the counter itself, the promotions being offered every three months, floor models, coop advertising' (Landis, 1981: S-6). As growth rates slowed in the 1970s, the industry edged toward both consolidation and diversification – the strong got stronger and the rest struggled. Inflationary media costs and soaring production costs for ads discouraged smaller firms from increasing their ad budgets, but as corporate giants (Revlon, Avon, Cosmair, Lauder) prevailed in the industry, a chief weapon in the struggle for market shares was advertising and marketing. The industry's rising star in 1985, Cosmair, spent $230 million per year on advertising and promotion.
5 An ad executive explains the positioning shift in *Aviance* perfume ads from the 'hard-driving sexual promise of "You're gonna have an Aviance night" to a "Touch of tenderness": in 1975, it was big news that a woman enjoyed sex. Well, there are other dimensions now. Aviance reflects a more tender relationship' (Landis, 1981: S-4).

6 Baudrillard (1981) sees symbolism based on ambivalence, while signs are rooted in equivalence. A 'passage' occurs from symbolic function to sign function; ambivalence is 'liquidated' via a process he terms 'semiological reduction.' But what does this mean in practice? Verbs like 'abolish' and 'liquidate' make for partial and one-sided analyses, and deny subjectivity. The *Vanderbilt* ads draw on a symbol to create a sign. A swan is photographically depicted floating, serene and beautiful, on moonlit waters. The caption privileges interpretation of the photo as an expression of female splendor and inner beauty. The ad works to transform the meaning of the symbol into a sign linked to the brand name. What is the relation, under these circumstances, between the swan as symbol and the swan as sign? Besides symbolizing beauty, purity and grace, the swan also carries ambiguous and equivocal connotations about gender and sexuality. Transforming the swan as symbol into swan as sign involves appropriating qualities associated with the swan's surface features, while deleting its ambiguous meanings and glossing its duality. Look at the first passage about swans in a reference book on symbols. The meanings the advertiser pulled out in order to establish a sign for the product are highlighted.

> A *milk-white swan floating on the water*, with the ineffably *graceful movements of its neck*, is *one of the most perfect creatures in nature*. Small wonder that *men have associated it with all things lovely, above all with women*. It was regarded as the bird of Venus, the goddess of love, and symbolized *love* and lust. But not only that: this spotlessly white bird could also stand for *chaste and chivalrous love*. That, however, is not the end of the swan's duality. The bird's turbulent aggressiveness suggested something masculine, an idea that found expression in the story in Greek mythology of Zeus visiting and impregnating Leda in the shape of a swan. 'Leda and the swan' became one of the commonest erotic themes in art, with the swan as the male. There is something ambiguous, not to say equivocal, about the swan as erotic symbol. It can represent both sexes, simultaneously at that.
>
> (Achen, 1981: 70-1)

Vanderbilt forms the swan *as sign* by linearizing, streamlining, rationalizing the meaning of the symbolic meaning. This abbreviation is accomplished not simply by condensation, but by making it partial and one-sided. Signs are formed by mimetically appropriating selected aspects of symbolic meaning. Symbols constitute metaphorical accounts of self-contradictory relations and feelings which are not necessarily reconciled. This sign, however, denies equivocality: it *is* rooted in equivalence, excludes non-equivalence, and hence elides the dialectic interplay between equivalence and non-equivalence.

7 Revlon's vice-president in charge of marketing *Scoundrel says*, 'Scoundrel is a woman who is past the aspiration state.' She is *not Charlie!* 'She has reached one level of success and expects to be at another in the near future' (Sloan, 1980: 1).

8 The advertising format that uses a mortise, pictorial image and framing caption is limited primarily to 'mass market' fragrances. In *Vogue's* November 1979 issue, nineteen fragrance ads used a mortise juxtaposed against a picture of a human subject, and all were for products aimed at a mass market. Among the seventeen ads for products aimed at an elite market, none used the mortise and only one depicted a human subject, although six relied on manifest textual statements of reification.

3

THE MORTISE AND THE FRAME
Reification and advertising form

How do advertisements mean to viewers? Advertisements are message systems designed to organize perceptions and 'create structures of meaning' (Williamson, 1978: 12). Advertisers draw sociocultural meanings from viewers' life-worlds and the mass media themselves, and embed these meanings in images which are then returned to viewers – now framed in relation to meanings of products, services or corporate identities. In national brand-name, consumer-goods advertising this process of articulating and correlating meanings is simultaneously (and inseparably) a process of producing and consuming sign values. Meaning is the fundamental and constituent element in all ads: the 'meaning process . . . is the basic process of all ads' (Williamson, 1978: 87; Berger, 1972). Advertisers direct this rudimentary process of 'meaning' toward the 'basic advertising function of linking the product and a quality or idea' (Williamson, 1978: 88).

A primary objective of advertising is to generate brand-name recognition. Thus a fundamental agenda in contemporary consumer-goods advertising is to link a 'positioning concept' to a named product (Ennis, 1982). This entails turning a minimum of two meaning systems in relation to one another. When institutionalized, the process of joining the meanings of named products to 'positioning concepts' builds up an elaborate currency system of sign values. Decades of cigarette advertising, for instance, connected meanings of cigarettes as commodity-objects to meaningfully arranged images of glamour, sophistication, popularity or rugged individuality. By methodically framing the meanings of commodity-objects in terms of social relations, advertisers contribute to a language of images *and* a currency of commodity-signs: e.g., *'The Marlboro Man'* or *'The Virginia Slims Woman.'* Cigarette advertising has so completely reconstituted the social meaning of cigarettes for women around images of feminine allure and elegance, that the American Cancer Society now presents counter-advertising aimed at deconstructing this general commodity-sign as unhealthy. Their ads invite viewers to examine reflexively their own participation in negotiating the commodity-sign construction process that takes place in cigarette ads.[1]

This chapter examines how a widespread advertising format – the *mortise and frame* – operates as a set of encoding practices. Tracing the relationship between these encoding practices and the process of producing commodity signs requires theoretically reconceptualizing advertisements as materially produced social spaces in which meanings are negotiated. Ads are not merely carriers of content about objects; they also comprise frameworks through which a world of objects is translated into a world of social relations. The materiality of the advertising framework as a context permits the transformation of meaning systems (as inputs) into hybrid meanings (outputs). Too often, ads are viewed as frozen, static thoughts (things sent, received, accepted or disposed of), instead of as a processual social space which when entered must be negotiated. Advertisers develop formats like the mortise and frame to maximize a 'preferred' direction of interpretation among audience members, but the nature of mass-mediated negotiations cannot be avoided, and a multiplicity of interpretations cannot be overcome by commodity-motivated discourse.

Although it frequently appears to be otherwise, advertising is not a communication form through which viewers passively receive and consume meanings. Rather, advertising requires viewers' participation in interpreting advertisers' arrangement of meanings. In the twentieth-century United States, interpretation of mass-mediated advertising images has evolved into an act of labor, the performance of which is necessary to produce and valorize both particular commodity-signs and a currency system of sign values. Ads provide a template and a set of instructions for steering construction of commodity-signs (i.e., they stack the deck), but it is the viewer who must complete the meaningful connections.[2] This matter of completing the commodity-sign is of critical importance to the political economy of corporate advertising.

MORTISE-WORK AND THE PRODUCTION OF COMMODITY-SIGN VALUES

The mortise has a long history as a tool and a method. For centuries, carpenters used the mortise and tenon system of joining materials. As a construction technique, the mortise and tenon joint involves cutting a cavity or hole into one piece of timber through which to receive the shaped end of another piece called the tenon (Tarule, 1979). This jointing method required development of specific tools such as the mortise chisel and mortise clamp. Eighteenth- and nineteenth-century mechanics adapted the method for building engines. Centuries earlier, the mortise provided a means of connecting images to church walls: 'Which Image was mortrest in a wall behynd the high altare' (Murray, 1962: 680). Printers devised a similar practice when they cut a hole in a printing plate for the purpose of inserting type. In the twentieth-century United States, advertisers took the printer's use of the mortise and made it a standard device for joining together images and meaning systems. In light of the transition to mechanically reproduced images (Benjamin, 1969), the significance of the mortise in material culture and production has shifted toward a means of facilitating the production and consumption of commodity-sign values.

Defined as a 'cavity, hole or the like, into or through which some other part fits or passes,' the mortise is employed as an element of layout and design in a significant portion of contemporary consumer-goods print advertising. As a transitive verb it means 'to join or fasten securely' (Morris, 1976: 855). In consumer-goods advertising, the mortise conventionally takes the appearance of a hollowed-out box insert containing a picture of a named, packaged product. This boxed insert functions to connect or join the named product to what is presented on the rest of the page (for an example, see Figure 3.1). In this joining and fastening function – the constituting of relationality between parts of the ad – the mortise pre-supposes an underlying set of interpretive rules or codes defining a logic of visual organization. The mortise is an encoding practice that conveys decoding instructions to viewers: as part of the advertisement's formal structure, it is a framing device that guides interpretation of the ad's content.

Mortise-work and the construction of commodity-signs can be sum-marized as follows:

(1) The mortise constitutes a formal device – a framework – used to steer and structure the assembly of meaning within an advertisement. Recog-nition of this framework is not accomplished by reading single ads in isolation, but draws on exposure to a system of advertisements.

(2) The mortise routes the connection and transfer of meanings within an ad. It exists for this purpose. As an element of advertising design, the mortise initiates the appearance of connection between a product as signifier and an image as signified. This makes possible a) a transfer of meaning from image to product; b) an appearance of inter-changeability between the product and the mediated visual imagery, such that either can come to stand for the other; and c) an appearance of a causal relation running from product to the visually signified meaning. In ads, the mortise constitutes a locus for producing commodity-signs: i.e., the joining of product as signified and image as signifier. As a device permitting a language of images to be turned to accommodate a language of value, the mortise literally becomes a 'production tool' in the articulation of sign values.

(3) The mortise-based advertising form steers viewers toward the perform-ance of interpretive procedures that include abstraction, equivalence

Introducing Aviance Night Musk. Put it on... and have an Aviance night.

Figure 3.1 The mortise as a means of encoding commodity fetishism

Source: Aviance Night Musk. Registered trademark of Chesebrough-Pond's Inc.

and reification. The mortise increases the probability these communi-cation-steering principles or *reading rules* will be observed in viewers' efforts to decipher an ad's meaning.

(4) Apart from the manifest ideological content imparted by any given ad's mobilization of a specific 'positioning concept,' contemporary advertising *forms* using the mortise reproduce an ideology and practice of commodity fetishism at a deep level of communicative competence. As a communication structure, the mortise-embedded advertisement makes the 'preferred' interpretation (Hall, 1980) of meaning contingent on using a fetishized code or grammar that requires 'consumers' participation in their own reification' (Herskovitz, 1979: 185).

This chapter looks at print advertising for consumer goods in mass-market magazines from 1979 to 1985, but the same technique is also found in television advertising, where it supplements a range of video editing practices. In television ads, the mortise appears most frequently in the concluding scene where it tends to be identical in construction to the structural layout of print ads.

FRAMING APPEARANCES

Advertisements employ *framing* techniques and devices as a means of guiding meaningful interpretations of images within the ad. As 'messages intended to order or organize the perception of the viewer,' frames permit the inclusion of certain messages and relations while excluding others (Bateson, 1972: 187). Frames constitute 'principles of selection, emphasis, and presentation' that organize the social construction of reality (Gitlin, 1980: 6). Frames and framing devices provide *coding instructions* about how to interpret an ad's organization of meaning.

The mechanical reproduction of photography has become such second nature to us that we forget photos are simulations; we become habitually unable to dissociate the meanings of objects represented from the meanings of their images. Though photographs carry the impression of depicting and reproducing reality, the photographic image is inherently abstracted from spatio-temporal relations. Advertisers work to reconnect images – abstracted or separated from original contexts – within a new context, itself shaped through the arrangement of other framing devices. In detaching images from contexts and resituating them within the context of an advertisement, advertisers modify or change the meanings of images. 'In the age of pictorial reproduction the meaning of [images] is no longer attached to them; their meaning becomes transmittable . . . an image will be used for many different purposes and the reproduced image, unlike an original work, can lend itself to them all' (Berger, 1972: 24–5). The meaning of every photo is framed. And every advertisement is an exercise in framing meaning. The fate of art in the age of mechanical reproduction appears in a *Charles Jourdan* ad (Figure 3.2) that isolates an image from Michelangelo's painting in the Sistine Chapel. This ad presumes that viewers have long since learned the framing codes of ads. The scene juxtaposes signifiers from dramatically different cultural worlds. A woman's smooth white legs wearing red high heel pumps stick out, oddly distorted, from behind the photographic reproduction of a cracked fresco painting of a nude male adolescent. Completing the image, a female hand with red nails curls around the male back. Because the two pictorial meaning systems are so disparate, viewers react by trying to place each referent system in their minds. The heavily abstracted feminine signifiers are easy – they signify sexual desire and female pleasure. But what about the meaning of the artistic 'reproduction'? When 'reproduction isolates a detail of a painting from the whole,' the meaning of 'the detail is transformed' (Berger, 1972: 25). Here, an image of an Ignudi – 'the Genii of the Soul' – has been ripped from the context of Michelangelo's spiritual vision in the Sistine Chapel. Some viewers can locate the source of the image, but for most it now signifies 'classical art' and the 'classic' image of the ideal male body. Viewers draw out this meaning because the image now appears in the *context* of an upscale shoe ad, in the arms of signifiers of female sexual attraction and desire.

Over the years, the mass media have evolved a visual language system based on the principle of isolating and then recombining images as signifiers and signifieds. This language system is in a continuous state of flux, driven by market interests and calculations. Professional image makers borrow from the well of past meanings to make and remake signifying images, producing 'semiological chains' in which significations drawn from daily life are instrumentally reduced to 'mere signifiers' in mass-mediated images, which are themselves, in turn, mined as signifiers for subsequent signifying images. The result is a 'staggered system of connotation' in which a derived and processed language of images, though at least a step removed from the language of daily life, nonetheless addresses viewers as a language 'in which' to speak about daily life (Barthes, 1972: 114–15). Of immediate sociological interest is the fact that viewers are *not* inclined to perceive this state of affairs as unusual or problematic.

As the fundamental unit of this 'second-order' language, the photographic image necessarily removes what is depicted from its context. The photograph is a frozen moment that 'isolates the appearances of a disconnected instant.' The inherent discontinuity of photographs

> always produces ambiguity. Yet often this ambiguity is not obvious, for as soon as photographs are used with words, they produce together an effect of certainty . . . . In the relation between a photograph and words, the photograph begs for an interpretation, and the words

Figure 3.2 Charles Jourdan
Source: *New York Times Magazine*, 7 March 1982

usually supply it. The photograph, irrefutable as evidence but weak in meaning, is given a meaning by the words. And the words, which by themselves remain at the level of generalization, are given specific authenticity by the irrefutability of the photograph.

(Berger and Mohr, 1982: 91–2)

Advertisements supply a context within which to restore the continuity of an image's meaning. But this restoration of meaning also changes it, since the image, itself an abstracted moment from history, biography or nature, is meaningfully reconstituted outside the life-world it purports to represent.

The meaning of an image is thus modified according to what meaning system is made contiguous to it. Advertisers have adopted the mortise and frame format to steer this process because using mortise, frames and captions (words) with photographs is a relatively efficient method of motivating interpretation of photographic images. The mortise mediates a relationship of mutual definition between words and photographic images, supplying the possibility of interpretive closure where it might not otherwise exist.

In advertising, both the choice of image and what is placed adjacent to it are dictated by the calculus of markets. Corporate profit has become the predominant motive influencing the production of meaning systems. In the twentieth-century United States the center of cultural construction

67

processes has gradually passed from the organic relations of daily life to an institutional apparatus organized by corporate capital. This institutional apparatus does not make culture per se, but channels and translates existing cultural forms into commodity format. To accomplish this, mechanisms are established to monitor and reflect the prevailing meanings and values held by carefully charted demographic segments of the population. Marketing functionaries use survey research methods to isolate salient meanings from the context of daily life and then stylistically rework those meanings to accommodate the sales agenda. Likewise, the collectively articulated symbols and sentiments of subcultures and social movements are *rerouted* into discourses linked to commodity consumption. A conspicuous example of this is *Virginia Slims* appropriation of the women's movement with 'You've come a long way, baby,' but the corporate rerouting of meaningful discourses is prominent in ads for fast food, soft drinks, beer, telephone carriers, greeting cards, chewing tobacco, bread, film and blue jeans.

As culture became industrialized (Enzensberger, 1974) and transformed into an array of products and services dispensed through markets as commodities, the signifying practices bound to social experience in daily life have themselves been converted into *raw materials* for corporately produced forms of culture. Corporate employees 'continually appropriate, dismantle and reassemble' (Brenkman, 1979: 105) the meaningful experiences of consumers into stylized discourses which, through the apparatus of the mass media, are then returned to the very audience of viewers that enacted the original signifying practices. 'Ads create an "alreadyness" of "facts" about ourselves as individuals' (Williamson, 1978: 42). Advertisers mine the cultural lives of demographically segmented audiences for meanings to associate with their products, and then rearrange those meanings through the framework of the advertisement, thereby positioning viewers to complete commodity-signs as if there were a natural, intrinsic association between the viewer's own meaning systems and the corporate products.

Early in the twentieth century, 'national advertisements constituted a new and bewildering code, a set of verbal and visual signs for which the referents were unclear' (Lears, 1983: 21). As frequency of exposure mushroomed, the underlying advertising codes become familiar, taken for granted and unproblematic. Since the 1920s, advertisers have incrementally streamlined their coding practices. Since the bulk of the population soon recognized an ad as such, ads became briefer and the codes abbreviated and contracted. Meanwhile, advertisers' practice of detaching visual and verbal signifiers from lived, organic contexts blurs the relationship between the material referent systems of daily life and this 'second-order' language constructed in the mass media. Splitting the unity of signifier and signified, advertising has built up a coding system, the form and content of which has grown progressively self-referential. Lefebvre (1971: 112) describes this process of substituting a self-referential language of reproduced images for the material referents of daily life as 'the decline of referentials.'[3]

THE MORTISE IN ADS

As a method of layout juxtaposition of photographic image and named product, the mortise 'metacommunicates' commands to viewers about how to interpret the transfers of meaning within the ad (Herskovitz, 1979: 182). As an advertising format, the mortise carries formulaic coding rules and instructions governing the spatial, sequential and thematic relationships between the various elements of an advertisement. Viewers' recognition of the mortise is a cumulating process in which prior acquaintance with its conventions provides the ground on which each successive generation of interpretations is made.

Although the mortise may be distinguished from other advertising formats used for consumer goods, it shares similar structural elements and, hence, similar 'reading rules.' The most striking structural similarity involves framing devices that spatially arrange relations between the ad's parts. The most obvious framing device is the literal frame – the use of visual borders – to differentiate parts of the ad from one another, while simultaneously providing a means of connecting the meaningful elements thus separated. Captions and headlines comprise another standard framing device used to define and select out what an advertiser considers the relevant thematic plane on which to interpret the photographic representation. Captions organize the relation between photographic representation and named product. From the advertiser's overly formalist vantage point, the reading of an ad is essentially *the reading of frames* arranged in relation to one another.

An example of a typical, straightforward mortise layout appears in the *Charlie* perfume ad (see Figure 1.1 on p. 28). Structurally, the dominant portion of the ad page consists of a photographically reproduced image in close proximity to the product name. Adjacent to the photographic image and mediating the product name is a verbal framing device – e.g., 'the gorgeous, sexy-young fragrance.' Captions or taglines select out a particular positioning concept chosen to market the product. Captions *privilege* a way of seeing these photographic representations, while excluding other possible meaningful interpretations. In this format, captions may work in both directions; they invoke double meanings, as they define both image and named product. Captions thus perform the function of *equivalence exchange*: making comparable otherwise incommensurate meanings. Another primary feature of the format is a bordered, rectangular cut-out space in the ad page. Placed inside this mortise is a photographic image of the product container.

By 1980, the mortise had become a taken-for-granted element in advertising layout. This had the effect of naturalizing the underlying operation of its code.

> The operation of naturalized codes reveals not the transparency and 'naturalness' of language but the depth, the habituation and the near-universality of the codes in use. They produce apparently 'natural' recognitions. This has the (ideological) effect of concealing the practices of coding which are present.
>
> (Hall, 1980: 132)

At the same time, pervasive use of the mortise became self-defeating for advertisers who vie to differentiate their ads and their products from those of competitors. As a result, variations in the layout have developed, each of which deepens and confirms the interpretive conventions entailed in the basic format. Advertisers can reverse the relationship between subject and object, with a mortise surrounding the subject's image while the product image occupies the rest of the page. Such reversals confirm the more general coding principle that the mortise sets up an axis of relational identity between subject and object. Viewer familiarity with format conventions permits advertisers to elide the actual graphic border around the product, allowing the photographic representation of the named product to carry its own implicit mortise. When the coding principle of the mortise becomes naturalized, non-box shapes may be substituted. Finally, photographic representations of both product image and signified subject may be collapsed into one simultaneous photographic space or superimposed over one another (e.g., *Polo*, see Figure 3.4). In such ads, the package as frame is made interchangeable with the (social) space within which its sign analogue is found. This technique may be reversed, as in a *Le Parfum* ad that places a mortise in the shape of an inverted male shadow around a smaller, conventional mortise containing the product package. A young woman lies prone on her back, gently touching her breast, absorbed in a reverie of sensuality. Standing above her is a male shadow apparently caused by a male 'intruder.' Across the shadow, and immediately beneath the conventional mortise the caption reads: 'An intrusion. Subtle, Sensuous. Surrender to Charles Blair.' Here, the mortise appears as the potential actor that casts its shadow because it contains the sign of *Le Parfum*. Act and product become one with the mortise. The woman's position is framed by her 'surrender' to the power of the 'intrusion,' *Le Parfum*-mediated masculinity. Thus we see the shape of the mortise can have both coding and ideological significance.

THE MORTISE AS A SET OF SPATIAL SIGNIFYING RELATIONS

The fundamental work accomplished within an advertising space is the connection and exchange of meanings between an object (a named product) and an image (another referent system). The form of an advertisement enables advertisers to translate 'the language of objects to that of people, and vice-versa' (Williamson, 1978: 12). The mortise is the 'motor' or catalyst of an advertising format developed to permit the efficient exchange and correlation of meanings. Again, the basic format consists of 1) the mortise; 2) a signifying photographic image of human subjects and/or metaphoric representations of subjects and/or feelings; 3) framing captions, headline and copy. This advertising format provides a 'meta-structure where meaning is not just "decoded" within one structure, but transferred to create another' (Williamson, 1978: 43).

What does the mortise 'do'? First, the borders of the mortise – its frame – separate and differentiate the product's packaged image from visual and verbal representations rendered on the remainder of the page. Second, the mortise cavity cutting through the plane of the page connects and associates the meaning of the product image to the selling idea as represented by a graphic image. Although the mortise invites the performance of what appear to be opposing interpretive moves, these are unified elements of a larger pattern of decoding. The caption is then directed toward the harmonious reconciliation and unification of the differentiated parts within the whole of the advertisement.

The mortise in the advertising format permits the joining of meanings separately constituted. The framework establishes formally equivalent spaces which the advertiser fills with content: in one space goes the image of a specific named product; the other space is filled with an image designed to evoke a particular positioning concept.

The relations established within this ad format may also be analyzed by analogy to linguistic grammar. This ad format consists of an axis of combination, i.e., the relationship between the product cavity (mortise) and the graphic signifying image; and an axis of selection, i.e., the caption or copy which uses words to draw attention to what is relevant (what is signified by the referent system). This advertising format structures the axis of combination as a

> Succession of equivalent spaces in which independent and immediately available meanings are free to interact with each other, unconstrained by the subordinating and distinguishing logic of syntax and discourse. Sequence is no longer casual but additive; it no longer processes a meaning but provides an arena in which meanings separately constituted are displayed and equated.
>
> (Fish, 1982: 189)

71

The axis of selection designates the positioning or selling concept. While the axis of combination necessarily differentiates the product image from the graphic image so that an exchange or transfer of meaning can take place, the axis of selection establishes an appearance of identity between the otherwise incommensurate meaning systems: 'the principle of equivalence [is projected] from the axis of selection into the axis of combination' (Jakobson, 1961: 358).

DECODING MORTISE-WORK

An ad for *Devin* (Figure 3.3) illustrates the mortise's operation as a meta-communication device. A men's cologne produced by Estee Lauder, *Devin* is targeted at a 'less urban-oriented individual than is *Aramis,* the city-life fragrance.' Inset on the upper two-thirds of the page is a squared frame with a narrow white border enclosing a photographic image. Set against a background of a sunlit field of tall, golden grass, a handsome young man sits with one booted leg propped over the back of a parked jeep. Across the vehicle's front seat stands a companion bird dog. Metallic gold in color, the vehicle is open, has no doors and is reminiscent of a safari vehicle. The man's hair is slightly tousled and his face is a portrait of satisfaction and contentment. His grinning gaze connotes affluence, a refined, comfortable sensibility and self-confidence. The caption beneath the picture reads: 'Devin. The Country fragrance for men. Rich. Relaxed. Fresh and Unhurried. From Aramis.' Situated immediately beneath the frame of the photo, the caption draws attention to three thematic elements in the photo: country living; wealth; relaxation. Pictured below both photo and caption is a yellow-gold bottle of Devin Country Cologne and the name *DEVIN*.

To the analytic observer there exists a puzzling ambiguity in this account. Is it country fragrance or is it the man that is rich, relaxed and unhurried? Surely these descriptive terms refer to the man. Is this not a picture of a man who possesses the wealth and refined sensibilities truly to relax in his leisure? Are these not qualities that refer to human subjects rather than objects? Yet, these descriptions are followed by the statement, 'From Aramis.' It must be that these descriptions were meant for Devin cologne. This should be confusing to most readers, but it tends to be unproblematic. Why? Because the ad builds around the mortise as a framing device, the very form of which provides a set of background assumptions that serve as an interpretive signpost to the ad's content. The presence of the mortise instructs viewers to: 1) recognize a relationship between the product's meaning and the signifying image's meaning; 2) differentiate the product and signifying image as parts of a larger whole. Pictures of the man and the cologne are visually arranged so viewers might assume the man wears the cologne.

Devin. The country fragrance for men. Rich. Relaxed. Fresh and unhurried. From Aramis.

DEVIN

Figure 3.3 Devin

Source: *Vogue*, November 1979

The presence of the cologne bottle as an insert permits an association to be made between the cologne and the imagery of a relaxed, self-satisfied, affluent man. A trained reader is able to take this association further by recognizing that the caption is meant to describe both the product and the abstracted referent system. The reader's acceptance of the advertising form makes unproblematic the caption's meaning, for the trained reader is able to read the caption by moving back and forth between the dual images on the page. Once this text has been deciphered, the association becomes one of equivalence. The apparent ambiguity of the verbal description dissolves when it is understood that man and cologne represent equivalent units of the same qualities. However, this impression of equivalence gives way when it is understood that the man represents what it is like to wear the cologne; the signified state of being – satisfaction, relaxation, affluence – is imparted by the cologne. Where the ad began by introducing the signifying imagery of a man relaxing in a sunlit field to give meaning to the product, it ends by implying that the product bears those qualities and is a conduit to achieving those qualities. Using an insert image of the cologne in combination with the framing caption and signifying photograph steers readers to utilize the cognitive practices of abstraction, equivalency and reification simultaneously as a means of deciphering the ad's meaning.

Examine the structural arrangement of meaning in the *Polo* ad (Figure 3.4). A photographic enlargement of an emerald green cologne bottle dominates the advertising page. Immanent within the frame of the bottle is a photo-realist representation of men on horseback as they play the sport of polo. Atop the container's frame, in glowing golden contrast to the green, is the bottle's crowning cap. The figure of the bottle and cap resembles an abstract outline of a male head and shoulders. The cap itself resembles a visored helmet. To the left of the neck where the golden crown joins the bottled frozen scene of a polo player in action is this sequence: 'Polo'/ symbolic image (trademark) of a mounted polo player/ 'Ralph Lauren.' On the right side of the neck-joint reads the phrase: 'A man's cologne in the Polo tradition.'

These captions define a relationship between the meaning systems of the cologne and polo as a male sport. Verbs are noticeably absent in each caption. Nevertheless, viewers are capable of making interpretations, because *the verb is contained in the structure of the layout.* The ad is set up to facilitate a series of equations through the doubling of meanings. To visualize how this works, survey the following overly mechanistic and linear map (see Figure 3.5). The term 'Polo' (1) on the left names both the activity depicted in the photograph (4) and the cologne bottle; in turn, (4) confirms (1). The trademark/symbol (2) exhibits a mimetic identity to (4) as it signifies the referential system of polo. 'Ralph Lauren' (3) ties together the semantic sequence (1/2/3); this sequence names both the cologne bottle by reference to the cap (5) and the framed scene contained below;

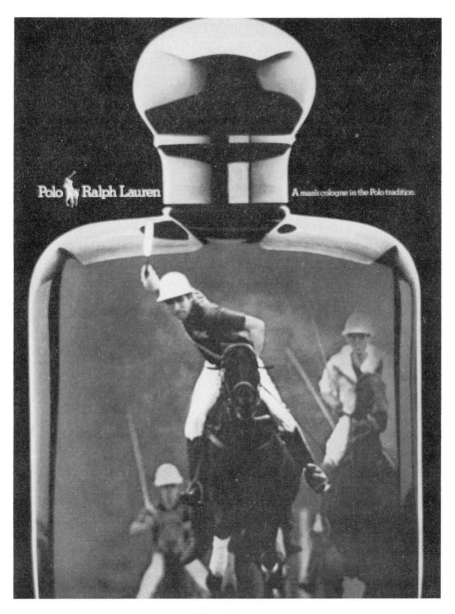

Figure 3.4 Polo

Source: *Vogue*, December 1985

situated at the joint of these two parts, the sequence (1/2/3) equates the parts even as it unites them. The doubling of meaning also generates ambiguity. The phrase 'A man's cologne in the Polo tradition' (6) amplifies the ambiguity as a means of reinforcing the identities already established. The first portion of the phrase 'a man's cologne' (6a) refers to both (5) and (1/2/3). 'In the Polo tradition' (6b) refers to both (1/2/3) and (4). This phrase on the right is made sensible by reading it as if there was an equal sign or verb running vertically between the crown and the scene inside the bottle's borders. Another equal sign/verb is made tacitly present by the horizontal line of the neck – since we read from left to right, the phrase on the right functions as a subtext for the bolder phrase to the left. Thus, a privileged reading would be 'Polo' (a man's cologne/this bottle entity) *made by* 'Ralph Lauren' *is* 'in the Polo tradition.' The words abstract from the photographic representation of a man playing polo to the universal condition of masculinity as mediated by this cologne.

To what does the 'Polo tradition' refer now? Is it the tradition of an upper-class sport played by wealthy horsemen? Or is it the tradition of Ralph Lauren's trademarked line of products? In the process of appropriating the meaning of polo as a referent system to create a meaningful sign for the product entity, the advertiser has blurred the direction of signification. Though resolved in the advertising text, the confusion generated by splitting the unity of signifier and signified has spilled over into the legal system. In order to defend and protect the self-referentiality generated by the marketing/advertising agenda of constructing sign values, Ralph Lauren filed suit against the US Polo Association for infringing upon his ownership of the mounted polo player as symbol and trademark. Lauren appropriated the referential system of polo to stand for his products, and was then compelled by the logic of the political economy of commodity-signs to seek to legally delimit use of the sign by those who gave it meaning in the life-world ('Lawsuits Filed' 1984).

An elaborated variation on the mortise is used with *Ciao* perfume (Figure 3.6). In the mass media, the term 'Ciao' has been associated with a young, hip, affluent, jet-setting lifestyle. The term has become a fetishized marker, a trendy 'in' way of closing conversations. This ad draws upon this currency as a means of evoking a glamorous, glittery way of life. Every element in the ad aims at augmenting and reinforcing this set of meanings.

Although the ad's message may be likened to a complex puzzle, the average reader deciphers the surface meanings of the message within seconds. This ad is an exercise in structured redundancy. The primary pictorial image in the ad spotlights a smiling, attractive young woman, her head turned to face the viewer. She is being nuzzled by a young man whose face is caught in profile and partially hidden from the viewer. Her face appears bright, a bluish-white that stands out in contrast to the gray skin tones of her male companion. This depiction of her expressive counten-

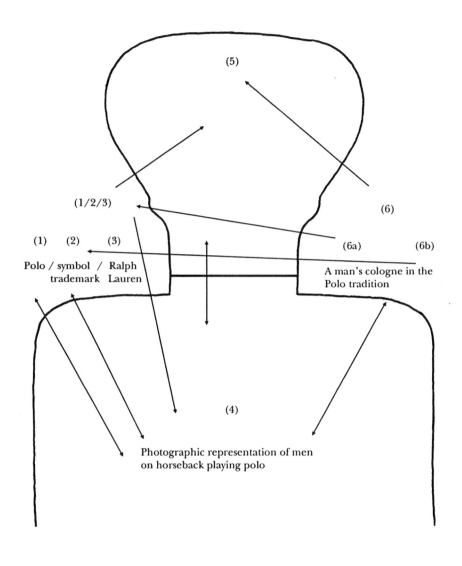

(5)

(1/2/3)

(6)

(1)   (2)   (3)

Polo / symbol / Ralph
trademark   Lauren

(6a)

(6b)

A man's cologne in the
Polo tradition

(4)

Photographic representation of men
on horseback playing polo

Figure 3.5 Polo ad drawn as a semiotic flow chart

CIAO
L'élégance de Paris
The vitality of New York
La dolce vita di Roma

Ciao Parfum, made and bottled in France by L'International Houbigant

Figure 3.6 Ciao

Source: Vogue, October 1981

ance is an attempt to reconstitute and capture her aura photographically, as the aura established by the perfume. Across his black jacket appears the name 'CIAO' underlined by a bold pink band. Immediately beneath this appellation is the caption:

> L'élégance de Paris
> The vitality of New York
> La dolce vita di Roma

The international flavor of the referents confirms the jet-setting connotation of the perfume's name. This image apparently designates a lifestyle encompassing Parisian elegance, New York vitality and Italian love-making.

Immediately to the right of the caption and directly in front of the woman is an elaborated mortise system. Standing in front of her aura the perfume bottle exudes a bright golden glow. Adjacent to it is a glass-encased picture frame which mirrors the scene above – capturing and echoing all the images seen in the ad. Caught in this photographic mirror is the reverse image of the model's joyful countenance, a reverse image of the perfume bottle and a triple superimposition of the appellation 'CIAO' (not reversed) designating the framed image. The pink and silver-coloured strands wrapped around the picture frame bind and connect the definition of this scene to the brand name.

The mirror integrates the three redundant meaning systems contained in the ad into a unitary meaning system framed as an ecstatic moment to remember and a reflection of our own possible futures. The ad equates this framed photographic reminder with the pleasurable moment of consumption and a lifestyle it purportedly represents. In defining the named object, *Ciao*, the ad actually describes a desired social relationship through the prism of the commodity form. In medieval literature the mirror was a metaphor for transformation via the transposition of images. The *Ciao* ad mirror *qua* mortise provides a method of reinforcing and intensifying the unity of commodity and sign. The mirror remains a metaphor for personal transformation, this time grounded in the articulation and consumption of commodity-signs.

PREFERRED AND NON-PREFERRED INTERPRETATIONS

More than any other mass media form, ads are shaped to accomplish 'preferred' interpretations. Advertisers employ rationalized formats to delimit fields of possible meanings, privileging certain interpretations over others. Ad formats consist of framing procedures which select out (and, hence, exclude as well) ways of seeing. Hall theoretically situates the hegemonic dimension of 'preferred' or 'dominant' meanings.

We say dominant, not determined, because it is always possible to order, classify, assign and decode an event within more than one 'mapping'. But we say 'dominant' because there exists a pattern of 'preferred meanings'; and these both have the institutional/ political/ideological order imprinted in them and have themselves become institutionalized. The domains of 'preferred meanings' have the whole social order embedded in them as a set of meanings, practices and beliefs: the everyday knowledge of social structures, of 'how things work for all practical purposes in this culture', the rank order of power and interest and the structure of legitimations, limits and sanctions . . . . Since these mappings are 'structured in domin-ance' but not closed, the communicative process consists not in the unproblematic assignment of every visual item to its given position within a set of prearranged codes, but of *performative* rules – rules of competence and use, of logics-in-use – which seek actively to *enforce* or *prefer* one semantic domain over another and rule items into and out of their appropriate meaning-sets.

(Hall, 1980: 134)

However, advertisers have *not* abolished non-preferred meanings or mis-interpretations. Try as they might, advertisers have been unable to produce 'perfectly transparent communications' (Hall, 1980: 136) which guarantee mirrored decodings. Furthermore, viewers tend to be neither static nor unmotivated in their encounters with advertisements. As noted earlier, every advertising message carries both a command about how to interpret the message and a level of content. The command portion of the message 'positions the receiver to adopt a particular attitude towards the report' (Herskovitz, 1979: 182). Herein lies the rub, for viewers do not merely decode content, they also react to being positioned. As viewers accumulate experiences of interpreting ads they develop 'vocabularies of motive' (Mills, 1967: 439ff) with which they negotiate the way ads address them.

Non-preferred interpretations are the result of many forces. Despite their efforts at monitoring audience perceptions and values, advertisers do make errors and not all are of equal competence. Encoding miscalculations occur – e.g., unintended ambiguities, unclear referents, poor execution of graphics, layout, design composition. In one 1980s fiasco, *Tab*'s campaign slogan 'Let's Taste' sounded like 'Less taste' to viewers. A 1986 *Kent* cigar-ette campaign elicited non-preferred meanings because it pushed the formulaic framework too far. The tagline 'The experience you seek. Kent' was superimposed, along with a picture of the Kent package, over a picture of two figures flying a kite on a grassy beach. The advertiser sought to appellate the viewer as efficiently as possible by literally inviting the viewer to step into the scene – by photographically emptying the figures of content so that they appeared as translucent, blue silhouetted outlines. But viewers

80

interpreted the image and the tagline in terms of background knowledge about the health risks of smoking. After all, in the context of a cigarette ad, the silhouetted figures connoted ghosts and the experience we seek with cigarettes seemed to suggest death rather than leisure relaxation.

Advertisers also, obviously, compete with one another, sometimes disrupting or discrediting the efforts of competitors to establish preferred interpretations. Other factors that generate non-preferred meanings lie on the decoding side. Undersocialized viewers have not fully acquired competency in deciphering codes and/or coding rules. Today, oversocialized viewers present greater problems: a) 'savvy' viewers operate as skeptics; b) bored viewers respond to the formulaic predictability of ads by sarcastically misreading (here, viewers supply 'creativity' to their interpretive project and thereby restore it as a leisure activity). Closely related is the willful misinterpretation that grows out of diffuse anger toward advertising per se, resentment at repeatedly being positioned, or specific disaffection for a particular product, firm or spokesperson. Finally, 'globally contrary' (Hall, 1980: 137) reinterpretation is practiced by those who supply an alternative theoretical framework within which to situate their decodings.

GRIST FOR THE POLICY MILL

Ads are messages motivated and structured by the aims of commerce. Advertisers seek to enhance brand recognition to facilitate additional product sales. To achieve this, they 'position' the meaning of their product to *differentiate* it from competitor products. Advertisers compete at mobilizing 'positioning concepts' that give products distinctive images and, hence, distinctive meanings.

In this market-motivated scenario, advertising 'is about social relations, not objects' (Berger, 1972: 132). Though advertisers may seek the sale of objects, they accomplish this by situating the meaningfulness of objects in terms of meaningful images of social relations. As Williamson (1978: 13) observes, when advertisements structure interchanges of meaning, they are really 'selling us ourselves.' Advertisers organize photography, narrative text and viewers' knowledge of a sociocultural life-world to *frame* stylized accounts of 'desirable' social relations. Establishing correlations between stylized social appearances and meanings of named commodities generates a currency of appearances. Ideally, an advertiser seeks to make the positioning concept and the commodity 'interchangeable as signifier/ signified' (Williamson, 1978: 31).

Recall that 'the meaning of an image is changed according to what one sees immediately beside it or what comes after it' (Berger, 1972: 29). Advertising may be conceived as a mechanized institutional form for rerouting the meanings of images. The mortise provides one practical structural method of regulating and steering the *relationality* between different meaning systems introduced within an advertisement. The mortise is a tool for articulating sign value: it positions viewers to superimpose a world of object relations over a world of social relations.

We have seen how ads draw upon already existent meaning systems: these are called 'referent systems' and they 'provide ads with [their] basic "meaning" material – a grist of significance for the ad mill' (Williamson, 1978: 19). Most analytic observers permit their gaze to be fixated on the surface content of these messages, and thereby ignore how the advertising form itself gives ideological substance to the discourses it organizes. The form is 'devoid of meaning, except in so far as meaning is constantly *assumed* through the form of its perpetual translation' (Williamson, 1978: 43). Advertisers decontextualize (or abstract) meaningful social relations from their actual locations in social formations, and then recontextualize images representing those meanings in the social space provided by the advertising form and the commodity form.

The process of disconnecting and reconnecting images and meaning systems is inescapably loaded with ideological consequences. 'A photograph isolates the appearances of a disconnected instant.' In removing an appearance from its mooring in a life-world, the photograph introduces an ambiguity of meaning – 'the abyss between the moment recorded and the moment of looking' (Berger and Mohr, 1982: 89). The advertiser's job is then to reframe, and thereby redefine, the meaning of a disconnected appearance in relation to their sponsor's product. This act of intervention, which advertisers call 'positioning,' invariably implicates advertisers in one ideological mapping or another.

This inherently ideological project gets compounded when we take into account how ads address viewers. The mode of address generally conceals the two-step dance performed by advertisers: the rupture of contextual continuity as a prelude to its reframing. At the most basic level, viewers expect to find meaning 'in every act of looking' at photographs in ads (Berger and Mohr, 1982: 117). Conversely, viewers do not look for ruptured meanings. Instead, the presence of verbal captions encourages interpretation as if the advertising form were a natural context. This mode of address legitimates an interpretive stance grounded in the suspension of rules of contextuality: a presupposition of 'abstract consumption' involves looking at relations between named products and product-mediated characteristics as potentially uniform, and not contingent on the position and attributes of individual consumers.

We have discovered that 'mortise' is a transitive verb. Transitive verbs express an action from the subject to the object, requiring a direct object to complete the subject's meaning. Within the world of the advertising page, the mortise functions as a transitive verb, but its grammatical function is inverted. As a tool for connecting, correlating and exchanging meanings, the mortise expresses an action that is carried from an object to a subject: it gives expression to fetishized social relations as if they naturally exist.

This argument about how ads get 'read' bears on questions of policy because it concerns what constitutes false and/or misleading advertising. The Federal Trade Commission's regulatory stance stands as an archaic reminder of an earlier historical epoch when commodities were presented as possessing straightforward use values and exchange values. Accordingly, an ad is deemed false or misleading if it can be shown to misrepresent calculatedly either the use/function of a good or service or the cost of said product. This standard deals solely with the evaluation of the surface content of advertising messages.

Structural changes in marketing and advertising practices have made this regulatory stance anachronistic. Advertising now anchors a sphere of political economy rooted in producing and consuming sign values. Today, relatively few national brand, consumer-goods ads remark on the cost of the commodity in question. Equally few detail the functional use of a product minus the interweaving of sign values. Appeals based on cost or function are, today, largely due to the advertising gambit of counter-positioning in a marketplace saturated by positioning according to image. Within this political economy of sign value the *form* of contemporary print ads systematically inverts relations between subject (the person as consumer) and object (the commodity).

These reified accounts represent a fundamental falsification of the relationship between human beings and the world of objects they name, and upon which they act. Nevertheless, the FTC does not address the *form* of advertisements in their calculus of what constitutes false and misleading advertising. By limiting themselves to a mechanical, legalistic review of surface content, the FTC assists in maintaining the hegemony of corporate interests: preventing questions about tacit ideological agenda-setting in ads from being posed; and sanctifying the daily articulation of a commercial grammar of reification as innocent and natural. It is hardly innocent: the advertising apparatus ceaselessly transforms our meaning systems as well as our desires into commodities, with vast sociocultural repercussions beyond whether or not an immediate sale is realized.

Where is this advertising/marketing apparatus located within the historical development of capitalist social relations? The mass-mediated encoding procedures and the feedback loop of market research that form the spine of contemporary advertising and marketing are geared to expanding surplus value by means of the internal colonization of meaning systems. The apparatus itself is an advanced capitalist institution that grounds the extension of the commodity form in the internal colonization of discourse and desire. At present, the realization of sign exchange-values is predicated on this colonization of our *culture*. Quaint distinctions between symbolic interaction and labor have thereby been shattered in practice in advanced capitalist society. The logic of capital has historically transformed the sphere of symbolic interaction into one more sphere of commodity production and circulation.

NOTES

1 The concepts of 'deconstruction' and 'semiotics' have been made unnecessarily difficult by the mystifications of French intellectual discourse. By 'deconstruct' I literally mean to take apart analytically that which has been put together – what has been socially constructed can be de-composed. This aspect of deconstruction is ruthlessly empirical. Adorno and Barthes held that any cultural artifact – be it a football game, an astrology column, an advertisement, etc. – could be *deciphered* like a text. A second prong to deconstruction derives from both structural semiotics and the logic of negation in dialectical theory (Marcuse, 1960). All meaning is built on *difference*.

2 This analogy between interpreting meanings in ads and the relations of commodity production should not blind us to a major difference: interpretation does become a form of value-producing labor but it is *not* wage labor. Interpretation of meaning in ads is a form of labor performed voluntarily (sometimes involuntarily as habitual reaction) in a time and space socially designated as consumption and leisure.

3 Reconstituting meanings within the framework of media logic involves viewers in a staggered system of referentials. A television ad for *Apple* computers compares the IIc to *IBM*'s PC Jr. After the announcer compares features of the computers, he asks, 'Now. Which would you rather take home?' and the curved end of a cane reaches out to select the *Apple IIc*. In depicting the cane, the advertiser's immediate referent is to *IBM*'s advertising use of Charlie Chaplin's image. The *IBM* ads, of course, drew Chaplin's image from the referent system of films such as *Modern Times*. The *IBM* campaign accomplished a 'semiological reduction' which ideologically reverses Chaplin's own emphasis on the relation between alienated labor and mechanization (Papson, 1990). Given the successive layerings of connotative meaning established via the mass media, when viewers decoded the *Apple IIc* ad, 'Charlie Chaplin' had been reduced in the form of the cane to a denotative meaning. The *Apple IIc* depiction of the cane was intended to subvert, via another ironic reversal, the correlation of meanings established in the *IBM* campaign between the cane and their products. In the *Apple IIc* ad, even the *IBM* sign (the cane) is made to signify the claimed superiority of the *Apple IIc*.

4

LEGITIMATION ADS

The story of the family and how it saved capitalism from itself

Expanded sales and control of market shares are not the only agendas at stake in corporate advertising. Corporations also seek popular legitimacy by joining cherished values and social relations to their corporate images. Corporate ads present the virtues of 'consumer freedom' as synonymous with 'democracy.' Advertisers seek to bolster corporate legitimacy by linking their images to institutions that represent the social ideal – say, the family. When ads *reframe* and *position* our meaningful relations and discourses to accommodate the meaning of their corporate interests, then, advertising intervenes as a potent political institution in mediating meanings of freedom, individuality, work and leisure, community and family life.

> If the connection between the product and the 'objective correlative' person or thing is made by us and in us, it is also made *with* us, in that we become one of the things exchanged (given the status of an object) .... [T]here are two axes along which the product '*means*': there is the process of its gaining meaning, in a transaction we make between signifiers (Catherine Deneuve and scent bottle, car and cigarettes); and now it appears to have a second replacement value: it replaces, hence signifies *us*.
>
> (Williamson, 1978: 45)

What happens when it is not a product that is made to mean, but the corporate name itself – when corporate deities hail us, then replace us, and signify our most valued relationships?

Whether their agenda is accumulation or legitimation, ads are never ideologically impartial. Treating meaningful activities as raw materials to be *re-worked* into signs in the interest of maximizing commodity sales inherently locates advertisers in the field of ideology. As we've seen, ads register an ideological impact by virtue of their framework or form. Implicit, but rarely acknowledged in consumer-goods ads, is the relationship between production and consumption. Ads tacitly presume the existence of wage labor, money as the reward for its performance and money as the necessary currency for purchasing the commodities on display. When they conceal commodity production, ads also hide class differences between people, substituting aesthetic distinctions publicized through the consumption of goods (Williamson, 1978: 13). And, virtually all consumer-goods ads champion patterns of corporate administration over daily life by presenting commodity consumption as an unproblematic, natural and rational way of meeting needs. Ads thus endorse the commodification of daily life as the means of attaining 'privatized utopias' without the messiness of political struggle (Gitlin, 1981a; Ewen, 1976).

Since the rise of modern advertising, however, these hegemonic representations have never fully sufficed. Advertising designed to reinforce corporate legitimacy started with *AT&T*'s pioneering efforts in 'institutional advertising.' Amid a climate of growing public mistrust of privately owned monopolies in 1908, *AT&T* initiated a campaign to represent themselves as a beneficent national monopoly. Advertising as a means of 'selling the system' grew more pervasive in the 1920s, as the nascent corporate advertising industry sought to deflect class consciousness among workers through the construction of a new political ideology of consumerism (Ewen, 1976: 51–9).

Modern corporations require a stable 'environment of confidence' (Barnouw, 1978: 83) in which to pursue their primary goal of capital accumulation. Yet, throughout the 1970s, pollsters charted a decline of public confidence in American corporations, dropping from 70 per cent to 15 per cent (White, 1978: 16). A diminishing faith in the nation's economic future aggravated a widespread perception of large corporations as greedy and unconcerned with the public good, placing many corporations on the defensive. Some corporate leaders perceived a general social malaise – a crisis of confidence – that corresponded to an erosion of modern social institutions and moral codes. This view of a 'moral crisis in American capitalism' (Wuthnow, 1982) surfaced in an *Ethan Allen* print ad titled 'What Ever Happened to "Home Sweet Home"?'

> The never-ending stream of news stories about divorce, drugs, rape, juvenile delinquency, murder, and muggings has us aroused. You, too, must be deeply concerned about the impact of all this on our children and about the erosion of the wholesome values and attitudes that have made us a great country. For generations, these values and attitudes were learned at home. Old-fashioned ideals like 'courage, honesty, respect for hard work, patience, love and regard for family and others' were taught by loving parents in the home and passed down for generations. Our homes . . . the fiber that holds our society together . . . are in dire jeopardy because we've become such a fast-moving high-tech society, losing touch with our families and

human values. The growing number of broken homes today and the traumatic impact on the children in those homes should shock us into action . . . yet we see countless people taking neither the time nor effort to keep their homes together.

This campaign was motivated by a concern to 'express our belief in the vital need to reaffirm and reinforce the importance of home for our families.'[1] Such appeals were calculated to secure a positive public image and build future credibility for the corporate firm. Advertisers' exhortation and cheerleading on behalf of 'the classical family of Western nostalgia' (Goode, 1970: 6) was organized to combat a perceived crisis of legitimacy and to boost sales by tapping into shared (and manufactured) ideals of what family life *ought* to be like.

This is *legitimation advertising*. Legitimation ads are an outgrowth of the culture industry's mass marketing of wish-fulfillments within a societal system fundamentally antagonistic to their realization. Ads concerning familial relations tap into a pool of unfulfilled desires and aspirations, channeling fulfillment of these desires through cultural commodities. On the other hand, these ads represent calculated attempts to restore confidence in corporate institutions while countering the erosion of 'old values,' 'social stability' and 'private moral standards' (White, 1978: 18).

Ironically, the decline of traditional values, disintegration of community life and unraveling of family life are by-products of corporate capitalist development. After World War II, the extension of corporately organized commodity relations (from shopping malls to nursing homes) cut away from the family's functions in social reproduction and 'freed individuals to pursue more individualized life courses,' while simultaneously contributing to an isolated family unit 'divided against itself.' State intervention into family activities (e.g., mandatory schooling; legislation defining parental treatment of children) 'provided external supports for the family' at the same time that it 'regulated its internal structure.'

> [T]he family increasingly became a way-station in a maze of more impersonal relationships. Family members passed through this domestic station, accumulating emotional and psychological sustenance from it, but using it ultimately as a staging area for a personal life geared to school, work, and consumption. Tragically, the nuclear family has sought the emotional and personal development that was its ideal at the expense of wider emotional and social satisfaction and growing dependence on the essential support of capital and the state.
>
> (Busacca and Ryan, 1982: 89–90)

As the State and corporate capital hollowed out the family's reproduction functions, the nuclear family turned into a center for emotional life isolated from the wider social bonds and supports of extra-familial settings.

Yet, 'we still cling to the "family" as a surrogate for "tradition" and make it an ideological totem' (Busacca and Ryan, 1982: 80). Corporate ads offer to solve crises of family life by resurrecting the traditional ideal of family life as an 'ideological totem,' while continuing to advocate the family be made into an *access* institution to the market. Of course, this latter arrangement has historically undermined the idealized domestic arrangements being mythologized.

TURNING PALEOSYMBOLIC MOMENTS INTO SIGNS

Corporate ads present our most valued social relations as emanating from the products and companies being advertised. Where the product is implied as the source of the relation, an ideology of commodity reification obscures the always contextual quality of human interaction, substituting for this reality the appearance of relations as the formulaic outcome of the interaction of objects that possess exchange and sign value. Where corporations situate themselves as defenders of treasured relations an ideology of corporate capitalist legitimacy is set forth. In practice, commodity reification and corporate legitimacy often intersect in ads. For example, in *General Electric*'s 'We bring good things to life' campaign, social relations appear to circulate about *GE* products. *GE* positions itself in gratifying relations of daily life, and edges viewers toward an interpretive stance of reification. Products bestow an aura of active agency on those who come near, and social relations take place among product-mediated actors. *GE* 'brings' optimistic familial relations into the lives of those who inhabit the *GE* world, the name '*GE*' representing both a corporate totality and specific products. Thus, *GE*, the corporate presence, takes credit for compassionate and fulfilling personal relations in the lives of people like us. As social alchemist, *GE* reduces those relations to the status of frozen auras – while concealing the actual relationships that create such auras. *GE* pictures its products giving substance to what is otherwise absent from the home – family life. In this way the 'family' is preserved as a consumption unit, and the institution defended, but only on terms that benefit *GE*.

Corporate advertisers turn photographic imagery of happy and wholesome familial relations into commodity-signs. An image of virtuous home life is detached from the total context of family relations and annexed to products so the image appears realizable through purchase and consumption of toothpaste, video games, electric appliances or soft drinks. The signified – having harmonious, loving family relations – has been separated from the actual relations within which they must necessarily take place and transformed into discrete images. If a *Hallmark* campaign is effective, when we think of greeting cards we think of secure and affectionate relations with our significant others, and images of these relations become associated with *Hallmark*.

In producing the commodity-sign, the sign's referent is itself transformed into a commodity. Commodity-signs convey the premise that consumption of a product carries with it access to what the sign represents. Marketers and advertisers thus translate the appearance of social relations of freedom, individuality, status, friendship and family life into commodity format. Just as cologne ads assert that feelings of independence can be gained ready-made by slapping on a cologne, ads for hamburgers suggest that experiences of fulfilling family life may be acquired upon entering the world of fastfood restaurants. Packaging social relations as commodities lies at the heart of marketplace competition today.[2]

Remember that detaching images from contexts and resituating them within the context of an advertisement permits advertisers to modify and redirect the meanings of images by how they arrange framing devices. Ad campaigns for *Bell Telephone, Pepsi, Coke, McDonald's, GE, Rainbow Bread, Luv's, Kodak* and *Taster's Choice* abstract emotionally significant moments and reframe them in relation to their product. 'What we're really doing is selling emotion,' says the advertising art director for *Bell Telephone*'s 'Reach Out and Touch Someone' campaign (Arlen, 1980: 98). Vignette-like scenes simulate moments from viewers' own lives as a means of evoking empathetic responses from viewers. These scenes stimulate a positive recollection that can be associated with a gratifying feeling-state. Affect-laden scenic understandings and the positive feelings they evoke are then connected to the commodity by means of framing devices. Hence, a complex commodity-sign is produced in which a *paleosymbolic scene* of an affect-drenched social relationship becomes the sign.

> On the sociological level, the paleosymbolic is part of the shared, ordinary . . . languages of daily life learned during primary socialization as children. The paleosymbolic, therefore, is powerfully associated with 'significant others' . . . . The language learned thus also becomes linked with images of such significant others, and with their relationship to the learner. The paleosymbolic level thus implicates central persons, nuclear social relations, and the affectively laden gratifications and securities associated with them.
>
> (Gouldner, 1982: 225)

Advertisers appropriate the abstracted details of private scenes and then reassemble them into filmed replicas as a means of tapping positive emotional valences among a target audience. Using vignette scenes in advertising steers the private, subjective forms of discourse encapsulated in paleosymbolic scenes toward the service of corporate ideological interests. Gouldner (1982: 224) described the paleosymbolic as 'a set of beliefs and symbols of restricted communicability . . . to be spoken in private settings, among those previously known to one another,' and thus distinguished from the necessarily 'public language' that constitutes ideology. This may have been true in earlier stages of liberal-democratic capitalist society, but mass-mediated culture and corporate image ads have collapsed the private language of paleosymbolism into the public language of ideology. This public language is, however, no longer constituted by actual public discourses, but as a serially connected collection of discourses about private life that have been decontextualized from social experiences and recontextualized in terms of commodities (Brenkman, 1979: 105–9). Ideological justifications covering the interests of corporate capital tap into the 'extra-rational support' elicited by the language of paleosymbolism. Advertisers attempt to orchestrate these sources of subjective, extrarational support to expand sales of products and foster images of corporate benevolence and legitimacy.

Corporate advertisers tap into viewers' memories of subjectively significant and gratifying experiences. Paleosymbolic scenes in TV ads are typified in a *Kodak* ad about a pregnant woman's relationship with her husband. An attractive young woman late in her pregnancy is shown picking and smelling flowers in a garden. A detached female voice, supposedly her own, narrates this vignette: 'I don't know who was more thrilled at having our first baby, Tommy or I?' This is paired with close-up shots of Tommy carefully watching her with proud affection. When she becomes momentarily weary, wispy and withdrawn (signified by placing her right hand lightly against her abdomen), she sinks into a lawn chair. Again she narrates: 'But when I'd get a little down, he'd be right there by my side.' The camera now reveals Tommy kneeling beside her.

Tommy: 'Know something?'
She: 'What?' she responds softly with eyes cast downward.
Tommy: 'You've never looked more beautiful,' he gushes.

She turns her face to give him a tender, affectionate look as if to say 'you're so sweet.' She moves forward in the chair, places her hand on his cheek and gently kisses him. This poignant, emotionally appealing scene is supplanted on screen by a frozen image of her sniffing a flower as she reclines amidst the background of a sunny, story-book yard. She quietly 'glows.' *Kodak* places the frame of a mortise around her image and a male voiceover invites the viewer: 'Shouldn't you trust your story to *Kodak* film? America's Storyteller.' A quick cut later the mortise containing her portrait contains instead an image of *Kodak* film, thus permitting *Kodak* to link itself to the dramatized intimate relation and the 'affectively laden gratifications and securities associated with it.' With the insertion of *Kodak*'s slogan, this 'biographical' (manufactured) memory and the photograph that evokes its recall are made to stand for viewers' own relations and memories. This narrative separates relations of intimacy and companionship from the structuring conditions of daily life in which they must take place, and resituates them within a context provided by the commodity and its corporate sign. While these scenes describe genuine personal affectivity, the implied message to potential consumers is that similar authentic relations are abstractly reproducible through the commodity.

An ideology of pseudo-individualism is embedded when joining such scenic frames to a commodity. *Hallmark* ad campaigns featuring vignettes about husband–wife, mother–daughter, grandmother–grandchild relations are smothered in this ideological process. Each story about a personal relationship steers viewers toward an understanding of *Hallmark* cards as vehicles for the private expression of affection and intimate feelings. In another husband–wife vignette the housewife surprises her doctor/husband with a birthday card expressing her love for him. Accompanying the decisive scene where the exchange of tender feelings is accomplished, a disembodied female voice (supposedly the housewife's) sings:

> So I'm giving you this *Hallmark*
> and hope that you will see
> what I'm really giving you
> is a part of me.

But no sooner has this statement of personal intent been uttered than a male announcer smoothly intervenes to counsel, 'This birthday give a little of yourself. Give a *Hallmark*.' His imperative tone, modifying the first-person declarations of song and scene, tell us that a lesson to be drawn from this ad is applicable to our own relations: it is appropriate and gratifying for you to demonstrate your affection for significant others through purchase and presentation of a commodity.

Paleosymbolic scenes in TV ads illustrate the intersection between a logic of reification, formation of commodity-signs, an ideology of pseudo-individualism and a corporate agenda for personal life. Paleosymbolic scenes are framed to yield commodity-signs in which the corporate logo assumes the role of protecting and nurturing our personal relations. These ads appropriate moments from our lives, taking our own best characteristics and selling them back to us in idealized fashion as promises. Dramatized photographic representations of moments from our lives are presented on the premise that they resemble experiences we might have if we become consumers. Exploitation of this emotional currency rests on abstracting salient social relations and emotions from actual interactions between people who possess biographical histories, and reframing them in the context of a corporate logic: 'Shouldn't you trust your story to *Kodak*'; '. . . give a little of yourself, give a *Hallmark*'; 'Times like these are made for *Taster's Choice.*'

A detailed interrogation of two *McDonald's* ads illustrates the thesis presented thus far: the institution of the family is defended as a means to another end, the legitimation of corporate capital.

91

McDONALD'S 'HISTORY OF THE FAMILY'

The first half of this 1978 *McDonald's* ad tells the 'history' of the American family. Sepia-tinted still photographs are edited together to establish a sense of historical chronology. Combined with contextualizing lyrics, the sepia tinting manufactures an artificial tradition of historical meaning. Counterfeit historical meaning is created by packaging static images of events ripped out of organic, historical context. Linking otherwise discontinuous photographic images as an apparently chronological series of events, this *McDonald's* ad exemplifies historiography in the 'society of the spectacle.' Several decades ago Henri Lefebvre observed that

> publicity acquires the significance of an ideology, the ideology of trade, and it replaces what was once philosophy, ethics, religion, and aesthetics.

(1971: 107)

Now we can add history to the list. By abstracting and separating photographic records of unspecified actors and actions from their lived, organic context, these photographs become signifiers in search of a signified. And the new unity of signifier and signified is imposed by *McDonald's*, which has selected the value of family integrity and stability as the signified.

The ad begins by scanning across a drawing of Pilgrim-like figures. This camera movement is repeated with the following photographs: a pioneer family standing in front of a covered wagon; sturdy farm laborers (a woman and two men) standing in a plains hayfield; a late nineteenth-century middle-class family portrait (parents and five children); a group of children on Flag Day circa 1900; and two scenes of southern and eastern European immigrant families. Drawing on an already existent – albeit simplistic – referent system of 'American history' (pilgrims, pioneers, farmers and immigrants), each photograph has been selected for its appearance and mood of authenticity and age. The photos' sepia texture encourages a sense of these images as an authentic recording of an earlier epoch. The arrangement of photographs and lyrics functions as a set of instructions guiding interpretation, positioning viewers to see these otherwise isolated and decontextualized images as a chronologically continuous and coherent sequence of events.

Coupled with cues about chronology, careful attention to details of dress (e.g., suspenders, shoes, pants) and milieu in the next scene situates it near the beginning of the twentieth century. But, unlike the preceding images, this scene of youth playing leap frog is presented in film format and is obviously a manufactured replica. Why does the advertiser risk contradicting and annulling the appearance of authenticity cultivated via the selection of 'real' photos? While the transition to film introduces potentially discrepant interpretive procedures, it is undertaken to create a bridge between the imagery of recorded history and a theme of 'living history.' To minimize the discrepancy and accentuate the theme of continuity the advertiser maintains a strong sepia overtone to the action film. The film gradually brightens as the ad progresses in its movement toward modernity, but remains dominated by browns and then reds. The ad also briefly oscillates between 'original' photographs and the filmed depictions of the transition to modernity. The first film sequence is immediately followed by another original photo of five black women – standing proud, erect and independent – with two children. This photo, in turn, gives way to the ad's most elaborate scenic reproduction: a mock-up of 'G. Watson & Son' family grocery store circa 1920. No detail has been spared: a period car is parked in front, a sign on the window reads 'Fruits & Vegetables: Farm to you,' and produce is arranged on open sidewalk stands. A young boy in knickers runs past. Watson beckons him back and tosses him an apple. The next scene shows three middle-aged women exchanging warm greetings at a family reunion in the 1930s, followed by a scene of a young woman holding a child as she welcomes home her soldier/husband at World War II's close. Lyrics and images have been integrated to spell out the relationship between the family and America's development as a nation-state.

> You, you're the one.
> So loving, strong, and patient.
> Families like yours
> made all the states a nation.
> Our families are our past,
> our future and our pride.
> Whatever roots we come from,
> we're growing side by side.

This version of history presents the family as the major force in the development of US society. This resembles a 'New Right' ideology of the nuclear family fostering the strength and love that make for a free and democratic society. As Jimmy Stewart said in his mini-address before the 1980 Republican Convention, the family is 'the core of the country . . . that's where it all begins.'

The ad's narrative appellates viewers, 'You, you're the one': this is 'your' family and 'our' history. The pronouns are not only inclusive, they become the means of joining *McDonald's* with US history; joining *McDonald's* with us – sharing our interests. The lyrics picture the family in terms of the melting-pot ideology – tolerance, diversity, pluralism and consensus. Synchronized to the first scene of an immigrant family at a railing preparing to disembark from a ship is the lyric 'families like . . . ' Although the lyric is completed by 'yours,' the image has shifted to a more prominent white middle-class family. While promoting its manifestly non-racist imagery of the melting pot, *McDonald's* latently identifies 'your' family as white and middle class.

Still, as a nation, we are really one big happy family – 'Whatever roots we come from, we're growing side by side.' Apparently speaking for all of us, *McDonald's* not only makes itself 'our' historian, it also implicates itself in its narrative of history. This is accomplished via a process of pronoun substitution, as the lyrics move from 'you' the subject to 'your' family to 'our' nation-state and history, until we = *McDonald's* + us (subject, family, state).

The stress is on continuity – the families that contributed to American ascendancy within the modern world-system were no different from our families. Responding to uncertainty about declining US influence and power throughout the world and the 'traditional' nuclear family in functional disarray, *McDonald's* propounds the counter-thesis that national integrity and the strength of the family as an institution remain, as ever, tied together. But *McDonald's* history of the family conceals 'all evidence of the upheaval and displacement in capitalism's transition from small businesses to multinational conglomerates' (Madison Social Text Group, 1979: 179). Because this excludes conflicts and contradictions to which family life has been exposed with the rise of corporate capitalism, it conveniently denies the ways in which capitalist development has imperiled existing forms of family life even as it has burdened the family with providing privatized emotional support. *McDonald's* nostalgic evocation of personal relations associated with the family-owned grocery store obscures the fact that such relations were negated by the development of corporate capitalism.

The ad's second part consists of nine tightly packaged (2–3 seconds each) *scenes* of contemporary families in ideal-typical form. In contrast to the prior sequence, these scenes appear contemporary and timeless. Chronology evaporates following the scene at the end of World War II: the entire history of *McDonald's* in post-war America appears as if cut from a single piece of cultural fabric. Sequencing this series of scenes in relation to the preceding narrative of family history, *McDonald's* superimposes its mythology of the past over the present. These scenes display the following social relations: 1) a mom, dad, brother and sister playfully pillow fight and wrestle on the bed on Sunday morning (the Sunday cartoons lie open on the bed); 2) a brother and sister in baseball uniforms walk home through a park; 3) a pregnant woman and husband stroll in a park-like setting; 4) a black father and young son share a warm embrace; 5) a modern middle-class portrait of a closely knit mother, father and two daughters in front of their home; 6) an elderly black couple rock on the porch as she peels apples and he playfully teases her; 7) a Chicano family – mom, dad, daughter and grandmother – collectively beam as they walk from church where they've celebrated the child's first communion; 8) an elderly couple celebrate an anniversary as they toast each other and blow out the candles

94

on a cake; 9) an attractive all-American couple stand together as the father lifts their infant child over his head.

Each scene frames the meaning of the nuclear family, addressing experiences that correspond to genuine needs in the family life cycle: expecting a child, having children, parents and children sharing affection, growing old together. These scenes uniformly locate the experience of harmonious familial relations in a context of leisure and home. Synchronized to the flow of the lyrics, the meaning of these framed photos seems immediately apparent.

> You, you're the one.
> You moms and dads and brothers, sisters and sons.
> We're stronger for each other.
> A family is a feeling that *together* is *more fun*.
> Looking out for one another
> That's the way our families run.

The family is defined as an *affective state*. These lyrics depict the family as a support group, a source of nourishment and security, and the means of securing commitment, stability and continuity. When the modern middle-class family portrait fuses with the lyric, 'A family is a feeling . . .,' the mock-up family photo places all members in physical contiguity, thus signifying the packed ('together') family unit as the natural site for intimacy and trust.[3]

Viewers are steered to presume that each scene in the sequence stands for the universal concept of 'the family.' Each scene is structured around the mobilization of paleosymbols.

> Paleosymbols are tied to particular scenes charged with drama and emotion. The paleosymbol does not provide or integrate holistic constructs such as the cross, the hammer and sickle, or aesthetic images that crystallize a wealth of meaning and significance; rather the paleosymbolic requires a whole scene where a positive or negative situation occurs.
>
> (Kellner, 1979: 16)

Manipulating paleosymbolic content in these scenes is designed to trigger *positive emotional valences*. McDonald's ad turns our subjectivity into their sign by connecting the affect generated by these paleosymbolic scenes with an ideological portrait of *the* American nuclear family that has already been converted into a second-order signifier of *McDonald's*.

How do paleosymbols, and the memories they spark, merchandise an ideological defense of the 'American way of life'? An appealing scene in the *McDonald's* ad centers on two children walking along a tree-shaded path through a sunlit park. The camera positions us so the children are seen

95

from behind as they move away from us. A small girl scurries to catch up with a slightly older and bigger brother. They are dressed in oversized baseball uniforms bearing the insignia 'Tigers' across the back, and they wear baseball caps with the bill turned backwards. The younger child half carries, half drags a bat almost as tall as she, while a catcher's mask is draped over her other arm. She is coded as adorable and idolizing of her brother. As she runs to catch up, her brother halts momentarily, turns to face her and waits impatiently but obligingly with his baseball glove perched on his hip. When she reaches him, she grabs hold of his shirt-tail, and still trailing him they start again down the path (away from the viewer and presumably toward home). The scene's visual structure is situated by keying it to the rhythmic strains of 'You, you're the one. You moms and dads and brothers, *sisters and sons*. We're stronger for each other.' The scene, which lasts less than three seconds, proposes an idealized vision of childhood that prompts viewers to compare their own experiences with this memorable image. The scene's structure invites viewers to interpret the ad in terms of the past (nostalgia) and the future (how you would like to see your children).

This type of scene can elicit an empathetic recollection of similar experiences. Warm feelings tapped by this scenic image spark a remembrance immediately appropriated by *McDonald's*, thereby cementing the emotional valence (and the meanings it triggers for any given viewer) to themselves and a broader notion of well-being. Advertisers consider the formulaic construction of such paleosymbolic scenes an efficient means of selling. A noted advertising strategist describes the technique:

> The total amount of information imprinted or coded within our brains is huge, and the associations that can be generated by *evoked recall* are very deep. Information available for recall includes everything we have experienced, whether we consciously remember it or not. The total body of stored material is always with us, and it surrounds and absorbs each new learning experience. Furthermore, it is instantly recallable when cued by the appropriate stimulus.
>
> (Schwartz, 1979: 325)

In *McDonald's* ad, post-war American society is a world of harmony and pluralism where stability, security and happiness are rooted in the American family. There is no tension and apparently no divorce in the world of the *McDonald's* family. Everyone smiles and nobody works. The family, it seems, consists only of affective relations conducted in the absence of all mediating relations – with the exception of *McDonald's*.

McDonald's affirms its faith in the strength and importance of the family as an institution by associating itself with the ideal American family they have decorated. This is confirmed by the yellow *McDonald's* frame that encloses the final photographic representation of the ideal-typical American family at the ad's end. An image of a radiant young couple holding their infant child is suddenly surrounded by the *McDonald's* frame, making it literally a picture in the family album – the *McDonald's* family album. *McDonald's* logo (the yellow-arched M) appears beneath the picture along with the slogan 'We do it all for you.' This frames the positive emotional valence as the experience of family life *brought to you by McDonald's* presence in our lives: 'We do it all for you.'

McDONALD'S REVISITED

Another *McDonald's* television ad (1982) celebrated the meaning of continuity in American life by presenting *McDonald's* story of family and community in contemporary urban America. An ideal-typical family has returned to Dad's 'Hometown' so he can show them the world he knew as a child. His memory hunting takes place in the family station-wagon Dad drives. With son and daughter in the back seat and Mom in the front, they cruise the old neighborhood streets. Anticipating his big moment, Dad informs the family his old house is 'just up the street here.' But a soprano voice in the background (functioning as *McDonald's* muse) warns that 'things have changed a bit since you've been around.' And, sure enough, the old homestead has been replaced by condominium apartments. From the back seat the son innocently inquires, 'What floor did you live on, Dad?' Disappointment washes across Dad's face as he realizes 'It's not there any more.' But he quickly reassures both himself and the family as he announces, 'Well, wait a minute. I'll show you where my old friend Shorty lived. Wait till you see the flower garden in the front yard. It was just . . . ' Dad's excited account of what once was ends abruptly as we discover his old friend's house is now a carwash. 'I don't believe it,' Dad sighs and the music sags. Now the daughter has had enough of Dad's fruitless search for his past, and from the back seat she asserts her needs, 'Dad, I hope that the place where you used to eat is still there, 'cause it's late and I'm hungry.' Without a word, Dad immediately responds by looking for his old eating haunt. Mom casts a faintly empathetic glance in Dad's direction, then turns her head toward the window and quietly looks away. Searching for the as-yet-unnamed eating place, Dad drives while *McDonald's* singing voice soothes, 'In the night, the welcome sight of an old friend.' Suddenly Dad's eyes widen, he breaks into a satisfied smile and points, 'There it is.' The camera cuts to their car pulling into *McDonald's* parking lot and the muse soothingly frames the experience, 'Feels so right here tonight at *McDonald's* again.'

This small dramatic sequence subtly unfolds a set of meaningful relations. The child expresses a want that conflicts with her father's desire to locate his 'roots.' However, the father responds by dutifully deferring/abandoning his wants and acting to meet hers. Mom reacts to the conflict-

97

tinged interaction in silence: she mediates conflict between other family members through silence. Her action acknowledges pre-eminence of the child's need *vis-à-vis* the father's while mutely expressing momentary sympathy for the necessity of Dad's parental sacrifice. This conflict is, however, fully resolved through consumption activities. Dad lights up when he spies *McDonald's*, and when the family enters *McDonald's* restaurant area in the next scene, they are all cheerful and aglow. Everyone's needs are satisfied at *McDonald's*.

The family is pictured in this scene as the 'symbolization of the family's social structure.'

> Turning to mocked-up families in advertisements, one finds that the allocation of at least one girl and at least one boy ensures that a symbolization of the full set of interfamily relations can be effected.
>
> (Goffman, 1976: 37)

As this portrait of the middle-class nuclear family nears the counter Dad explains to the countergirl (and to us) the personal significance of the occasion. 'I (uh) had my first Big Mac here,' he gestures. The countergirl – young, cute and effusive – asks, 'May I get you another one?' 'All around,' replies Dad, as the singer draws out the last phrase of the previous lyric – 'again' – to cover (and meaningfully situate for viewers) the salience of this interaction. Nothing changes at *McDonald's*, it's like being home again. A quick cut turns our attention to a close-up of a bespectacled man's face. Something across the room catches his eye. Surprise and disbelief register on his face. Rising from his table, he wonders aloud, 'Curly?' The camera pulls back to show him approaching the family's table, where Dad is animatedly recounting a story about growing up. As the man nears the table Dad interrupts his story, turning his head to see who it is. Dad does a double take, then stands to meet the smaller man, and peering intently at the man he ventures in a quizzical voice, 'Shorty?' ['Is that you?']. The question confirms what we have already suspected, and Shorty opens his arms and affirmatively exclaims, 'Curly!' The old friends laugh delightedly, reunited in a joyful embrace punctuated by the lyrics, 'To *McDonald's*, tonight at *McDonald's*.' An image of *McDonald's* golden arches seen through the window, immediately adjacent to the image of old friends embracing, frames the feelings of reunion as being available at *McDonald's*, derivative of *McDonald's* presence.

The final scene is a close-up of son and daughter, literally set within a yellow *McDonald's* frame, across which is written the slogan, 'You deserve a break today.' Having absorbed the reunion scene, the girl leans toward her brother and inquires with suggestive irony, 'Curly?' Her brother responds with a passive shrug and roll of the eyes. As a joke about their father's balding condition, this sequence is premised on schisms in generational experiences. The generational distinction is amplified by the structure of this scene. For the first time in this ad the children are presented in their relationship to each other as siblings. And, situated between and in front of their faces is the only prominent display of a hamburger in the ad. The children neither share in, nor care about, their father's reunion. Their needs are more immediate, and what connects them together is that *McDonald's* hamburger sitting between them. *McDonald's* curiously acknowledges here that the family unit they have idealized is actually bound together by serialized consumption relations. Or, to put it in advertisers' terms, this family is composed of market segments. Sound marketing strategy dictates that *McDonald's* offer each market segment – parents and children – an appealing incentive for coming to *McDonald's*. But to actualize this strategy, *McDonald's* end up tacitly subverting their claim that *family* is defined by the rich and empathetic sharing of common experiences.

What is being sold here? The viewer knows – and is presumed to know by the advertiser – because of prior acquaintance with *McDonald's* that fast food service is being sold. Yet there is only one mention of a 'Big Mac' (and that, to connote the idea of *McDonald's* as an old friend), and only one conspicuous visual display of a hamburger (deployed to anchor another social relation between the children). In fact, this ad is a sustained attempt *to sell social relations*. In a world characterized by instability, upheaval and the impoverishment of conditions favorable to primary social relations, *McDonald's* depicts itself as a 'haven in a heartless world.' Against the backdrop of commercial urban upheaval, *McDonald's* endures, there to repair the splits in our lives. *Angst* prompted by the absence of stable communities and friends is supposedly healed by *McDonald's*. *McDonald's* is the 'old friend' that remains, solid and reliable, to soothe our wounds and bring us together with 'lost' friends. Although the moment and need the ad taps are authentic, the resolution it provides is false.

Is *McDonald's* really a countervailing force against privatized rootlessness and continual social and geographic separation from family and significant others? In fact, the injury they claim to heal is fostered by corporate capitalist institutions that exhibit a greater concern for maintaining internal labor market requirements and corporate balance sheets than for the well-being of local communities (Bluestone and Harrison, 1982). In the late 1970s, one out of four persons in the working population was fired, laid off or transferred every year. When they compel constant geographic mobility that is antithetical to forming stable networks of friends, relatives and neighbors, labor market practices promote social instability and fragmentation in individuals' lives.[4] Thus

the expectation that one will live in a stable neighborhood with a stable group of friends becomes increasingly unrealistic. Plans are made, futures are decided, and identities and relationships are established on the narrowest of social bases. Nothing else can be counted on.

(Smith, 1981: 282)

McDonald's seizes upon anxieties stimulated by separation and isolation, and implies these can be annulled and overcome through consumption of *McDonald's* as a commodity-sign (*McDonald's* = community of kinship and friends). This ideological resolution is possible only by separating consumption relations from production relations. This fiction is compounded when considered in the light of ads' unspoken premise – that a product and its sign are available in exchange for a monetary equivalent. And how is that monetary equivalent obtained? – for the vast majority of the population it is gained through the sale of labor.

McDonald's offers a resolution consisting of commodifying family and community. When they assert that dissolution of family and community can be countered through consumption at *McDonald's*, the experience of a convivial family life is transformed into a ready-made sign. For this to be so, the fiction must be established that experiences of family life are the same across all family units. *McDonald's* resolution to the crisis of personal life is only possible if the family is abstracted from the complex contextual features of daily life. And the only place where that is possible is in the *McDonald's* ad.

IDEOLOGICAL IMAGES OF FAMILY LIFE

Corporate ads offer ideological justification and support for the sanctity of family life. Ideologically, these ads validate 'the family.' Images of a universal family form mask the multiplicity of kin groups based on social class, ethnic, racial or lifestyle affiliations. Where blacks, Chicanos or working-class whites appear in the homage to the American family, they are typically shown in white, middle-class family suits. Another *McDonald's* ad featuring the black family as the building block for black community illustrates how stereotypical cues about black culture are used to construct an image of the virtuous black family that, upon reflection, is impossible to differentiate from the homogenized white family in mass culture. In *McDonald's* 'history of the family' ad, images of minorities are brought forward for the sole purpose of demonstrating that all families are fundamentally the same. Thus stereotypes of Hispanic families as multigenerational and the anti-stereotypical depiction of a black father–son relationship in the *McDonald's* ad have this in common: each takes a problematic (from a middle-class perspective) family relationship and resolves it by placing the actors in the context of corporately sponsored consumption relations.

100

Imagery of a generic family draws upon a myth system of images built up by the culture industry over seventy-five years. The standardized and conformist family seen in TV ads replicates the imagery set forth by Disney Studios and Disneyland, where the streamlined family of 'Tomorrowland' is the same as the family typifying the 1920s. In mass culture, the same picture of family structure recurs throughout human history – each era being distinguished only by style of dress and degree of technological development. Corporate TV ads repeatedly plug in a cleansed, nondescript clone of this manufactured view of family life. This family is held together by its consumption of commodities – toothpaste, soft drinks, detergents and video games. An *Atari* ad represents the comfort, security and satisfaction of a father–daughter hug as the immediate outcome of playing video games in the living-room. It is a family unit integrated by the market and composed of serial relations 'in which the members are connected with one another . . . insofar as they are isolated from one another' as supposedly free and privatized consumers (Brenkman, 1979: 100).

Relations that constitute family life are situated in terms of consuming named brands, while set against the background of commodity consumption in general. A mother–child embrace thus appears contingent on the presence of *Cannon* towels by placing a frame around the image of the hug and fixing beneath it the tagline '*Cannon* touches your life.' Mother–child hugs appear in a *GE* ad as outgrowths of a refrigerator and a dryer, while father–child hugs are associated with a microwave oven, outdoor lighting and a TV. If nothing else, the *GE* ad campaign repeatedly counsels that gratifying parent–child relations require a physical infrastructure made up of commodity-objects (see Figure 4.1). Parent–child embraces are the culmination of intensely stirring dramas in *Coke* and *Pepsi* ads. *Coke* freeze-frames the hug in relation to the forcefully shouted lyric '*Coke* is It!' while *Pepsi*'s framing lyrics pulse, 'Come on, come on, and have a *Pepsi* day!' The same relation is shown repeatedly, devoid of any biographical history or context. Having watched all these parent–child displays of affection we are unable to distinguish one from another. Each roughly equivalent scene has been made to stand for ourselves and the relations we desire. Beyond the immediate message of each ad, that *GE* 'brings you closer to the ones you love,' or that *Polaroid* 'means Love,' the interchangeability of signifiers requires that viewers be able to generalize interpretively from any specific message the principle that commodity consumption is the necessary condition making possible the meaning of family life.

Invariably, the family is situated in, and associated with, leisure and consumption activities. Only where the family is depicted as rural do contemporary family members engage in laboring activities. Otherwise, TV ads show families systematically severed from work relations and production activities. Ads not only dissociate the context of family life from work activities, they situate the conduct of family life outside the framework

Figure 4.1 General Electric (TV) 1982

of economic relations. There is a kernel of truth in this, for family relations have become physically segregated from work activities. But the generalized description of family life as untainted by market relations serves primarily to emphasize the promised quality of unalienated activities within the family. Asserting that non-market values predominate over the terrain of family relationships, while partially the case, obscures the relationship between the family and other institutions. It also legitimates the family (aided by the corporate distribution of products) as the primary site in which non-instrumental relations can be had.

A consumptive and not a productive unit, the typical ad family is defined as the private sphere. The images that compose this family demarcate it as a haven, a retreat, a place where one can engage in affectively supportive relations. This is amplified by treating the family as a feeling-state. *McDonald's, Hallmark, Coke, GE et al.* ideologically portray the family as a private, protected site for affective individualism. Not only do these ads appropriate the most gratifying and hopeful private moments from people's lives, they also unhesitatingly entangle their corporate presence in our achievement of intimate moments. They offer to sell us back idealized images of ourselves as we would like to be (or think we ought to be). Thus, an ad for *Cannon* cotton products orchestrates a sequence of paleosymbolic images of satisfying, privatized family relations. Wrapping each scene are the soprano-sung lyrics, '*Cannon* touches your life.' The sequence opens with parents and child asleep together; an open book in dad's hand signifies they have fallen asleep while reading together. The sequence concludes with children gleefully scampering about a front yard, spraying each other and the family dog with the garden hose. A loving mom enters to wrap a wet daughter in a towel.

Within this privatized setting, the family is shown as child-centered. Since the 1920s advertisers have stressed that 'needs of the young should occupy the first place in parents' thoughts' (Lasch, 1979a: 20). Recall *McDonald's* 'Hometown' ad where the daughter's statement of need took immediate precedence over the father's needs. Stress on the primacy of children's needs expresses a historical trend toward greater individuation; it is also a source of internal conflicts within the family as it promotes a family composed of competing sets of individual needs. But in TV ads, personal conflicts are instantly resolved by further consumption of commodities and the presence of corporate logos.[5] Instead of resentment, parent and child are bound together in an apparently mutually satisfying process of consumption, where the valuation of children (and their relationship to parents) receives expression in terms of commodities: 'Choosy mothers choose *Jif*.'

Running throughout the depiction of family life in mass media advertising is the tendency to invest the family with the task of preserving society by reproducing a vaguely defined, but symbolically salient, moral order. Though the family is cast as the private sphere, it is consistently asserted that making the family strong 'again' will restore the integrity of a public sphere that has wilted. This theme is addressed by the *Ethan Allen* advertising campaign that linked societal problems to a pervasive erosion of values and posed the necessity of reconstituting the home as the 'nurturing ground for the wholesome values and attitudes that made our country strong.'[6]

SOCIETY'S CORNERSTONE?

Under capitalism, the sphere of family life has been excised from the realm of production functions, leaving the family essentially as a locus for intimacy and personal life. Drawing ever inward, the family has been made a private space where emotional support may be derived, and opportunities for individual and interpersonal development pursued. But as responsibility for overcoming the poverty of subjectivity in both public life and the workplace became centered within the family, so too it became overburdened as the sole space of personal fulfillment.

103

Within the capitalist epoch, the family unit became a necessary means of reproducing labor power as wage labor at the same time that it was partitioned from the relations of production. Structurally the two spheres were integrated, while ideologically separated. For decades, advertisers have encouraged an understanding of family life as radically separate from production relations by disseminating an image of a congenial family in which intimacy and personal fulfillment are achieved through the consumption of commodities. In this way, advertisers have unintentionally contributed to an overburdening of the family by promoting impossible expectations of it as a private, conflict-free haven within which to achieve social and individual fulfillment. In practice, this kind of family life pits needs for individuated fulfillment against needs for a strongly fused nuclear social unit that might function as a bastion for emotional support and a counterbalance against depersonalization. Consequently, this kind of family often tends to be experienced in terms of intensely contradictory demands for individuation versus otherness and independence versus dependency.

The narratives about family life in ads for *McDonald's, GE, Kodak, Coke et al.* are doubly misleading. First, this advertising style grew even more prevalent at a time when the United States was in the midst of a deep recession and high unemployment. A weighty disparity appears when utopian images of a conflict-free family unbound by the economy are considered in relation to the actual social conditions that exist when unemployment and its repercussions strain families to the breaking point. Second, these ads falsely identify *moments* (snippets) from daily life as equivalent to the whole of family life. Advertisers appropriate, remove from context and then reassemble in the ad's context the signifying practices of family life. These ads are effective only if viewers perceive in them some *echo* of their own subjectivity; but it is a subjectivity robbed of its subject, a subjectivity externalized and projected back on the subject through the form and the sign of the commodity. It is thus a subjectivity objectified in the form of pre-digested commodified meanings.

Depicting the interior of family relations as a realm of private and subjective matters (home, emotion, intimacy) independent of production relations, ads propound the primacy of the private sphere. Private life is no longer offered merely as a compensatory haven from alienated work relations, the abstracted private sphere becomes represented as identical with the general quality of life. Such claims conceal how political economic forces condition family life. But while the manifest ideological theme of corporate ads is the independence and primacy of family life in relation to production relations, the tacit ideological theme moves in the opposite direction: the inner workings of family relations are exposed in idealized fashion to impart the understanding that true, virtuous family life outside capitalist social relations (outside the relations of commodity consumption) is inconceivable. Here the structure and the ideology of family relations converge in the penetration of family life by market, i.e., commodity relations. These ads promote and celebrate the extension of commodity relations into family life even as they decisively divorce family life from the world of the economy. In this way, image ads preserve the family as a consumption unit and defend it as an institution in terms that benefit capital in general. Although corporate ads depict the abstracted family as a wonderful end in itself, the very form of the ads instrumentalizes the family, making it a means to another end: namely, the legitimation of corporate capital.

NOTES

1 Such corporate ads steer audiences toward one-sided accounts of contemporary social life as they exclude, and conceal, institutional contradictions. Family life and wholesome values are endangered by the advent of 'high-tech society' according to INTERCO (Ethan Allen's parent company). They conveniently omit that multinational corporations such as INTERCO contribute to social changes that play havoc with the home and its 'old-fashioned ideals.'

2 In October 1981 *McDonald's* switched advertising agencies, moving from Needham, Harper & Steers to Leo Burnett Co. Other fast-food chains had been copying 'McDonald's advertising style of family vignettes and studies showed consumers were confusing the ads' (Cox, 1981: 44). In a market saturated by virtually identical products, competition centered on images of family life. However, when the marketplace became saturated by images of the family that interfered with product differentiation, then images of family life were discarded as positioning concepts – i.e., as signifiers of the product. The corporate allegiance to family life did not outweigh the imperative of accumulation.

3 Differing moods and meanings of family life are conveyed by *McDonald's* mock-up of a contemporary middle-class portrait and the putatively 'authentic' middle-class portrait chosen to represent the 1890s. Four children appear in the 1890s photo compared to two today. The 1890s portrait spaced each family member at a distance from one another, whereas the *McDonald's* portrait crowds family members together, thus conveying a sense of greater personal intimacy among family members than where each family member is posed as a discrete figure. In the 1890s portrait the seated husband/father occupies a higher elevation than does the seated wife/mother, whereas the contemporary portrait shows the kneeling husband/father and wife/mother even in height. The father exhibits a stern expression in the 1890s photo, while the later photo shows father with a softer, smiling expression. If we accept Goffman's thesis that relative positioning, head and shoulder cant and facial expression are coded indicators of superordinate–subordinate relations between men and women, then the *McDonald's* photo suggests a decline of patriarchal dominance in the family.

4 Many people welcomed the opportunity afforded by the development of regional and national labor markets to escape their experience of suffocating family relations (Sennett and Cobb, 1972).

5 'As consumption becomes the personal mandate, children move ever more to center stage. The child loses his/her functionality in the household and becomes a pure consumer . . . . With this the child-mind in everyone becomes

celebrated, as indeed it should be by the managers of society, who . . . sense in the infantile mental organization a possible way out of the crisis instigated by the glut of commodities. However, the child as consumer is in an inherently antagonistic relationship to the parent as provider, so long as the desires of the one are yoked to infantile yearning, while the largesse of the other is bounded by the impoverished reality of capitalism. This antagonism, rooted in the deepest assumptions of capital, is responsible more than any other factor for the schism between generations that afflicts late capitalist society; and in a fundamental way it enters into the kind of emotional disturbance now prevalent' (Kovel, 1981: 121–2).

6 The Ethan Allen campaign presents an explicit corporate ideology of family life as a counterweight to social crisis. Under the heading, 'Have You Thought Seriously About The Importance Of Your Home?,' Nathan Ancell, Chairman of Ethan Allen, spells out a vision of the 'furnished' contemporary family.

(1) Your *Home Is Your Nest*
    where babies are conceived, diapers changed, scraped knees bandaged and children's tears dried . . . where stories are told and histories unfold . . . where your young ones thrive on parental love and learn the real values of life . . . where love and respect between husband and wife are nurtured.

(2) Your *Home Is A Classroom*
    where you must show your children the ways of the world and teach them right from wrong, because our overburdened schools can no longer do it . . . where they learn the old-fashioned virtues of beauty, truth and cleanliness.

(3) Your *Home Is A Retreat*
    from the elements, the frustrations of daily life . . . where you can shut out the world and its traumas. It's a haven you children can run to, not run away from . . . where worries *are* calmed and weary hearts and minds renew their strength and courage.

(4) Your *Home Is A Stage*
    where the drama of your life is played . . . where a warm environment and beautiful furnishings can provide a rich fulfilling setting, but the true story comes from the love and spirit of you and your family.

(5) Your *Home Is Your Piece of the World*
    the most important investment you'll ever make in your life . . . one that says 'this is ours' while it provides the warm inspiring environment you want for your loved ones.

5

ENVY, DESIRE AND POWER
Gender relations and the dialectics of appearance in ads

A growing proportion of 1980s consumer-goods advertisements stressed women's expanding opportunities for achieving success and parity *vis-à-vis* men. Ads more and more depicted men and women in relations of formal equity, but on different footing. *Secret* deodorant, for example, presented itself as strong enough for a man, but made for women. Gender difference was relocated and justified as taking place in nature: women's perspiration biochemically differs from men's. Television ads presented women playing and competing with men at men's games, and winning, while in the end reaffirming their traditional (i.e., natural, 'god-given') gender traits – looking attractive. The message: women make active choices, both in competing with men and selecting a scented deodorant that leaves them feminine, pretty and fashionably stylish. Redressing the power imbalance in gender relations was invariably cast in terms of commodity consumption and personal appearance: change occurs not through politics, or strikes, or challenges to the legal system, but through individuated commodity consumption.

Ideological themes ran the gamut from valorizing a professional woman image in campaigns for *Visa, American Express* and *E.F. Hutton*, to cosmetics and perfume ads that articulated a mythic superwoman figure. *Visa* and *American Express* ads exploited role reversal techniques to tell of women's newly achieved equity within the socio-economic system. These ads positioned an accompanying male who is subtly threatened by the woman's enhanced professional status and economic power. In each story-line the woman recognizes his perception of threat (the man in the *Visa* ad feels reduced to second-class status because she, and not he, received the special 'Gold' card) and then moves to dispel his anxiety that her new-found power will upset the proverbial applecart.

The other end of the spectrum featured the superwoman myth, aka the 'fabulous new woman' – sublimely self-confident and secure, poised, effortlessly beautiful, she moves with a style and grace called 'presence.' She is independent and successful; liberated, yet feminine and romantic; modern, yet traditional at the same time.

Keeping up with our changing new world is me.
But so is holding on to the good, old values. (*Me*)

You're tough, you're smart, you're driven.
You're soft, you're warm, you're loving.
You go from day to night, without missing a beat.
You've become the person you were meant to be. (*Charles of the Ritz*)

Everyday you win. More independence. More success.
But you still love to cry at sad movies.
You still believe in the power of love at first sight.
And you think fragrance should be all flowers and feelings.
Because being a woman – is everything. (*Pique*)

These commodified definitions of liberated women are ahistorical and fictional: magically reconciling and unifying the culturally contradictory relations of independence and ultrafeminine romance.

But simple debunking does not get at the motor force of advertising's ideological grip on women. Advertisers have tried to harness the ideological currency of feminism, rerouting feminist critique for the purpose of extending commodity relations. However, these ads also reveal a real social moment – namely that gender power is now partially lived out at the level of appearances. Advertisements frequently represent women taking control and power over their lives and relationships through their commodified articulation of feminine appearance. This model of social power proposes that autonomy and control can be obtained through voluntary self-fetishization. A dialectic of desire, envy and power is embedded in these advertisements' form of address and the currency of appearances they endorse: disentangling it reveals how the ad/reader (encoding/decoding) circuit has sublated the judging power of the male gaze into a self-policing narcissistic gaze.[1]

METAPHORS OF CONTROL

The *L'Eggs* pantyhose ad in Figure 5.1 appeared in *Glamour*, May 1983. The top half of the page contains a photograph of a woman's figure inclined at nearly a 45-degree angle against the front edge of a large, spare desk. The image is cropped so the woman's face and head are missing – so the viewer herself might imaginatively 'fill in' the woman's identity. We assume she is talking on the phone, which is a simple but stylish, streamlined design. The woman wears a long-sleeved, blue jersey dress cut just above the knees and belted at the waist. Caught in this manner, her body could likewise be described as streamlined. The focal point for the advertising agency, given

Figure 5.1 L'Eggs

Source: Glamour, May 1983

its sales agenda, is her calves. Her left leg extends straight to the floor to form a flawless line with the rest of her body. Her right leg is bent at the knee and angled so that her toe points straight toward the floor. She wears black, mid-heel pumps, and presumably a pair of *L'Eggs* pantyhose. Beneath this photograph's outer frame is the caption: 'Being in control never felt so good.' This is printed to approximate the appearance of handwritten script. With the caption, the photograph can be interpreted as that of a young female executive in her office. Carefully arranged visual signifiers in the photo confirm this reading: a leather briefcase on the floor behind her; the corner of a portfolio pouch on the desk; and a legal pad and pen on the desk. The pad and pen in conjunction with the handwritten caption below might lead viewers to surmise the caption has been penned by this woman to describe her own situation.[2]

To what, then, does 'being in control' refer? Thus far, the possibilities include a) she is in charge; this is her office; a woman on her own merits has risen to the top in a man's world; b) she is in command of her immediate environment and job; there is a calm, uncluttered order to the scene depicted. But this does not exhaust the meanings of 'being in control,' since thus far we have employed the artifice of examining only the top portion of the advertising page. How does the meaning of the caption and photo change when viewed in relation to the bottom portion of the page? Pictured at lower left are four product containers named 'Control Top.' These are the familiar oval-shaped packages that appear in displays in stores across the country. Adjacent to this is a block of copy in smaller print: 'With L'Eggs control-top style pantyhose, you've never been so comfortable being in control.' Punctuating this copy is the product slogan, 'Nothing beats a great pair of L'Eggs.'

Our assessment of what is meant by this image framed by the concept of 'being in control' must now be revised. 'Being in control' is apparently also a function of the pantyhose she wears. 'Being in control' refers to the *L'Eggs look* – attractive calves, the smooth, slim lines of her waist and bottom. By investing 'being in control' with multiple meanings, the advertiser steers viewers to connect the meaning system of a woman gaining control over her life in the work world (a woman not subject to the commands of others) with the meaning system of pantyhose that give *your* legs a flattering look while comfortably holding *you* in. In both ad and fact, control-top pantyhose pull in the stomach, making the mid-section appear flat. This leaves the impression of not having been, or perhaps not intending to be, a childbearer. She appears 'in control' of her biology and, by extension, no problem to her employer because of maternity.

When understood in contrast to traditional bourgeois-patriarchal accounts of success, this caption works at the level of irony – binding together themes normally opposed to one another. Whereas in the past, men were advised that control came at the cost of renouncing pleasure, women are here advised that the path to control – so long blocked to them – is available via the route of pleasure. At still another level of meaning, women's traditional task of controlling their figures, so long achieved by means of patriarchally enforced self-torture (girdles, corsets), has now become a supposedly pleasurable activity. However, the cultural shift in locus of control from externally motivated methods (corsets) to internally motivated methods (the 'will-power' to diet and exercise) creates a new potential for self-abuse. The current scenario makes women morally accountable for making their bodies comply with an idealized image trumpeted and managed by the mass media. A new form of oppression emerges as women go to war with their recalcitrant bodies. Failure to exercise appropriate self-restraint becomes internalized as a character flaw. For many women, a daily ritual of anxiously validating and revalidating self's physical appearance is performed in front of the self-scrutinizing voice of the mirror and the bathroom scales.

Control over one's bodily appearance is correlated with control over one's socio-economic environment, and the correlation ratified as positive: it 'never felt so good.' This phrase is comparative, but the referent is left unspecified – 'so good' as what? If a viewer goes to the trouble (and most viewers indicate they rarely do) to read the small print at the bottom of the page, the latter phrase refers to comfort – these pantyhose do not bind and are not tight. The meaning of this subtext might better be expressed as, 'Looking great [beautiful] in these pantyhose does not feel uncomfortable.' But, it is now obvious that this strand of interpretation stands neither alone nor in the foreground. This interpretation in conjunction with the framed photographic image presupposes a condition of feeling good about self. And, if we return to the other set of meanings about rising to a position of control and esteem, then 'feeling good' might refer to the gratifying emotional state that corresponds to being on one's own and not being subservient any longer. 'Felt so good' refers both to tactile sensations and to a socio-emotional state. The unspecified comparative referent directs viewers to infer from the foreground/background composition of this frozen pictorial frame a narrative action bridging past, present and future.

Viewers' grasp of this narrative movement hinges on a relatively superficial social knowledge of changes in men's and women's roles: that the workplace has been historically segregated by gender, with women occupying structurally and monetarily inferior positions. As a narrative sequence, the ad pivots on juxtaposing and connecting the conventional with the unconventional: the unconventionality of a woman executive is matched by the conventionality of the model's pose. Though the caption steers us to perceive a 'present absence' of subordination, this pose is not atypical of the photographic gender displays which have suffused our lives with mappings of female subordination. The bent knee, pointed toe and

111

semi-reclining body cant are familiar poses in fashion displays. The posture does not usually indicate a serious demeanor (a male executive would never be depicted in this posture), connoting instead a more playful, dreamy attitude toward self. Though it need not be exaggerated, the semi-reclining posture is often used in ads to encode the possibility of sexual availability (cf. Goffman, 1976: 41–3). Certainly, the framing of the product-mediated woman as 'a great pair of L'Eggs' introduces meanings which, at least on the surface, seem to contradict those of control and authority.[3]

Although she is shown alone, the model's posture suggests 'she is offering up her femininity as the surveyed.' But to whom is she offering it? In the western tradition of painting and in contemporary pornography, women have been depicted 'responding with calculated charm to the man who she imagines looking at her – although she doesn't know him' (Berger, 1972: 55). While we cannot discount the absent male gaze as a constitutive element shaping this pose, the advertiser's agenda and audience differ materially from that of the traditional male artist or pornographer. Marketing surveys conducted by the fashion industry repeatedly conclude that women today calculate their appearance in terms of what other women think.

Given this agenda and the framing of the pose, can we hypothesize that the model who stands for the female viewer is made the 'spectator-owner' of her own appearance? The woman's stance suggests she is aware of the appearance of her figure, the pose permitting a narcissistic self-observation. Who is the surveyor? Again the absence of the face is pivotal – detachment of the face encourages a detached view of the viewer's self as it might be mediated by this attire. Like most consumer-goods ads this ad's image addresses the viewer as 'you.' Cropping the woman's persona invites the viewer imaginatively to insert herself: she becomes both surveyed and surveyor, both spectator and potential owner.

Her appearance is loaded with meaning. This photographic image, at this juncture of our cultural history, validates an idealized female figure. 'Trim,' 'fit,' 'slim,' 'shape' – adjectives that now double as popular magazine titles – are not only the meanings signified by this female figure, but also the topical agendas around which mass audiences are organized by mass media practitioners. Remember, this ad appeared in the same magazines which announce on their covers similar agendas: e.g., 'Making it big at 30!'; 'Ways to make the job you hate the job you love'; 'the sinner's diet'; 'terrific clothes'; 'Is There Sex After Success?'; 'How to be your own woman – making love, money, friends, decisions.' This stylized image of a female body now signifies a type of persona that repeatedly appears in the pages of these magazines. This persona corresponds to the ensemble of meanings that Ewen (1976) calls the 'commodity self' – a self composed of product-mediated parts. Calling it a 'commodity self' draws attention again to how these meanings correspond to markets: fitness centers, spas, bodybuilding, the fashion industry, shoe industry, low-calorie food industry and diet centers, cosmetics and the magazines themselves.

What, if anything, does possessing a shapely feminine figure have to do with success and parity for women in a male corporate world? A seemingly paradoxical claim, regularly made in consumer ads, has women enhancing their social and economic power *vis-à-vis* men by presenting themselves as objects of desire. These ads endorse a notion that femininity as defined by commodity consumption comprises a route to control, security and power in relations with men. An ad for *Cosmopolitan* magazine in the *New York Times* (Figure 5.2) pictures a 'Cosmo cover girl' with her testimony:

> Three dates in I got the non-commitment speech. 'You're wonderful but I'm not ready for a relationship.' Fine, I said, and we kept dating. One night I had to cancel because of a heavy meeting the next day. He was astonished. Two weeks later I went on a business trip to France. He was in shock. Two months later – right this minute – he's the most attentive man I've ever known. I didn't plan to be hard to get . . . I really *have* been *busy*. My favorite magazine says don't play games . . . just play your career for all it's worth and a lot of things will fall into place. I love that magazine. I guess you could say I'm That COSMOPOLITAN Girl.
>
> (*New York Times*, 17 September 1984: D16)

What moral can be extracted from this story? She turns the tables on him. Playing at his own game, she turns his attempt to control distance in their relationship against him, domesticating him. Following *Cosmopolitan*'s philosophy, her pursuit of a career (in France, no less) makes her less accessible, which in turn heightens his desire for her, which gives her greater control in the relationship. When this moral is situated in terms of the Cosmo heroine's accompanying glamour image, we see how many ads and magazines address women about increasing their social power by willingly engaging in self-fetishization. Ironically, our past cultural heritage of patriarchal predominance has been hegemonically sustained by fetishizing the female anatomy and persona.

A DIALECTIC OF DESIRE AND POWER

John Berger (1972) presents an interpretation of advertising and the construction of envy. Two excerpts represent his argument.

> Publicity is always about the future buyer. It offers him an image of himself made glamorous by the product or opportunity it is trying to sell. The image then makes him envious of himself as he might be. Yet what makes this self-which-he-might-be enviable? The envy of others.

Three dates in I got the non-commitment speech. "You're wonderful but I'm not ready for a relationship." Fine, I said and we kept dating. One night I had to cancel because of a heavy meeting the next day. He was astonished. Two weeks later I went on a business trip to France. He was in shock. Two months later—right this minute—he's the most attentive man I've ever known. I didn't plan to be hard to get...I really have been busy. My favorite magazine says don't play games...just play your career for all it's worth and a lot of things will fall into place. I love that magazine. I guess you could say I'm That COSMOPOLITAN Girl.

One of my most satisfying relationships is with a magazine.

COSMOPOLITAN

A PUBLICATION OF THE HEARST CORPORATION

Figure 5.2 Cosmopolitan

Source: New York Times, 17 September 1984

Publicity is about social relations, not objects. Its promise is not of pleasure, but of happiness: happiness as judged from the outside by others. The happiness of being envied is glamour.

The spectator-buyer is meant to envy herself as she will become if she buys the product. She is meant to imagine herself transformed by the product into an object of envy for others, an envy which will then justify her loving herself.

(Berger, 1972: 132, 134)

Let's pursue Berger's insights via the decoding of two ads. The *L'Oréal* lipstick ad (Figure 5.3) in *Mademoiselle* (1981) epitomizes the commodified glamour relation between men and women. Berger and Goffman note how the arranged demeanor of women in works of art frequently sets up women as objects of display for the admiration and exploitation of the spectator-owner. The *L'Oréal* ad magnifies the depiction of woman as fetishized parts. Because the eyes and identifying features have been shielded, the lips, made to stand out because of their bright red glow against a predominantly white setting, constitute her as a subject. Shielding the eyes and the rest of the face creates a kind of anonymity that is not anonymity at all, but a coding suggestion that viewers fill in the rest of the woman based on the signifiers of the lips and the surrounding accoutrements.

This colorful image appears as a framed work of art hanging on a museum wall. What does this image signify? Along with the broad-brimmed, lace-trimmed hat, the ear-ring, white ruffled scarf and perfectly smooth facial skin, the red, full, slightly parted lips stand for an ideal of feminine pulchritude. It is also an obviously veiled suggestion concerning the promise of oral sexuality. Stationed in front of this mounted image stands an apparently admiring male, his back turned to the viewer. This scene is labeled 'The New Spirit of Chic' and the model's face identified as an admired art object. At the same time, the ad transforms the named lipstick into the means of producing the art image. Artistic agency is renamed 'L'Artiste.'[4] An equivalency is drawn between the red lips and possession of a social power. The ad's language incorporates an elitist appeal to glamorous elegance – words like 'chic,' 'Paris' and 'L'Artiste' in combination with the abundant clean white empty space in the ad layout contribute to an impression of cultured elegance.

This fetishized art object is evidently worth admiring. But the unknown man does more than admire. We may infer that he desires this beautiful object represented by the super-realist painting. Indeed, placement of his hands in his pockets suggests the possibility of sexual arousal by this fetish. Here we encounter a complex dialectic of desire and power. Another way of addressing the woman's depiction is that she is placed on a pedestal. Such a representation clearly makes her vulnerable – she becomes not simply an art object but an object of consumption, an object of the male

115

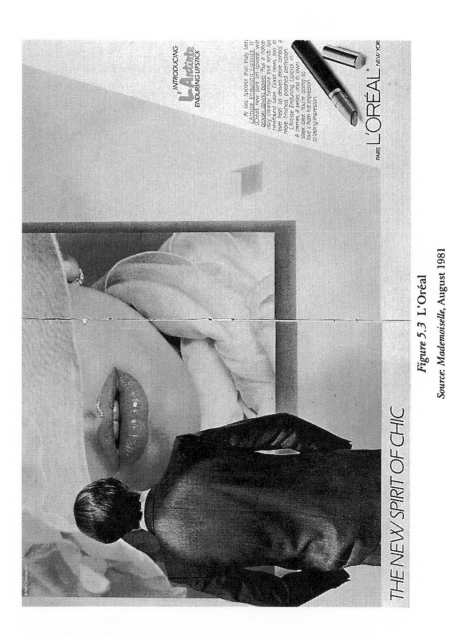

Figure 5.3 L'Oréal

Source: *Mademoiselle*, August 1981

gaze. And yet, her desirability – her social power to command his attention – is contingent upon occupying this position. Her image is elevated above him where she commands his attention. This ad speaks precisely to this fantasy: by turning yourself into a glamorous object of envy and desire, you can have power over the man of your dreams (i.e., the man who dreams of you). This may be accomplished through use of this named commodity, painting her (your) lips with the 'L'Artiste' brush. The relation of art objects (red lips) to named product to consumer-as-self-portraitist is sealed by the color connections of lips to logo to mortise, and by the display of the product in the mortise as being an artistic tool open and ready for the consumer to paint her own 'image' and thus her own relations with men.

This ad reinforces a prominent ideological account of woman defined by the male gaze. Running beneath the textual account of gender relations in this ad is a narrative of male power, but the manifest claim made is that woman's power over man is constituted through a fetishism of appearances. Just as in daily life, men stare at women – they scrutinize and evaluate women's reified parts. The ability to survey is based on power, but here the female look confers power. Woman's power over man is thus ironically depicted as a function of her willing acceptance of her vulnerability and powerlessness *vis-à-vis* men. Here, the woman as paragon of beauty commands the male's attention by making herself *an object* of desire. By emphasizing the fetishized self as the conduit to power and control, the ad obscures the fact that feelings of control gained through impression management are literally purchased at the cost of self-alienation. Furthermore, fetishism as her source of power – her enhancement of herself as currency – entails a more immediate vulnerability, i.e., the male accusation that appearance is a justification for violent rape.

The accompanying text defines the abstracted lipstick-mediated lips as a reified object capable of effecting a particular social relation, that of a 'lasting impression.' The ad directs viewers to construct a commodity-sign – *L'Oréal* lipstick/mesmerizing lips – which becomes part of a currency of looks. Ads like this set up an equivalence between the object of desire and the self (Williamson, 1978). The currency is complete when ads for jewelry, watches, shampoo feature similar lips as a sign carrying the expressive connotation of 'sexy.' The lips as a visual object of desire work on the assumption that such lips are desirable to the absent 'male gaze' situated in front of her. Self is represented here as an appearance made into an object of desire, and quite naturally a fetishized visual signifier of self is used to communicate this message. The sign, lips, has become an abbreviation for fetishized desire, even while made to stand for an idealized woman that you want to be.

Content analysis of lipstick ads from 1946 through 1977 revealed that, whereas in 1946 most ads showed the whole body of a woman, by 1977 most ads showed only the body part. The transition was accompanied, of course, by a learning process whereby readers came to accept the part as standing for the whole. This *L'Oréal* ad addresses the reader, and asks the reader to position herself as the image of self shown on the page. The ad invites the reader to abstract from the model's likeness to their own possible likeness when mediated by use of the cosmetic. Simultaneously, the reader is encouraged to envy herself as she might become (the abstracted visual image on the page). But here envy and desire get mixed up in the wake of gender relations. Viewers may internalize the male gaze and accept the premise that if these lips attract the male, such lips may be worthy of envy. But female viewers could also read the lips as an object of desire to be had not as a means to males but as an end in itself.

> Being envied is a solitary form of reassurance. It depends precisely upon not sharing your experience with those who envy you. You are observed with interest but you do not observe with interest – if you do, you will become less enviable . . . . It is this which explains the absent, unfocused look of so many glamour images. They look out *over* the looks of envy which sustain them.
>
> (Berger, 1972: 133)

Now we can expand our explanation of why the eyes of this woman are shielded. It not only permits the viewer to read herself in, it also sustains the power of her glamour, for she does not observe with interest. The ad reinforces this by removing the woman *as* lips from direct interaction via her placement as a painting. This impersonality, as Berger suggests, preserves the illusion of power.

An *Ultra Sense* pantyhose ad (Figure 5.4) appeared in *Glamour* in April 1984. Against a blue background stands a pair of legs from just above the knee down. Shown from the back and occupying the entire length of the page, these legs are free of hair and wear a pair of pantyhose and red and black high heel shoes. Along the right edge of the page a male hand is shown pulling – between thumb and forefinger – the pantyhose away from the leg. A female hand is positioned immediately above the male hand and parallel to the right calf. The female hand is encoded as a gentle, 'feminine' touch, with the tip of the female forefinger barely touching the male forefinger. What does this image mean?

Running across the page and over her legs is the framing headline: 'With Ultra Sense You've Got Pull!' Beneath this in the space between the female ankles is an additional subtext in smaller print that explains: 'Beautifully sheer like some department store pantyhose, but even better. Because Ultra Sense won't pull out of shape. Fabulous look! Fabulous fit!' Beneath this is a small image of the product package. And below this is still another textual comment, this time in bolder type than the passage above, but less bold than the main headline: 'When fashion sense makes good sense . . . that's No Nonsense.' Paired with the headline and picture, the wordiness

Figure 5.4 Ultra Sense

Source: *Glamour*, April 1984

of the subtext seems to draw out the primary positioning angle chosen by the advertiser – these hose will not pull out of shape. But observe how this manifest meaning of 'With Ultra Sense You've Got Pull!' is actually based on a reversal of linguistic and pictorial meaning.

The headline utilizes a familiar colloquial phrase, 'You've got pull,' which signifies the possession of power relative to someone else, i.e., personal influence. This meaning seems, at first glance, to be clearly in opposition to what is depicted in the picture. In this staged picture, the male hand does the pulling. Yet, it is the woman/you who supposedly has the pull. Let's examine this apparent contradiction by looking at the visual meaning of the relationship between the female legs (clothed as they are), the male hand, the female hand and the pantyhose. A male hand pulling the pantyhose differs in significance from a woman's hand in the same pose and same act. The latter pose might be said to have a strictly demonstrative purpose. The male hand does serve a similar demonstrative function – calling the viewer's attention to the hose's stretching capacity, indicating that even under duress the hose do not run – but its presence is more than demonstrative. Indeed, the male hand in relation to the woman's leg and hand may actually distract attention from the demonstrative purpose.

The female fingertip (nailtip) barely touches the male forefinger. What does the cant of her hand, and this touch, signify? In conjunction with the coding cues of the bracelet and the polished fingernails, the way the hand is held designates 'femininity.' The delicate touch may signify permission giving, while it also silently controls and manages the male hand. To put it more directly, her hand's gesture suggests neither anger nor defensive action – she is not slugging him! Surely, in the real world the act of a male pulling skin-hugging pantyhose from a female leg would be regarded as threatening – an intrusion into personal space and a threat to personal safety. Yet this hand is not agitated or threatened, but rather calmly in control.

Here one meaning of 'you've got pull' is that the woman gains attractiveness via the product. The product-mediated legs generate attractiveness, and attractiveness thus generates *power* over the unseen, but filled in, male libido. The male hand pulling the pantyhose would ordinarily presuppose a position of male dominance. Nevertheless, the advertising copy and photographic imagery of the female hand in relation to the male hand redundantly imply that this product (commodity) places the female in control of the relationship.

Pictorially, the ad encodes the female leg as an object of desire. The leg *qua* 'fabulous look' is made into an object of desire by framing it within the meaning systems of hosiery and high heels. Mediated by the 'beautiful sheerness' of the 'Ultra Sense' hose, the objectified leg becomes the visual source of pull – the power generated over the male by virtue of the desire evoked in him.

Once again, woman gains power by participating in the fetishism of commodity appearances. By actively mastering the currency of looks (smooth hairless legs in sheer hose with high heels)[5] a woman may hope to acquire power over men – she makes herself an object of desire in order *to bring him to his knees.* Note well that, for the male hand to occupy the position it does, the male would have to be either supine or on his knees. In either case, she stands over him.

Again, noticeably absent are the visual means of identifying persona (both male and female). Hence, the encoding of the legs and female hand nearly demands that female viewers infer a typology of a whole woman. This relation between heavily coded body parts and persona presumes an acquaintance with a system of advertising texts (intertextuality influences both encoding and interpretation), and rests on the performance of abstraction as an interpretive principle. It also relies on the individual viewer's willingness to be appellated and step into the mirror space of the ad, where she is positioned to read herself in as the subject to whom these legs belong (Williamson, 1978). This, of course, is not you, but a potential you – the desired you (as *Clairol* ads put it, 'You. Only Better'). The woman viewer is encouraged to envy these legs for what they might accomplish – the upper hand in relations with men.

WHOSE GAZE?

Ads continue to address women about themselves as malleable surfaces that can be adorned with objects that carry desired attributes via commodities' powers of signification. They encourage and perpetuate a pattern of seeing women as collections of body parts. Like pornographic representations, these ads abstract body parts from the whole person so that each part carries its own sexual persona. While many women cringe at the thought, there is only a difference of degree between the fetishism encoded in these ads and that promoted in 'girlie' magazines. Ads encourage women not merely to adorn themselves with commodities, but also to perceive themselves as objectified surfaces.

> Femininity is recuperated by the capitalist form: the exchange between the commodity and 'woman' in the ad establishes her as a commodity too . . . it is the modes of femininity themselves which are achieved through commodities and are *replaced* by commodities.
>
> (Winship, 1980: 218)

An ad for the *Fit Self-Improvement Series* (Figure 5.5) epitomizes this representation of the female self as a commodity whose value can be actively enhanced as a set of appearances, perfected via the specialized expert guidance contained in the series. Equating 'healthy' with 'looking great,' self-improvement becomes a matter of increasing the value of one's parts

Figure 5.5 Fit Self-Improvement Series

Source: Fit, February 1984

in the interest of securing admiration of one's appearance, hence popularity, hence validation of self. In the mass media, and particularly in advertising, this commodification of appearance is endorsed as the route to 'control,' 'power,' 'strength' and 'success.' Sometimes this theme gets carried to extremes, as in a recent rock video fantasy entitled 'She's Got Legs,' where a young woman overcomes her victimization and oppression and turns the tables on her oppressors by having her legs repackaged into objects of desire.

This much is not new. For decades, a pervasive theme in advertising aimed at women has been the notion of *woman as capital.* The principle of 'possessive individualism,' once the exclusive domain of men, has now been extended to women through the sphere of consumption. Crudely put, the principle works like this: the individual has a right to all that is accrued by virtue of her ownership (her proprietary relationship) of her body. Her appearance is her value, and her avenue to accumulating capital. Ironically, men once dominated women on the basis of proprietary claims made on the body of woman; today, male domination gets reproduced on the basis of women acquiring proprietary control over their own bodies – or, over the appearances given off by their bodies. Feminists have observed how questions of feminine appearance have previously hinged around competition among women for the 'best' available men in marriage markets. When this is the agenda, then woman's social power does depend on management of her 'beauty assets.' These ads differ in that they now confuse this form of motivated competition with an agenda of women actually competing against men in labor markets. This ambiguity permits advertisers to perform a sleight-of-hand: though they ostensibly address women in terms of new gender roles embracing new-found 'freedoms' and life-chances, those new roles are made no less contingent on the same old scenario for gaining power – using appearance to simulate, and stimulate, desire.

Ads' ideologically loaded representations of gender and power derive as much from what they conceal as what they make visible. These ads conceal diverse forms of terror experienced by women who objectify themselves. There is the mundane psychic terror associated with not receiving 'looks' of admiration – i.e., of not having others validate one's appearance. A similar sense of terror involves the fear of 'losing one's looks' – the quite reasonable fear that aging will deplete one's value and social power. A related source of anxiety involves fears about 'losing control' over body weight and appearance. The neurotic obsession with body and food has become the scourge of young women. And, there is the very real physical terror which may accompany actual presentation of self as an object of desire – the fear of rape and violence by misogynous males.

Where determinations of personal rarity and value are grounded in continuously made invidious comparisons, the many must be invalidated.

Thus, it comes as no surprise that these ads which offer to put women 'in charge' of their lives, actually stimulate among women a fear of their own female bodies. In a 1984 survey for *Glamour*, 76 per cent of the women surveyed said they were 'too fat.' Susan Wooley, author of the study, found women were unhappiest about the 'distinctively female parts of their bodies.' Many women feel their inability to manage their body parts reflects upon their moral worth as individuals. This model of envy-based personal power pushes some women toward hatred and rejection of their bodies and themselves.

What is the object of desire targeted by these ads – sexiness or sexuality? Though 'sexy' represents the image of sexuality, it is not identical to sexuality. Indeed, for all the talk of how ads promise sexuality, they do so primarily by refracting that promise through a set of appearances. Commodity-mediated appearances are made to comprise an avenue to an individual woman's power *vis-à-vis* others; and it is a currency maximized by withholding possession from others. Here, the more a woman is able to elicit desire via presentation of self as a valued commodity – valued by her rareness/availability – the more powerful she feels.

Advertisers construct consumer-goods ads to maximize the likelihood of preferred interpretations. This requires them to overdetermine (to make redundant) the encoding process as a means of steering viewers in pre-ferred directions. And yet, these messages are neither simple nor mono-semic. Representations of women in ads carry both a message and a set of instructions about how to make sense of it. The structure and format of an ad, along with its mode of address, communicate instructions about how to interpret the ad's meaning. Who does it address and how? These ads try to position viewers to exclaim 'Hey, that's me' or 'Hey, I wish that was me.' Often, the wording is explicit, as in a TV Guide ad which features a woman holding her young daughter over her head, facing the caption, 'People like you . . . ' Such proposed relationships between photographic represen-tation and self provide a subvocal precondition for understanding the ad. 'People like you' as a mode of address 'assumes both a coherent ego, one that is in a position to compare itself to other egos, and an implicit "non-youness" – a system of differences' (Williamson, 1978: 60).

A real interpretive confusion or ambiguity exists at precisely this juncture – over whose gaze is presumed as constituting woman's essence in these ads. One reading present in these ads involves an absent male gaze that remains paramount in defining women's representations. Some ads (e.g., *L'Oréal*) are premised on women having internalized the male gaze so that 'women are invited . . . to respond to themselves through the imagined fetishes of men' (Winship, 1980: 219). Advertisers appropriate images of women as independent and 'in charge,' harness them to their sales agenda and reproduce a logic of female subordination in the process. When a female-mediated male gaze is presupposed, the model's photographic appearance may be read as standing for the viewer's own commodity-enhanced appearance, where the object of desire is the appearance that will make her an 'object of envy for others' and thereby generate desire on the part of 'that special male.'

The form of address repeatedly built into these ads presupposes another kind of motivated gaze on the part of viewers – the *mirrored gaze*. Although the subtext of the male gaze remains, another layer has been called forth, built on a structural relationship between privatized audience members and marketers linked together through demographic-based marketing practices. Advertisers address population segments with the aid of advanced market research which divides people up into consumer profiles, social and personality types – e.g., from 'Achievers, Societally Conscious, and Belongers' to 'Inner Directeds and Outer Directeds' (Atlas, 1984). This better permits advertisers 'to sell to values' of dispersed, individuated 'person-centered' consumers. The continuous rationalization of consumption has created a circuit between audience and advertiser that invites a narcissistic gaze which becomes differentiated from the male gaze. As this marketing loop is repeated time after time, it feeds a cultural transformation in which the cultivation of appearance is no longer merely a means to other ends (to maximizing chances in a competitive 'marriage market'), but also an end-in-itself. The desire becomes to *own* the appearance, *and to be owned by it*, i.e., to be judged by it. The object of desire is to possess *the look*.

This mirrored gaze rests on a tacit interpretive understanding that ads mirror desired ego packagings. This is plainly visible in ads where body shape is pursued because it says something important about you. The pose in 'Woman: A New Definition' (Figure 5.6) presents a narcissistic ideal motivated by a desired gratification that comes from a self-admiration contingent on the imagined admiration of others. This photographic definition of the 'new' woman rests on the relationship between her body image and the viewer. Another headless body in search of a self appellates viewers in conjunction with text that is about her, but addressed through 'you' the viewer.

> You're rewriting the book on what it means to be a woman – and we're getting the message. Pleasantly plump is out. So is fashion-model skinny. Today's body is defined by strength. You're saying to the world: 'I'm strong. I'm healthy. I'm in charge of me.'

Here the viewer must be able to assume simultaneously a subjective and an objective stance. The viewer is asked to insert herself imaginatively, but it would be a physical impossibility to view that side of one's figure without the artifice of photography or strategically placed mirrors. Ads such as this and *Danskin* (Figure 5.7) address 'you' about Self as seen by Others: 'You're saying to the world . . . ' or 'All the world's a stage.' Ads address women about their bodies *as* signs. Not only is the female body a sign, it also works

Woman: A New Definition

You're rewriting the book on what it means to be a woman—and we're getting the message.

Pleasantly plump is out. So is fashion-model skinny. Today's body is defined by strength. You're saying to the world: "I'm strong, I'm healthy, I'm in charge of me." And you're doing it with **chrome dumbbells by Joe Weider.**

Joe Weider's Chrome-Bells. Hi-tech hand weights in four sizes.

3 lb. Chrome (WC3) · $19.00
5 lb. Chrome (WC5) · $27.00
8 lb. Chrome (W28) · $40.00
10 lb. Chrome (CD10) · $45.00

Each set includes a full-color exercise program. AVAILABLE AT FINER DEPARTMENT STORES EVERYWHERE ... or you may order direct from **Weider Health**

& Fitness. Shipped postage collect. California, New Jersey and Missouri residents, add applicable tax. Please include code number for each item with your order, and mail to: **Weider Women's Division**, Dept. SGCD11, 21100 Erwin St., Woodland Hills, CA 91367. In Canada order from: Weider Institute, 2875 Bates Rd., Montreal, Canada PQ H3S 1B7.

Credit card customers call toll-free: 1-800-423-5713. In California: 1-800-382-3399.

Figure 5.6 Woman: a new definition

Source: Shape, November 1984

Figure 5.7 Danskin

Source: *Vogue*, March 1988

as a meta-language that 'talks about' (literally behind her back) the self as seen by others. Indeed, the text's voice is located not in the head/mouth/brain, but *in* the body. With this voice, the goal is to elicit envy in the eyes of other women and desire in the hearts of men.

The *Danskin* ad illustrates the fusion between the spectator-buyer, the spectator-owner and the object of desire. Interpreting this ad as yet another narrative about the male gaze, we encounter the profound moment of photographic discontinuity – the abyss of meaning – that advertisements try to turn from ambiguity into currency. At first glance, we cannot tell whether the male on the skateboard is coming or going. His moment of arrest coincides with ours. He seems to be striving for one last, long gaze of admiration and desire – he cannot help himself, he must look back for one more sight of her. His gaze is directed at her derrière as 'the object of desire.' Her gaze is averted from his, focused instead upon the same object of desire – her own fanny in a *Danskin*. Looking away from him averts the completion of his gaze, putting her in the driver's seat to control the circuit of power and desire. But looking away has another, equally significant, meaning to it. The ad collapses the subject and the object of desire. The circuit between the male gaze and the female object of desire has been contracted and compressed. The male is allotted a curiously ambiguous status. He no longer commands patriarchal status, rather his primary significance is now merely that of a signifier of the male gaze. He has been made redundant, reduced to an ornament included in the scene simply to attest to her desirability. In fact, absorbed in the narcissistic pleasure of admiring her own fetish, the female spectator-buyer has momentarily displaced the male spectator-owner.

Like most consumer-goods ads, these ads address 'you' as a subject with a coherent ego, invited to compare the photographed body as an object of desire to your own possible body. In turn, this triggers another comparison, this one made in front of the subject's mirror. These ads encourage a narcissistic model of self-realization, wherein actualizing interpersonal power rests on evoking desire and envy through the details of one's appearance.

Feminists have attacked this commodified model of ego development as an impossible mythology. Though 'the look' is a mythology, its practice in daily life constitutes a precarious zero-sum mode of self-realization predicated on a scarcity of value/recognition. The same corporate firms which sponsor this ideology also structure the built environment of consumption in urban daily life. In these impersonal social spaces, discontent and anxiety become continual companions when personal well-being hinges on being judged by appearance. Not only is the commodified model of perfectibility perpetually elusive, but Self can never be entirely sure how she is being evaluated by Other. When the circuit of recognition is disrupted in even minor ways, there may follow crises of Self. One response is to retreat to be alone, to be safe – with the 'flawless you.' But the mirror is no safe harbor, for when Self substitutes for Other as judge, it can be far more critical in castigating flaws. Envy of Others and periodic disgust with Self are the self-contradictory social fruits of basing self-realization on the trade in appearances.

Where unequal and segregated labor markets and patriarchal rule have prevailed, women have learned there is a kernel of truth to claims that social power hinges on their ability to evoke desire through appearance. Becoming an object of desire supposedly makes a woman more valuable in the eyes of others, and hence more valuable to herself. If successful, men will desire you and women will envy you. But to be valued in such terms is to stand out, and the process of judging is based on the premise of invidious, competitive comparisons with other women. Hence in a competitive political economy of sign-value, the hyper-critical individual is beset by an ever-present sinking feeling that she is not performing as well as others at controlling and managing their appearance. For the rare few, a real social power is gained; but it is gained at the expense of the many and it does nothing to challenge the male power to scrutinize and judge.

NOTES

1 'Sublate' is one of very few English words that capture the dialectic process that the German critical theorists express with the term *Aufhebung*. *Webster's Unabridged Dictionary* defines sublate thus: 'from the Latin *tollere* to take away, lift up, 1a: negate, deny b: cancel, eliminate 2: to cancel but also preserve and elevate (an element in a dialectic process) . . .'.

2 It is a peculiar feature of advertising that unless our attention is directed to it, we do not dwell on the human agency that shapes the textual message. Here, the staged use of handwriting as an encoding device calls attention to the question of agency – *who wrote it*. This use of handwriting falsifies the *agenda* within which it is used, because it conceals the origin of the message.

3 Women may also be anxious about 'being in control' in terms of occupying a power role, because they may be perceived as aggressive, dominating, castrating, a bitch (all negative stereotypes of women in control as projected by male anxiety about the meaning of losing feminine receptivity). Perhaps this accounts for the pose: 'being in control of one's control without being controlling.' In this sense, the commodity is positioned as an anti-anxietant.

Interpretively, the semi-reclining posture might be revalued once the gaze is redefined as the female viewer's. If revalued, we have an image enacting before women a role played with men, but also the nonchalance of being 'laid back' – a typically male way of displaying ease with one's own power.

4 This confuses objectification of self with active agency – 'you' become the object created by the agency of the product – 'L'Artiste.'

5 In each ad, the absence of hair has been focal. In the western tradition of art, the woman's skin is stripped of hair to 'appeal to [the male viewer's] sexuality, not hers.' 'Hair is associated with sexual power, with passion. The woman's sexual passion needs to be minimized so that the spectator may feel that he has a monopoly of such passion. Women are there to feed an appetite, not to have any of their own' (Berger, 1972: 55).

6

COMMODITY FEMINISM

Pop feminist criticism of advertising mounted throughout the 1980s, and by the late 1980s, many advertisers were bidding to reincorporate the cultural power of feminism, while domesticating its critique of sexist mass media. To stay competitive in the hunt for market share, advertisers adapted to female consumers who had grown hostile to how advertisements continuously positioned them to envy the body or the look conveyed by model images. Contemporary women have been so inundated by photographs of beautiful women that they often react to the images with feelings of anger. Ad campaigns in the latter 1980s like that for *Pantene* acknowledged the problem of women competing with each other in terms of image. The caption 'Don't hate me because I'm beautiful' aimed at appeasing women's anger about being addressed in terms of unattainable images of glamour. Responding to women's resistance to being framed as objects of desire, advertisers devised aesthetic responses to the male gaze and the customary mode of address. Advertisers also pursued a wide range of superficial ideological grafts that spliced together signifiers of feminism with the consumer narrative of femininity as envy, desire and power.

Advertising representations of women have become a significant part of the historical circumstances that condition women's consciousness of everyday life. Parallelling advertising's ideological shifts, the category of 'postfeminism' emerged during the 1980s to designate a new generation of women who take for granted the victories secured by their elders, presuming their right to equitable treatment both in the workplace and at home, while shunning the label of feminism. Postfeminism 'describes the simultaneous incorporation, revision, and depoliticization of many of the central goals of second wave feminism' (Stacey, 1987: 8). Mass media advertising to women represents an aesthetically depoliticized version of a potentially oppositional feminism. It is a feminism tailored to the demands of the commodity form.

COMMODITY FEMINISM/FETISHISM

The pun, commodity feminism, is a reminder that commodity relations turn the relations of acting subjects into the relations between objects. The process of turning feminism into sign values *fetishizes* feminism into an iconography of things. When advertisers appropriate feminism, they cook it to distill out a residue – an object: a look, a style. Women's discourses are thus relocated and respoken by named objects like *Hanes* hose, *Nike* shoes, *Esprit* jeans. Sign-objects are thus made to stand for, and made equivalent to, feminist goals of independence and professional success. Personality can be represented, relationships achieved and resources acquired through personal consumer choices.

The motor force of commodity culture rests on joining otherwise disparate meaning systems to generate new sign values. *Punning* furnishes an efficient method of joining meanings by simultaneously differentiating, collapsing and recombining at least two clusters of meanings. The pun's motion invites readers to realize double meanings and thereby generates a new meaning for a product look or fashion style. 'Commodity feminism' represents the process of punning used to double and join the meanings of feminism and femininity. In today's marketplace, the identity of a magazine or a fashion product is conditional on its *sign-difference* from comparable commodities. Advertisers compete to bridge the difference between {feminism/not femininity} and {femininity/not feminism} in order to establish differentiated commodity-signs (e.g., *Esprit*/'neo-feminism').

Women's magazines in the late 1980s touted an apparent detente between femininity and feminism. Since the early 1970s, advertisers have tried to connect the value and meaning of women's emancipation to corporate products. First 'femininity [was] recuperated by the capitalist form,' now feminism has been similarly recuperated. Women's magazines tried to redefine feminism through commodities, rendering the everyday relations women encounter and negotiate into a series of 'attitudes' which they can then 'wear.' To carve out *differentiated image niches* for their products, advertisers compete at translating women's discourse back to themselves as spectators. In mass advertising, feminism takes on a plurality of faces, but its potentially alternative ideological force is channeled into the commodity form so that it threatens neither patriarchal nor capitalist hegemony. Feminist morality, along with the tensions it contains, has been turned into yet another 'raw material' in the never-ending drive to renew and expand the commodity-sign values of consumer goods. Feminism has been reduced to the status of a mere signifier, so that it may be re-encoded by advertisers as a sequence of visual clichés and reified signifiers. This produces visual abbreviations – second-order signifiers – that gradually eclipse the original referent system of feminism. The visual signs focus meaning intensively, but at a cost of hermeneutic reductivism. Feminist values including self-

131

definition, equal treatment in labor markets, control over one's body and personal freedom have been semiotically transformed into what signifies attractiveness to men.

Change, in these representations, has no history, but is simply a marker of novelty, or difference, represented in fetishized form by special commodities. Commodity feminism *elides* the social dimension which conditions the contradictions experienced in daily life. Feminism becomes 'depoliticized' as ads turn 'feminist *social* goals to individual lifestyles' (Rapp, 1988: 32).[1] When framed by ideologies of individualism and free choice, feminism put into commodity form *forgets* its origins in a critique of unequal social, economic and political relations.

A close critical reading of ads in a representative cultural text, the September 1987 issue of *Mademoiselle*, addresses this reframing of feminist discourse. Interrogating these ads aims at re-articulating the ideological contradictions concealed by the daily routinization of the commodity and advertising *forms*. This critical decoding aims at repoliticizing the depoliticized – bringing back into the picture the social, cultural, political and economic relations which these ads refer to, but gloss.[2]

'FEMININITY,' 'FEMINISM' AND 'MARKET SHARE'

Mass-circulation magazines like *Mademoiselle, Glamour, Vogue* and *SELF* cultivate and promote commodity relations and exchanges wherever possible. A glance across the magazine covers in the supermarket checkout line reminds us that no part of our lives escapes the corporate formula of commodified solutions for needs – e.g., '17 ways to beat stress'; 'get your rear in gear – 5 firm moves'; '100 looks for love and work.' These items, like the ads inside, hail the individual reader, either explicitly naming 'YOU,' or implying 'you' and letting readers fill it in for themselves. Magazines proclaim themselves as the voice of 'expertise' – addressing readers in an imperative voice as well as that of an intimate friend engaging us in personal dialogue.

In the twentieth century, advertising has evolved a distinctive mode of address toward women that articulates a vocabulary of visual signifiers which define the meaningful universe of 'femininity.' Goffman delineated the gestures and poses used to signify 'femininity' in ads – e.g., licensed withdrawal (a wispy, self-absorbed aura) or 'the touch.' The mass media signify femininity by visually emphasizing the line and curve of the female body along with a code of poses, gestures and gazes. This visual lexicon has become so familiar that we now accept the isolated signifier – the close-up curve of a calf or the hip or an ear lobe – as standing for 'the feminine.' Femininity has become widely synonymous with the intensive scrutiny of signifiers created by visually dissecting the female body into zones of consumption – lips, eyes, cheekbones, hair, breasts, hips, waist, thighs, skin, hands.

132

To signify feminism, on the other hand, advertisers assemble signs which connote independence, participation in the work force, individual freedom and self-control. *Commodity feminism* presents feminism as a style – a semiotic abstraction – composed of visual signs that 'say who you are.' Since the early 1970s when *Virginia Slims* and *Revlon* began to capitalize on changing attitudes among women, marketers have grown attentive to what women 'want to hear about themselves.'[3]

> By now, the housewife/mother is a despised figure – most despised by actual housewife/mothers . . . . Since these viewers now prefer to see themselves represented as executives, or at least as mothers with beepers and attaché cases, the *hausfrau* of the past . . . has largely been obliterated by advertisers.
>
> (Miller, 1988: 50)

A generation after the women's movement scored victories with anti-discrimination suits, advertisers routinely address women, and their daughters, in a voice which acknowledges these changes. The culture industry now carefully tracks the demographic paths and attitudes of women as a method of positioning products to target audiences. *Mademoiselle* owner, Conde Nast, is a corporate conglomerate that calls itself 'a family of magazines' – a family defined by market analysis. Survey research guides Conde Nast's efforts to assemble women into audience packages that can be sold to advertisers. Corporate marketers take aim on 'market share' by dividing and subdividing women into market segments. Competition for audience and market share often centers on how marketers and editors position their product *vis-à-vis* ideologies of feminism. In the 1980s, marketers could no longer confine themselves to asking simply 'what do women consumers want?' They now had to ask '*how do we address our target audience woman?*,' since domesticating the mode of address is an essential ingredient in synthesizing 'postfeminist' signs.

Advertisers' efforts at bridging the ideological distance between feminism and femininity have spawned new ideological contradictions. Meanings of choice and individual freedom become wed to images of sexuality in which women apparently choose to be seen as sexual objects because it suits their 'liberated' interests. The female body gets reframed as the locus of freedom as well as sexual pleasure. A tacit theoretical concept of individual freedom of choice lies at the center of commodity feminism. The commercial marriage of feminism and femininity plays off a conception of personal freedom located in the visual construction of self-appearance. Body and sexuality emerge as *coincidental signs*: the body is something you do to validate yourself as an autonomous being capable of will-power and discipline; and sexuality appears as something women exercise by choice rather than because of their ascribed gender role. The properly shaped

Figure 6.1 SELF

Source: *SELF*, 7 March 1988 © The Conde Nast Publications Inc.

LTHY and WISE

Today's women are tuned into more than their bodies. So is the magazine they read: *Self.*

Self readers are successful career women, used to making decisions. And *Self's* award-winning journalism gives them an edge.

Timely articles on medical breakthroughs. In-depth fitness and nutrition coverage. New fashion and beauty ideas. Advice on finance, careers, relationships.

So, be wise and invest in this important group of consumers.

Now can you see yourself in *SELF?*

female body is taken as evidence of achievement and self-worth. Magazine editors and 'experts' endlessly counsel that achieving this body freedom is a significant personal accomplishment, requiring sustained acts of goal-directed will-power.

> The sleek, smooth, tight butt is a badge, a medal asserting that anal compulsiveness is an unalloyed virtue. Perfect thighs . . . are an achievement to be admired and envied. They signify that the woman has made something of herself, that she has character and class, that she is the master of her body and, thus, of her fate.
>
> (Douglas, 1988: 19)

CONSTRUCTING AND ADDRESSING THE AUDIENCE AS COMMODITY

Before turning to *Mademoiselle*'s editorial environment and product advertising as they choreograph a *postfeminist* unification of feminism and femininity, consider how women are portrayed in ads which market women readers to media buyers. Publications such as *Advertising Age* contain the pictorial flip side of turning women into commodities. They foreground what is usually background or subtext: the political economy of consumer product advertising as it conditions editorial and advertising messages in women's magazines.

Women's magazines prosper as vehicles for advertising messages.[4] These magazines compete for advertising revenue by delivering demographically identified segments of the women's market. When women buy a magazine, they become part of a 'package' the magazine has sold to companies that advertise in its pages. Women readers, as potential consumers, are marketed to media buyers just as other goods are sold. Using images of femininity and feminism combined with specific descriptions of purchasing power, household income, age and lifestyle characteristics, women's magazines make their pitch to potential advertisers in the pages of trade journals. A magazine's appeal to readers is putatively based on editorial content; the appeal to advertisers is based on the audience whose attention (and buying power) it can command.

Ads for *SELF, MS.* and *Cosmopolitan* appeared in *Advertising Age*. In each ad, the magazine positions their 'product' – the woman reader/consumer. The commodity sold here is an *audience* of women.[5] The two-page ad for *SELF* magazine (Figure 6.1) features a young woman reclining against a white background.[6] Across the top, the caption reads 'HEALTHY, WEALTHY, and WISE.' The woman's body is photographically segmented into three corresponding zones, each clothed and accessorized to signify the different spheres of consumption in her life. Hiking boots, wool socks and jeans on her feet and legs signify a healthy outdoors lifestyle. This is spliced to a photo of her mid-section clothed in nylons, a red satin dress and silver bracelets on her sun-tanned arm – all signifiers of a woman of means and sensuality. From the shoulders up she wears a black and white business dress, accessorized with gold jewelry, pen in hand and glasses lying in front of her on an open magazine. This offers a carefully constructed visual representation of marketers' compartmentalized vision of young women.

Note how a magazine that purports to speak from a feminist perspective markets itself to readers and advertisers. The *MS.* pitch to advertisers (Figure 6.2) makes 'buying power' the motive for postfeminism.

WHAT DO YOU CALL A WOMAN WHO'S MADE IT TO THE TOP?

MS.

> She's a better prospect than ever. Because we've turned the old Ms. upside down to reflect how women are living today. And you're going to love the results.
> The new Ms. is witty and bold, with a large-size format that's full of surprises. Whether it's money, politics, business, technology, clothing trends, humor or late-breaking news – it's up-to-the-minute, it's part of the new Ms. So if you want to reach the top women consumers in America, reach for the phone . . .
> THE NEW MS. AS IMPRESSIVE AS THE WOMAN WHO READS IT.7

Pictorially, the new *MS.* woman is literally turned on her head. In a lighthearted moment she reclines over a couch so that a collection of identifiable items spill from her pockets. These include a passport; Tictac breath mints; a child's drawing; calculator; keys; American Express Card; perfume atomizer; gold charm bracelet; a crumpled $100 bill; Anacin; and a business card. These material artifacts signify the mix of interests and accomplishments of the 'new 80s women' who look to *MS.* for direction. Each significant *relation* is encoded in commodity-object form.

Though *MS.* is usually cast as the ideological opposite of Helen Gurley Brown's *Cosmopolitan*, note the similarity of their pitch to media buyers. *Cosmopolitan*'s campaign (Figure 6.3) works off the tagline 'The power behind the pretty face.'8

> You assume she likes to get around. To her, that means a new set of wheels. You figure she likes to keep in shape. She knows that includes exercising her mind. The truth is, the Cosmo girl knows more, does more, earns more, spends more.
> THAT'S POWER. THAT'S THE COSMOPOLITAN GIRL.

Behind her back, the Cosmo Girl holds her collection of objects, remarkably comparable to the signifying objects of the *MS.* woman: American Express gold card; make-up brushes; Pan Am World air travel card; Hertz Rent-a-Car card; compact disk (Mozart); portable Sharp calculator; motor-

Figure 6.2 MS.

Source: Advertising Age, 7 March 1988

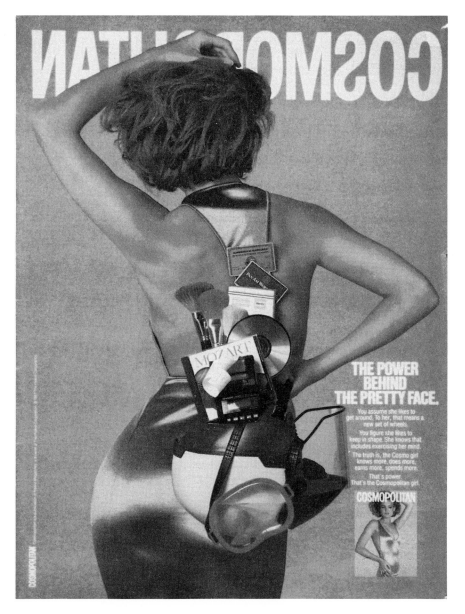

Figure 6.3 Cosmopolitan
Source: Advertising Age, 7 November 1987

cycle helmet; scuba diving mask. Both *MS.* and *Cosmopolitan* represent their 'woman' as a consumer of objects that symbolize the worth of emancipated women – signifying lifestyle leisure activities, disposable income, professional and personal roles, concern for appearance and travel.

The Conde Nast package of women's magazines included *Mademoiselle, Vogue, Brides, Glamour* and *SELF.* Like its competitors, Conde Nast sold women as active leisurers packaged in unabashedly commodity metaphors (Figure 6.4).[9]

26 MILLION WOMEN IN A PACKAGE.

Critical Mass. 26 million high-gear women readers set wheels in motion, get ideas rolling. Their sources are Vogue, Glamour, Mademoiselle, Brides and Self, the magazines of the most dynamic force in women's media, The Conde Nast Package of Women. To shift tastes. To drive sales curves uphill, get the particulars on The Conde Nast Women's Package, the Critical Mass.

In Conde Nast's commodified family of women, *Mademoiselle* is the magazine for *Strong women with a weakness for fashion and beauty.*

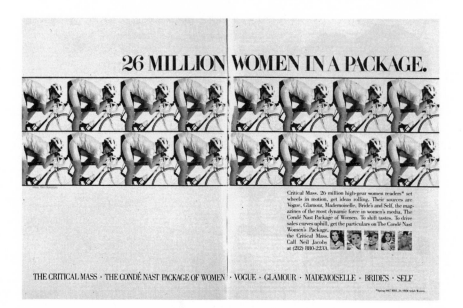

Figure 6.4 Conde Nast

Source: Advertising Age, 7 March 1988 © The Conde Nast Publications Inc.

ADDRESSING THE GAZE

Mademoiselle readers are addressed by a cacophony of voices, each competing to differentiate itself aesthetically from the others. This would appear at first glance to be disorganized pluralism, but remember that all of this is still contained within a framework defined by the logic of commodity consumption and the logic of the advertising form. From the late 1940s to the early 1980s, ads painted a world that contained no ideological contradictions. By the 1980s, advertisers who spoke to women could no longer get away with this line of address. Advertisers learned that many women had grown to resent images of objectified body parts paired with the male gaze. Motivated to recapture the attention of estranged readers and compete in narrowly defined market segments, advertisers began to *vary* their mode of address. The September 1987 issue of *Mademoiselle* contains a wide spectrum of gazes. An ad for *Coca-Cola Watches* (Figure 6.5) typifies the standard, all-American cheerleader male gaze. It's so spelled out that we can even see reflected in her sunglasses the admiring male gaze one might win with the benefit of this look. But we cannot read her eyes – she is an appearance who can command admiring gazes but does not necessarily return the gaze. A twelve-page *Georges Marciano* ad spread represents the male gaze at its zenith, but gives patriarchy and the male spectator-owner an ambivalently sleazy look. The *Marciano Guess?* ad campaigns are notorious for the uneasy way in which they exploit cultural contradictions, piling equivocal meanings of rebellion, risk and sexuality into a single photographic scene. These pages include provocative scenes of young women in the company of an affluent older man. They kneel in front of him, sit on his lap or permit him to nuzzle their ear. With this dirty old man scenario, *Guess* 'is associating an edge of danger with its brand name, a strategy that plays directly on the urgency and ambivalence of adolescents' sexual impulses' (Moog, 1989: 155). Though the young women in these scenes are photographically posed in sexually vulnerable and subordinate positions, they address the camera and the viewer with gazes that suggest indifference. As a fantasy about being an irresistible object of desire, they still possess enough cool detachment to remain aloof and in control. Who is exploiting whom here? Perhaps these photographic representations are ambivalent and contradictory because they target young women whose selves have been socialized within the contradictions of patriarchal and capitalist relations – told to be simultaneously objects of desire and subject in control of their social situation. In stark contrast, the *Joan Vass, USA* ad (Figure 6.6) targets an upscale, disaffected market with models who reveal no affect; they are emotionally distant and withdrawn, posed like statues and mannequins. The commodity has finally purged the subject from the body, leaving only the commodity-styled shell. The de-centered subject now sits outside herself surveying with us her object-

Figure 6.5 Coca Cola Watches

Source: Mademoiselle, September 1987

Figure 6.6 Joan Vass, USA
Source: Mademoiselle, September 1987

image. Is this nihilist posturing a self-indulgent presence calculated to give pleasure to the self as an absent spectator-owner? Or is it a statement about the death of fashion, death of sex – the end of desire? Rounding out the assortment of gazes is a *Nike* ad (Figure 6.7) that appellates women athletes with a gaze that says this look is not about, or for, men. It might even be that her gaze invites viewers to eschew femininity.

Each ad hails viewers through its mode of address, asking us to insert ourselves when the model fits – when we perceive an 'alreadyness.' Invited to see a potential 'self' in the mirror of the ad, we are bidden to perform a critical interchange of meanings. Most advertisers prefer to stay with a mode of address constructed around the framework of the conventional male gaze. Consider a *Nivea* face cream ad (Figure 6.8) with its caption 'Is your face paying the price for success?' The viewer is appellated, but the query is situated in relation to a photograph of a blonde woman in her mid-20s holding the hand of a female child on an urban sidewalk as she peers into her reflection in a glass window. Whose face? – there is no confusion if we recognize the model's presence as an imaginary subst-itution for ourselves. This woman's attire exemplifies how a set of visual signifiers can be made to function as a sign for 'feminism.' Let's unwrap the relations signified by this photo. The child whose hand she holds we presume to be her daughter. Her other hand holds a signifier of her professional rank and status – a briefcase. Drawing attention to the brief-

Figure 6.7 Nike

Source: Mademoiselle, September 1987

Figure 6.8 Nivea

Source: Mademoiselle, September 1987

case, the advertiser has visually masked whether she wears a ring. Though we may infer she is married, the centrality of a man in her life is left open and we might also infer that she is a single mother. And yet, the relationship with her daughter seems almost incidental, because her primary relationship is with herself as she looks at her reflection in a store window. Her blouse, open at the neck, with a tailored, double-breasted jacket and matching skirt suggest her to be a fashion-smart woman who has achieved professional success in a formerly male-dominated work world while also devoting herself to her family.

Despite reading the caption, most readers label this woman as 'pretty.' Yet, this penetrating self-examination in the mirrored store window suggests her fearful recognition of lost beauty through premature aging and stress. The caption alludes to the real world where women who work and parent encounter a double dose of physical and emotional stress. We see a woman who, we are led to infer, has practiced the work ethic and suffered to gain success while balancing the demands of family. As a result, however, she/you may be 'paying the price' in diminished *face value*. The price of her success in the labor market may cost her what she values most – her beauty, because that is what makes her of value to the market.

But she has already managed *stylishly* to wed together the worlds of mother and professional, and here is yet another commodity solution to her concern about maintaining her labor market value and her face value (cf. Lakoff and Scherr, 1984). Her priorities, values and status have changed, but there is an amazing similarity between this ad and 1920s ads aimed at women defined as housewives and competitors in the marriage market. Now, as then, the emphasis is on insecurity and anxiety about how she looks as she *surveys* herself in the mirrored window. The advertiser set up this scenario about the anxiety of a diminished self in order to offer a commodity solution, in this case a scientifically formulated skin cream (cf. Ewen, 1976: 34–48). We may now take another interpretive whack at the relationship between the caption and picture. Perhaps the woman depicted has already used the product and, despite her penetrating survey of herself, has withstood for another day the threat to her youth. She's the you that you might be if you too use *Nivea*.

A *Vanity Fair* bra ad uses a scalloped border to frame the direct gaze of an attractive young woman wearing/modeling a full-figure bra. Ringing her image around the edge of the page is a string of words printed in irregular lettering. The layout of the frame indicates that these words constitute her internal monologue.

CLIENT MEETING black dress? Blue dress. Cancel Lunch. Mom, when you said I'd have to wear big, ugly bras all my life . . . I'm glad you were wrong. Weekend agenda: RELAX!

We thus infer she has a professional career and is an independent person. The male world of commerce and status forms a silent, but present, party to this dialogue. She has entered this world, but still frets over 'feminine' details such as what to wear. 'Mom' had counseled that daughter's fate lay in 'big, ugly bras.' 'Mom' stands for a generation of women whose fatalistic and limited expectations can be contrasted to our more modern views. The proof lies in this 'pretty' *Vanity Fair* bra which contradicts Mom's traditional view: 'Streamlined construction hugs the body for absolute comfort, ideal support and freedom of movement.' Though each term supposedly describes the product line, each also conveniently refers to social ideals sought by today's woman.

Mom was wrong, you can have freedom of movement without suffering constraint. Unlike men, who have sought success through the formula of hard work and a willingness to endure discomfort, today's woman can not only succeed in a man's world, but manages to retain a balance between an implicitly successful professional career and feminine tastes, between work and leisure/play. She can be equally at home in the business world and in her sensuous, narcissistic appreciation of her own visual beauty.

Men constitute a referential absence in this narrative. She works, *supports* herself; men may fit into her leisure life, not into her plans for economic survival. In a sense, indeed, the bra replaces the male – after all, it supplies her with comfort, support and freedom, and she can 'forget' it. Despite her outward independence, the *Vanity Fair* woman continues to indulge the pleasure of her body/breasts. Women's magazines have always located femininity in terms of a visual lexicon of *pleasure*. Her gaze fixes us and invites us to share in this potential pleasure. Here, as throughout advertising, femininity as pleasure has been defined in terms of woman's privileged access to her own sensual body surface. This derives from the frame of the 'male gaze' which has historically premised interpretation of pictures of women in magazines. Within the parameters of the male gaze, women's pleasure symbolizes men's leisure (Winship, 1987: 52ff).

COMMODITY DIFFERENCE: POSITIONING THE MEANING OF EMANCIPATION

Competition within product categories such as jeanswear centers on establishing a differentiated positioning concept for each brand name that integrates, in a singular way, the meaning of feminism with femininity. The unity and diversity of the 'many faces' of commodity feminism are particularly evident when examining ads within a single product category.

Lawman (Figure 6.9) instructs that 'No one has the right to pressure you into anything that hurts your body, clouds your future, or robs you of your *self respect.*' There is no submissive posture here, but a spirited young woman ready to become all that she is and can be. Positioning *Lawman* as

Figure 6.9 Lawman

Source: *Mademoiselle*, September 1987

an agent of freedom, rather than as an agent of coercive containment, creates a paradoxical conjunction of terms unless one shares in a conservative mythology of 'lawman' as the champion of individual rights. Ironically, the jeans which sponsor this young woman's bill of rights draw their name from the agency which enforces the legal relations of a capitalist/patriarchal State – the very State which historically enforced women's second-class status. Today, young women can gain and protect their freedom by binding their bodies in '*Lawman.*'

The *Lawman* ad presents a cheerleader-like celebration of postfeminism. When joined to the list of inalienable rights, this picture sums up postfeminism – a generation of young women who take for granted the rights gained through the struggles of feminists. This humanist 'declaration of independence' depoliticizes these rights into individualized lifestyle options. A model posed in a moment of liberation – taking off into an unalienated future – is made to represent and express the meaning of '*your self respect.*' The *Lawman* ad ideologically celebrates the field of lifestyle consumption as 'an autonomous playful space beyond determination' (Featherstone, 1987: 58).

Get Used projects a very different image of independence for young women. Ads for *Get Used* clothing hail defiant young women who want to hit the streets to teach mom and dad a lesson. The names 'Bonwit Teller' and 'Macy's' in the bottom corner are familiar as upscale department stores, but the pictured denim shirts and jackets look like prison work-farm attire. What meanings might readers derive from their pose as modified by the framing concept 'Get Used'? While, in most ads, the commodity is made to embrace a way of life, can this be the intent when showing two apparently alienated, upscale young women hanging out on the street at night? This is an independence of another sort – a feminized 'James Dean' brooding rebelliousness. Textured black and white photography draws on the 'new ad realism' – its grittiness is palpable. Joined with the name, this texture suggests an anti-fashion statement. Perhaps the girls' rebellious posture represents a defiant anti-consumer statement – 'Get Used'! This would seem consistent with the billboard motif in the background that appropriates the aesthetics of graffiti culture. But the very nature of the ad repudiates such a claim, suggesting instead that this is an instance of ideologically recovering resistance to the corporate control of culture. Shot on the street and not in a studio, we see how 'anti-fashion' is turned into a fashion statement.

There are no men in the picture, though their presence is ambiguously implied. 'Get Used' may connote the girls as sexual objects, or we might even infer they 'get off' on the thrill of potential sexual violence. Yet, this places the ad outside the boundaries of conventional middle-class morality. Such a reading also evokes risk, danger and vulnerability. Are these girls street-tough? Do they appear threatened? Or inviting? Coldly desirable and defiant or merely brooding? Are they posed for an absent male gaze? Why would an advertiser address young women with this imperative, one meaning of which is 'sexual abuse'? No single interpretation seems to prevail here. This ad builds on intentional ambiguity, letting viewers fill in their own solution to the riddle of this pun and its disconcerting context. There is an attention-getting shock value in naming the product 'Get Used.' Is there also a semiotic reversal available in here: by consuming *Get Used* jackets, the consumer can inoculate herself against 'getting used'? One mixed message is 'put on "Get Used" and you'll be strong enough to stand cool and steady. You're sexual, but you control your choices.'

PHOTOGRAPHIC HYPERREALISM: DE-GLAMORIZATION AND 'NEO-FEMINISM'

Advertisers once differentiated themselves via their tagline themes; by 1987, they also positioned themselves by how they address viewers through photographic style about questions of what is 'real' and 'authentic.' *Mademoiselle* readers would likely have encountered *Esprit* ads before. Consumers know *Esprit* by its minimalist, no-frills advertising style featuring 'real people' with diverse interests and lifestyles just being themselves. Subject matter and photographic style foster a sense of 'simple, unpretentious quality.' *Esprit*'s 'real people campaign' positioned the brand as joining with viewers in rejecting the usual advertising fictions about commodity selves. Their ads disclaim any link to 'pseudo-individuality' – the advertising premise that a woman can truly become herself by owning the mass-produced commodity in question.

As much as anything, *Esprit* (Figure 6.10) stands out from the advertising clutter by how the women are posed and positioned on the page. The women's portraits are cropped so the frame breaks off in the middle of their foreheads. This sharply contrasts with a conventional *Clairol* ad on the preceding page that centers model face and hair on the page. Women in the *Esprit* ads also appear minimalist in their make-up use. In her full-page photo, Ariel O'Donnell addresses us straightforwardly, her shoulders and head squared toward the camera/us. A simple blue workshirt accentuates a squared look, de-emphasizing the line of her body. Seated with her legs crossed, we can see little of her from the waist down. Tiny print, framed within a black band ¹/₈ th inch high, lists Ariel's vital statistics:

Ariel O'Donnell San Francisco, California Age: 21 Waitress/Bartender, Non-professional AIDS Educator, Cyclist, Art Restoration Student, Anglophile, Neo-Feminist.

Repeat the list again with each referent's semiotic function in parentheses: 'Waitress/Bartender' (her employment, which we may recognize as temporary); 'Non-professional AIDS Educator' (indicates her social consciousness);

149

Figure 6.10 Esprit

Source: Mademoiselle, September 1987

'Cyclist' (her athletic recreation – her leisure); 'Art Restoration Student' (connotes her intellect and a possible professional future); 'Anglophile' (her quirky, purely personal interest); 'Neo-Feminist' (her philosophy).

On the next page, another biographical blurb repeats these symbolic categories, but in a slightly varied order, to define Cara Schanche. Like Ariel, she is identified in individualist and non-conventional terms.

> Cara Schanche Berkeley, California, Age: 23 English Literature Student, Part-time Waitress, Anti-Racism Activist, Beginning Windsurfer, Friend of the Dalai Lama.

Unlike Ariel, and perhaps indicative of *Esprit*'s 'personal touch,' Cara is posed in a tight close-up shot of her face and neck. There is no tilt to her face – her chin is level and her eyes greet the viewer straight on. We see a blue-jean/denim jacket collar about her neck, but that is all. With no make-up on, Cara emanates an image of naturalness/realness. There is no place to hide here, as she – unflinchingly, maskless – confronts the camera. There is none of what Goffman called facework in the way her face addresses the camera/us. She apparently has enough ego-strength to be seen as herself. Her clothes don't define her, she defines her clothes. Joining together this meaning of ego-strength with the image of the *Esprit* label immediately opposite her eyes valorizes the sign value of *Esprit* jeans.

Other *Esprit* ads convey similar 'neo-feminist' themes – e.g., 'Successful, Independent Woman' or 'Future News Anchorwoman and Mother.' Young women are pictured as achievers, *not* as stereotypical, vacuous fashion models. They are obviously smart and not so self-involved as to be unconcerned with questions of social consciousness. As multi-dimensional personas, these 'real' young women stress their non-stereotypic feminine roles, preferring instead the active pursuits previously associated with males. There is nothing delicate or dainty about them.

Opposite Ariel's photo is a white page with an *Esprit* canvas beige jeans tag angled across it. Likewise, at the bottom of the page the words '*Esprit* jeans' appear with the brandmark printing of 'E.' There seems to be no sales pitch here – the jeans are not the primary photographic focus, and only the sign appears opposite Ariel's portrait. And something else is missing too – the viewer has not been conventionally appellated.

The page facing Cara's picture has a black background and a predominating image of blue denim in a sequence of grids. The top three-quarters of the page is divided into twelve bordered blocks – each block equals one-sixteenth of the page. At top is the *Esprit* tag on the back of blue denim jeans. Like the picture of Cara, this photo of the jeans is a close-up 'super-real' shot that permits viewers to see the rows of threads in the denim. But gazing at the texture of *Esprit*, we perceive an apparent distortion in the way the blocks fit together. Nine of the blocks would be perfectly contiguous if the black rectangular grid lines had not been drawn through the photo. But box #4 is a different scale shot of a side pocket and box #5 contains the front button. Sewing together back pocket, side pocket and front button into a single flattened plane creates a visual distortion. Box #12 contains a wallet-size photo of Ariel's cropped face. Her presence is juxtaposed against the *field* of *Esprit* denim/product in which she is situated. Below Ariel's photo is this block of text:

Esprit Jeans – A Modern Concept

Because denim and jeanswear are such social equalizers today you don't necessarily need silks and satins to be elegant. Elegance is now, curiously enough, anti-fashion and anti-luxury. This new elegance has become a *de-*classification process that puts what you can do – your style and abilities far ahead of what you can afford. Now you don't have to be rich to be elegant.

Esprit raises – as it simultaneously obscures – questions of social class. *Esprit* self-consciously does what 99 per cent of ads refuse to do – they bring up the categories of gender and class. They do so to declare dead the tyranny of class and gender limits – *Esprit* claims to be the motor of this *de-*classed new age where heroic young women are free to do 'what you can do.'

This ad presumes reader familiarity with 'the meaning of *Esprit*' and the world of fashion advertising. Savvy readers who possess such intertextual familiarity, recognize *Esprit*'s claim to stand for unembellished quality and value, and its corollary, an absence of pretense. So too, because their ads deviate from advertising conventions, *Esprit* can claim to stand for the interests of 'anti-fashion and anti-luxury.' *Esprit* claims as its sign what it is not.

Until the final wallet-size photo of Ariel and the block of text below, the advertiser has avoided appellating the viewer in all the usual ways. But now at the end of this anti-ad dedicated to social equalizing, the viewer is finally named – and invited to insert herself for Ariel in the mirror-space in the *field* defined by *Esprit* jeans.

> What the advertisement clearly does is thus signify, to represent to us, the *object* of desire. Since that object *is the self*, this means that, while ensnaring/creating the subject through his or her exchange of signs, the advertisement is actually feeding off that subject's own desire for coherence and meaning in her self. This is as it were the supply of power that drives the whole ad motor, and must be recognized as such.
>
> (Williamson, 1978: 60)

Esprit attempts to differentiate itself by inverting the usual juxtaposition between woman and product image so that the woman (Ariel) becomes a sign for the product/*Esprit* name. But this only has value for *Esprit* if, once named, the reader imaginatively inserts herself for Ariel.

In the inverted logic of advertising, a commodity, *Esprit* jeanswear, is portrayed as the agent of progressive social transformation. *Esprit* constitutes the framework (the sign-universe) within which 'neo-feminism' exists – where *you as a modern woman* can a) transcend the constraints of patriarchy and *choose* to define yourself; b) smash the inegalitarian pretense of fashion and luxury; c) redefine 'elegance' and 'style' in terms of 'what you can do' and not what money can buy. According to this doctrine of 'neo-feminism,' *praxis* is relocated in the act of autonomous consumption.

'PLURALISM' AND THE CONTAINMENT OF DIFFERENCE

Contemporary commodity culture 'contain(s) difference or antagonism' by constructing superficial polarities that supposedly correspond to real differences (Williamson, 1986: 100). Commodity culture, in its mass-mediated form, continuously reproduces the appearance of difference, validated in terms of 'pluralism' or 'individual freedom of choice.' The conjuncture between *difference* and *individual freedom of choice* is located in the positioning concept of Style. Style domesticates real political differences *within* the field of commodity choices, masking ideological contradictions and asymmetrical social relations.

The field of Style contains the antagonism between feminism and femininity when both are turned into a series of commodity-signs that women may select to try on, wear, display and even own. Femininity and feminism become presented as interchangeable alternatives, as do the many interpretive permutations generated by the logic of market segments and product differentiation. And since ads stress the individual freedom to interpret the advertisement, in the land of democratic pluralism, each woman can choose to consume her favorite philosophic pastiche of femininity and feminism.

Conventionally, 'femininity' in ads has been synonymous with markers of home, love, sex, 'otherness' and 'naturalness.' Certainly, a majority of ads in this September 1987 copy of *Mademoiselle* continue to address women in and about the language of beauty. This language presumes that universal sexual differences overshadow class, race and ethnicity and women are defined as *not* money, work and power (Williamson, 1986: 103). Commodity feminism appears, at first glance, to take possession of those domains previously declared out of bounds to women. 'Femininity' as both a material and ideological category was once central to the reproduction of capitalist/patriarchal relations. In contrast, the new commodity blends of 'post-feminism' define access to the realm of money, work and power as legitimate. And, paradoxically, the female body has become the mediating element between the constructed domains of femininity and feminism – the domestic sphere and the world of work. Commodity feminism declares that control and ownership over one's body/face/self, accomplished through the *right* acquisitions, can maximize one's value at both work and home. As far as corporate marketers are now concerned, this new 'freedom' has become essential to the accumulation of capital – to reproducing the commodity form.

NOTES

1 Depoliticizing and privatizing feminist demands for greater autonomy and control for women is *not* new. Nancy Cott (1987: 172) shows that, in the 1920s, the nascent consumer industry translated the rhetoric of feminism into the 'consumerist concept of choice' based on packaging 'the modern woman' in commodity form.

2 This reading presumes that ads must be deciphered by viewers. The structure of ads requires viewers to participate in negotiating their own ideological formations. Women bring widely varied 'vocabularies of motive' to interpreting ads, and our analyses cannot possibly give voice to every privatized interpretation available in these texts. People tend to look at ads in areas defined as personal space (hence the probability of privatized and idiosyncratic interpretations). Viewers vary by lifestyle, age, social class, race, education, politics and religion in how they interpret ads. Some women 'make over' the culture of women's magazines into an extension of their own cultural space in opposition to masculine hegemony; some younger women contest every ad that confronts them, and resent the way ads address them. These women react to advertisements as a political affront, but many more claim to find them a bore, and the

majority tend to take ads and the whole reading process for granted, because ads so saturate our environments that the mode of reception becomes habituated, 'distracted' and routinized.

3 See Judith Williamson (1978) about the *Virginia Slims* ads.

4 The 1987 year-to-date figures through November showed 36,256 ad pages in women's magazines. 'Consumer Magazine Ad Linage,' *Advertising Age*, 16 November 1987: 81–2.

5 See Smythe (1977). The images assembled in these ads mirror the uncertainty of those who work in advertising about how to speak effectively to women. Advertising 'agencies and clients are having trouble appealing to women who work as well as to those who stay home . . . . "The majority of women out there aren't neatly typecast, so it's very difficult to develop strategies to reach a large number of them."' See 'Despite Less Blatant Sexism, Ads Still Insult Most Women,' *Wall Street Journal*, 1 August 1985: 19.

6 *Advertising Age*, 7 March 1988: 30–1.

7 *Advertising Age*, 7 March 1988: S-7.

8 *Cosmopolitan* belongs to the Hearst Group which pushes '*Woman Power.*' This is defined as 'bring[ing] together 53 million women. And joins the forces of the five best editorial staffs in the business . . . *Cosmopolitan, Good Housekeeping, Harper's Bazaar, Country Living* and *Redbook*, all in one . . . what you can buy like one magazine is actually five of the most powerful *editorial environments* around' (*Advertising Age*, 7 November 1987).

9 *Advertising Age*, 7 March 1988, inside cover.

7

THIS IS NOT AN AD

THE POST-MORTISE STAGE OF ADVERTISING

When this study of advertisements began in the late 1970s the advertising industry was extensively engaged in streamlining the advertising form initiated in the early twentieth century. Decade by decade, ads underwent a process of abbreviation, as the ratio of text to image was reversed – text was deleted, its meanings tacitly compressed and abbreviated into framing conventions. By the late 1970s, standardized formulas such as the mortise and frame had become overdetermined in pursuit of achieving perfectly transparent preferred interpretations. But already the commercial avant garde was trying to differentiate itself from the crowd by adopting eccentric framing techniques or pursuing the logic of frame reductionism to its minimalist limits. Through the 1980s, more and more advertisers opted to acknowledge to viewers the nature of the framing process in ads. By the end of the 1980s, the hippest advertisers were gravitating not toward transparency in their messages but toward opacity.

Constant pursuit of differentiated sign positions in the 1980s led to a positioning category I call 'this is not an ad.' This type of ad has been designed to look as if it is not an ad, as if it has foresworn the agenda of ads – to sell us a commodity-sign. This style of advertising, it must be emphasized, is only effective to the extent that it remains a minority method of advertising.

In print advertising, the not-ad structure evolved from early incarnations such as the media-hyped *Dior* campaign featuring a pretentious serial about a pretentious *ménage à trois*. Soon, however, the strategy shifted to an avant-garde minimalism that elided formal boundary and coding markers. *Calvin Klein* and *Ralph Lauren* and *Donna Karan* affected this minimalist style in print ad campaigns. Upscale designers could rely upon widespread recognition of their name and utilize a *post-mortise* format that slurs and omits the product image altogether. Leaving out the usual framing techniques could

155

Figure 7.1 Calvin Klein
Source: Vogue, December 1985

throw viewers into minor interpretive quandaries – turning away from such ads wondering 'what does this mean?' Could viewers accustomed to framing markers and the expectation that images bear coherent meanings interpret images which lack borders or lines or words? *Calvin Klein* pressed ad minimalism forward with a campaign that featured sensual and eroticized embraces (see Figure 7.1). As with the subsequent *Calvin Klein Obsession* campaign, the only textual frame was the product name, but the instructions and cues necessary to interpreting the ad had been condensed into the frame/format of the ad. Viewers were thus impelled to complete the advertising narrative by supplying the missing equation between the product and the signifying relationship. Still, *Calvin Klein*'s early forays into minimalism produced little interpretive mystery because they were so highly charged with visual sexual meanings. The later *Calvin Klein Obsession* campaign courted intentional ambiguity with a style of representation that featured scenes of frozen blue passion under the name 'Obsession.' A textured photographic veil clouded nude bodies intertwined, limbs akimbo like pieces of modern sculpture. The blue veil made problematic the exact number and meaningful relationship of body parts. How does this photographic style steer the meaning of obsession – as fetish, fixation, preoccupation, control, monopolization, domination or phobia? Without further framing directions such ads resist interpretive closure, although abstracted body surfaces placed beneath a superimposed or adjacent designer name can still be interpreted if it is understood that subject and product have been collapsed into a single semiotic plane where the subject as signifier and the product as signified are no longer differentiated.

Advertising has historically signified the commodity self by the visual abstraction of body parts. We are accustomed to equating persona with unblemished components of the human body – most notably the expressive surfaces of the eyes, mouth and hands. And, of course, American media culture has abstracted female breasts so relentlessly that they are often treated as if independent of the person who bears or 'wears' them. In the 1980s the sleek, smooth and tight buttock and thigh emerged as a paramount signifier of female beauty. But, in the latter 1980s this style of centered photographic abstraction was simultaneously extended and violated by placing extreme microscopic close-ups in asymmetrical relation to commodities. The conventions of the commodity self required both a recognizable appellation structure (the subject must know that she has been invited to make an exchange with the subjectified object) and a centered, symmetrical relationship between subject and commodity. Deciphering the equation for the commodity self became more problematic when a photographic slice of an elbow or the sole of a foot or the trace of a thigh appeared on the margins of the page or screen. A 1988 *Donna Karan* ad campaign illustrates this style of photographic *ultra-abstraction* without subverting the representational claims of the photographs. The campaign features (Figure 7.2) full-page, tight, fuzzy close-up shots of the body part the Donna Karan commodity is meant to service and display. The sparse minimalism flatters viewers that they are already among the cultural elect who can decipher this text and appreciate a commodity that is not visible. Conversely, perceptive viewers now feel insulted by crude versions of the commodity self because they implicitly recognize the pseudo-individuality involved. This ad features a surfeit of visual signifiers without a corresponding richness of signifieds. We recognize feet, a pointed toe, part of a sheet, a background out of focus, a graceful turn of the wrist and hand, a fuzzy photograph, a soft filter and the absence of a product. These material signifiers may furnish weak connotative hints of sensuality, grace, realism and romance; but, the only overarching signified is 'you' even though there is no immediate signifier of 'you.' In fact, 'you' is signified by viewer recognition of the advertising metastructure and its coding instructions. Discerning viewers may pat themselves on the back for having been able to reconstruct the circuit of pseudo-individuality without a map.

Ralph Lauren's 1985 television ads shown in New York City pursued a comparable minimalism that never mentioned consuming a product, but, unlike other designer ads mentioned above, these ads were neutered and de-sexed. Motivated to differentiate itself from the sea of advertising clutter, one commercial shot entirely in black and white made no reference to clothing or even the name 'Ralph Lauren' until the very end of the piece. Both video and sound were tinkered with so they would not have the *feel* or *texture* of an ad. The soundtrack consisted of an unfamiliar tune (i.e., it brought no currency to bear) performed by an unrecognizable voice and a tinny-sounding acoustic instrument. Just as the music bore no mark of a recording studio, the video images seemed like amateur home movies rather than professionally manipulated film stock. The absence of narrative markers or superimposed framing devices forced viewers to search for coding cues. Without such coding cues, no apparent commercial agenda could be identified, and the point of the sixty-second composition was an enigma. Just as bothersome was the absence of any obvious appellation process. Until the name 'Ralph Lauren' appeared on the screen at the end to clue viewers that this was an ad, the point of the text seemed as aimless as the pick-up truck and the dirt road depicted in both song and image. The name permitted viewers to deduce that the narrative which went nowhere actually points to the sign of Ralph Lauren: the high status and style of Ralph Lauren clothing requires no artifice, but reveals its superior status by producing an avant-garde, artistic ad that isn't an ad at all. The sign of Ralph Lauren is *the subject* who has no need for signs. Indeed, the claim to high status no longer resides simply in the clothing worn, but in the fact that the consumer has enough savvy and class to consume the non-ad.

Subsequently, adventurous advertisers have stretched the omission of coding cues in conjunction with intentionally ambiguous photographic

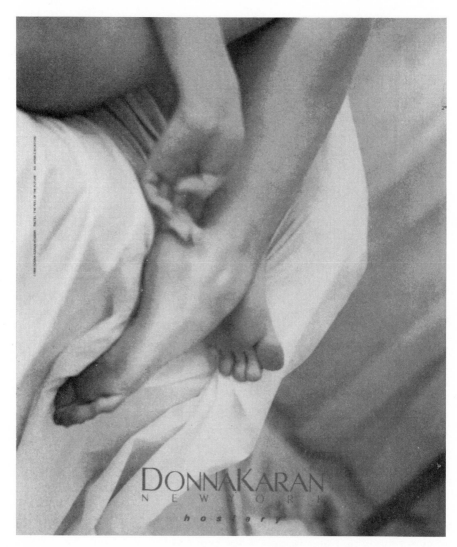

Figure 7.2 Donna Karan

Source: *Elle*, October 1988, photograph by Peter Arnell

images to make the decoding process appear arbitrary and open-ended. An ad from *Vogue* (March 1988) for a product called *Comme des Garçons* (Figure 7.3) features a two-page photograph of ballerinas caught in mid-flight. Tiny print in the upper right-hand corner credits the photograph to Andre Kertesz. Despite this acknowledgement, it feels as if Kertesz's picture has been stolen, directed toward an end in which it had no interest. But what end is that? Very few viewers are likely to recognize either Kertesz or *Comme des Garçons* (an upscale, avant-garde clothing line designed by Rei Kawakubo).[1] What is the relationship between the product name and the photographic content? Since no product image is apparent (unless the product is ballerina dresses) and the product name is unfamiliar, we fall back on where the ad is found and deduce the product to be for women. Still, why would a visually absent clothing line available in chic international boutiques feature a Kertesz photo that has no obvious relevance to clothing? The pool of signifieds is nearly infinite, but exceptionally shallow. Is this enforced polysemy or gibberish?

> Here the simple notion of reading as the revelation of a fixed number of concealed meanings is discarded in favor of the idea of *polysemy* whereby each text is seen to generate a potentially infinite range of meanings.
>
> (Hebdige, 1979: 117)

Figure 7.3 Comme des Garçons

Source: *Vogue*, March 1988, © Estate of Andre Kertesz

Hip and avant-garde not-ads aim to create a style that equals *the meaning of* polysemy. They aim to stand out by creating 'obtuse' semiotic riddles that have no answer. These ads consistently disregard the 'near-universality' of visual codes that govern recognition of mass-mediated images in our culture. While this may initiate ideological reflexivity about the constructedness of habituated coding practices (see Hall, 1980: 132), in these ads the question of hermeneutics becomes an increasingly private matter: the advertiser only cares that privatized polysemy becomes the sign for their commodity – e.g., the triangular logo/sign of *Guess?* by Georges Marciano can accept any meaning *you* want to give it. The new rule of thumb is that iconic photographic representations and apparently definitive photographic meanings are considered plebeian, while perplexing and insoluble images are associated with art and elite boutiques. After all, anyone can decipher the mortise and frame, but only cynically sophisticated subjects can identify themselves as members of the artsy totem group.

Over the years, advertising practices of photographic abstraction have escalated by degrees until some refuse to obey the codes of realist representation and intentionally defy our expectation that photographic images have meaning. Another ad from the same issue of *Vogue* for the *Helmut Lang Collection* initially appears as a Rorschach probe. The grainy shadings of black and gray are barely recognizable as an extremely abstract photographic image – no immediate denotative referent and no direct connotative significance leap out. Within our culture, this does not register as an iconic representation. Like a Rorschach test, this ad requires that viewing subjects supply a subjective interpretation. Though a committed viewer may pursue a closer examination in an effort to identify the 'natural' history of these images, it really is not important that we figure out what the image was, because ads like this move beyond questions of representation. The severity of the abstraction process in conjunction with the absence of conventional recontextualization turns the photographic substance into a sign of pure aestheticism.

Artsy ads like these point, whether intentionally or not, to the arbitrariness of signs and question their motivation. Processes of photographic abstraction are normally taken for granted and so we rarely question the practice of lifting meanings out of context and transforming them into free-floating signs chained arbitrarily to one another. But here the exaggerated severity of the abstraction process draws attention to this arbitrariness. Ads like these for *Comme des Garçons* and *Helmut Lang* challenge the expectation that we will find a meaning in an advertising image by relying on conventional coding rules; they also disclose the capricious and arbitrary juxtaposing of images to create commodity-signs that routinely takes place in ads. If nothing else, these ads indicate a totally random relationship between signifier and signified. But, of course, the question of motivation is fudged. If viewers can find no relationship between the referent systems that appear in an ad, the only motivation is to be found in the framework of the ad as a metastructure – by the interest in creating a sign value.

IS THIS AN AD?

A TV ad for *Honda* motor scooters in 1988 was indicative of both the intense pressure to differentiate ads and the desire to confuse and scramble meanings. Against a grainy black background, a series of white handwritten queries flash past (see Figure 7.4). There is no voiceover or musical soundtrack to steer interpretation of the questions which burst and streak by on the screen. These are accompanied by a strident cacophony of discordant background sound-effects: screeching, scratching, breaking glass, haunting screams, dropping bombs, explosive cracks and shots, wind howling, tearing, a child's laughter followed by frustrated screams.

who am I?
why am I here?
what's a quadratic equation?
can dogs think?
why is there war?
am I ugly?
how does a thermos work?
is there truth?
is there justice?
is there any pizza left?
who am I?
why does love end?
should I buy a vowel?
how long is eternity?
who am I? [flashed 3 times]
why am I here?
did I floss?
why are there zoos?
do giraffes sneeze?
what if I'm captured?
are they laughing at me?
should I pierce my ear?
who
can dogs think?
pizza

From this blizzard of questions slashed across the screen, the scene cuts to a shiny red Honda scooter as a male announcer intones in a baritone voice

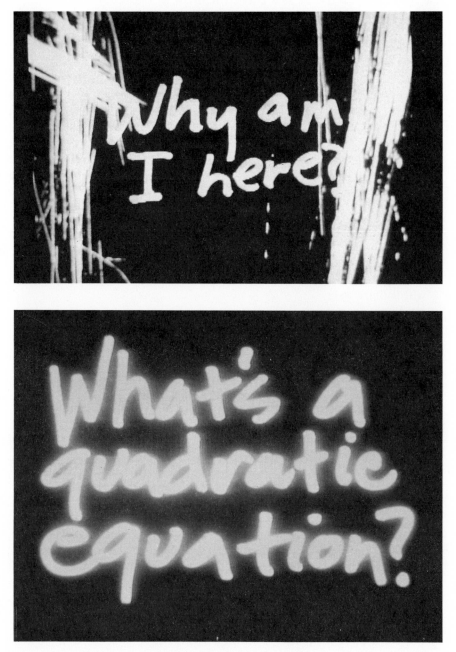

Figure 7.4 Honda (TV) 1988

Source: photograph courtesy of American Honda Motor Co., Inc.

The new Honda Elite 50.
If it's not the answer,
At least, it's not another question.

There is a significant pause composed of sharp cracking sound followed by another scream before his voice reverberates

Another question.

The ad is noisy, perceptually stressful and cognitively disturbing. The discordance defies sense making, positioning the text to sympathize with teenage viewers who are daily bombarded by a stream of questions. Our cultural codes arrange categories of discourse in a hierarchy of importance, but the *Honda* ad seems intent on subverting this code. The questions, serious or not, are all given the same weightlessness. The video text begins with trite questions about self-identity and cosmology. The next question seems out of place – isn't this a school question? And why do the white-lettered words sometimes pulse on and off three times? But there is no time to wonder because another child-like query about animal psychology has already streaked past. Flashing through this stream of consciousness, we race from an anxious adolescent preoccupation with appearance and self-identity to open-ended philosophical musings and metaphysics that oscillate with the mundane routine of daily life ('is there any pizza left?'), the banality of media trivia ('should I buy a vowel?') and the ridiculous ('do giraffes sneeze?'). As the ad propels along, the speed of the questions accelerates until it is impossible to recognize all the questions without slowing the tape of the ad. Of all the questions, the anxiety-laden 'what if I'm captured?' and 'are they laughing at me?' are the most fleeting and the most viscerally disturbing. The fragments of consciousness which dribble out at the end seem an apt metaphor for media implosion.

The *style* of the ad is non-formulaic – the words on the screen vary in size, proportion and placement. Hand lettering connotes the absence of machine standardized and perfected writing. Because the words are not vocalized by a voiceover, and are sequenced in no apparent narrative order or relationship to one another, viewers are pressed to try and read the words. The ad eliminates familiar framing markers that viewers usually rely upon to give direction to the interpretation process. In fact, the ad is designed to ensure multiple viewings if viewers are to piece together the anti-logic of the ad.

Photographic graininess has been drawn out and made as visible as possible. The stray white streaks of light denotatively resemble photographs of particle decomposition in nuclear accelerators or trajectories of disintegrating bullet fragments. The streaking offers a way of meta-communicating to viewers that what is seen has been *produced, made, put together* – we no longer stand in awe of media simulations because OZ has now been exposed of all its media

165

tricks. Grainy photography invaded ad-land in the late 1980s, part of a broader effort to signify *the real* and deny participation in *the bogus* world of media distortion of the world. Exposing the grain of the film/video supposedly exposes the veneer of photo-realist simulation.

FRAME REFLEXIVITY

Ads such as the *Honda* ad have become acutely self-conscious and self-reflexive about their own status as advertisements. Ads now feed on the culture of advertising in the never-ending search for differentiated signifieds that can be used as currency. Various styles have emerged that mock and parody not just the ads of competitors (sign wars), but the very field of advertisements themselves. *Moschino* ads *obviously* satirize the fashion system and the arbitrary construction of sign values: one ad places a model of a fighter jet on a mannequin's head and labels it COUTURE!

Confronted by bored and jaded viewers who scorn the vulgarity of the typical appellation process, some advertisers have gravitated toward reflexively acknowledging and foregrounding the process of framing and the related issue of how the viewing subject is positioned *vis-à-vis* the commodity ideal. In ads directed at women, these questions may be joined to the now fashionable pose of 'denying the [male] gaze.' All of these concerns are raised in this *Matrix* ad (Figure 7.5), which is jarring even for those jaded by too many advertisements. A young woman's sultry appearance is partially enclosed by an art frame, captioned *how to control your fantasies* and punctuated by the banner of *Matrix* hair products. What does this mean? The image is simultaneously straightforward and ambiguous. At first glance, her look seems like the male gaze in toto. The codes of patriarchy are all there. And yet, unmistakably, across her body she holds a long, sharply pointed blade. And why the artifice of the ornate museum art frame suspended around her image but not containing it? Though her look and her position as an object of desire are coded to appeal to the absent male spectator-owner, the knife blade conjures up a fantasy about castrating (disempowering) the spectator-owner. The blade is symbolically presented as a double articulation – simultaneously representing both the terror of the phallus and the instrument of its removal. Now she has the look and she controls it – she symbolically controls the frame.

This ad overflows with contradictions. The text below states: 'Hair. Threads of imagination, from which can be woven patterns that reflect our secret dreams. *Matrix*.' Though written in the language of symbolism, viewers are schooled to read that *Matrix* hair styling products have a use, that is to control your hair. 'The tools of the trade for those who dare to weave.' *Matrix* represented here as both subject and predicate. Embedded in this discourse lie decades of accumulated ideological presuppositions about the relationship of the commodity self to heterosexuality. Like so

166

Figure 7.5 **Matrix**

Source: *Glamour*, May 1988, hair and conceptual design Dwight Miller, Intl Artistic Director, Matrix Essentials Inc.

many ads before it, this ad equates the potential subject's desire with the fantasy look that is the stereotypically male-defined heterosexual object of desire. In the routine 'mirror-phase' of advertising the self is confronted by an image of the Ego-Ideal and the fictional promise of a unified self-identity (see Williamson, 1978: 60–5). By breaking the field of the frame and disturbing the mirror relation, the *Matrix* ad problematizes the search for a unified self-identity orchestrated by advertising through the exchange of self for a better commodity self. The torn edge of the picture (i.e., somebody took this picture and somebody tore it) and the frame suspended in mid-air each call attention to the process of framing. Foregrounding the framing techniques introduces momentary uncertainty about the power relation a) between the advertiser and the viewing subject who is positioned to enter the space of the ad to complete the exchange of meaning; and b) between the female subject and the absent male spectator-owner (the male gaze).

> What the ad can do is to *misrepresent* the position of the subject, and misrepresent its relation to [her]. It disguises its symbolic nature in offering you a unity with the sign, a unity which can only be imaginary, and hence a denial of the Symbolic.
>
> (Williamson, 1978: 65)

Though the *Matrix* ad acknowledges the usual misrepresentation of the subject's position, it cannot let go of Desire as a wellspring of exchange value. Since '[desire] blindly strives after the unattainable, constantly replenished because never fulfilled' (Williamson, 1978: 65) it is perfectly suited to the never sated reproduction demands of the commodity form. So the *Matrix* ad simultaneously unmasks the fiction that the image of desire is identical with desire itself (the picture is not the thing-in-itself) while it fetishizes desire as style like a zillion ads before it have done. The unmasking gambit is designed to motivate viewers to participate in the exchange and transfer of meanings between the self (the viewing subject) and the Ego-Ideal (the model), between signified and signifier. By disturbing the meta-communicative framework, the *Matrix* ad denies positioning the subject to make false assumptions. Though the ad tacitly acknowledges the anger of the female subject who has been repeatedly positioned to seek satisfaction in becoming an object of desire, it does so to deny any complicity in the power relationship inherent in positioning the subject to engage in false assumptions. *Matrix* exposes the meta-messages that underlie this system of distorted communication in order to reposition the subject/viewer to participate in the process of alienated self-exchange essential to transforming signifiers into signifieds and vice versa (the exchange of meanings between self and commodity-sign).

Reflexivity in such ads exposes the meta-discourse that constitutes the code so that sophisticated consumers can then consume their own savvyness. Reflexivity of this sort turns meta-discourse into a signifier that can be joined with a commodity to become an object of consumption. Though reflexivity may interrupt the ideological circuit of the ad, the means of signifying reflexivity can be recuperated quickly. Witness the appearance of rips or tears in advertising pages. The simulated torn edge of an image has moved from signifying a radical disruption of advertising space into a mere signifier of difference. The ripped edge is turned into Myth, in the sense that Barthes speaks about it: 'myth can always, as a last resort, signify the resistance which is brought to bear against it' (1972: 135).

SEMIOSIS AS A SECOND-ORDER SIGNIFIER

A relatively new breed of ad is the self-conscious and self-reflexive semiotic ad. For example, a recent *Pepe* print and television campaign (Figure 7.6) cleverly plays with re-motivating signs it has set in opposition to one another. Simple in design, the ads playfully introduce referent systems which are normally thought of as having nothing to do with one another. But then in characteristic semiotic fashion it reveals deeper levels of meaning in the relationship between the two apparently random photographic signifiers/signifieds. One ad shows a picture of jeans with the word 'def.' below it and a small framed image of an atomic mushroom cloud with the word 'dumb.' below it. In today's youth culture, the term 'def' means hip, while the signifier 'dumb' beneath the atomic cloud clearly defines opposition to nuclear war.

Pepe jeans/def (hip): nuclear bomb/dumb (unhip).

There is a shock value in this semiotic opposition since it is rare that an ad will risk including an overtly political statement. Appeals to consumerism (looking cool in jeans) ordinarily seek to depoliticize referents they touch, but this ad unequivocally seeks to differentiate itself from competitors by linking the consumption of *Pepe* jeans to the politics of 'no nukes.' This is actually a safe risk since the youthful target audience holds idealistic anti-nuke sentiments.

The mortise containing the logo/name in the bottom right corner identifies the product. Reversing the technique of showing no product image, here the subject has been left out. The jeans appear to stand alone minus any perceptible appellation structure. Viewers are invited to step into the jeans only by way of the descriptive equation of non-equivalence written along the side of the ad. To decipher this, viewers must turn the page ninety degrees and read the 'facts' from left to right: 'Atomic bomb. About 14 megatons. Men's and women's jeans. About 14 oz. Macy's.' An interpretive playfulness is at work here. Comparing apples and oranges, atomic devices and jeans, is accomplished by indicating a numerical identity between their vastly contrasting weight units. The jeans are thus

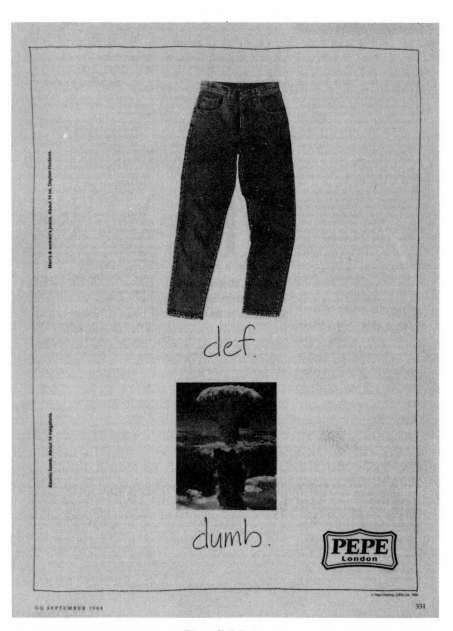

Figure 7.6 **Pepe**

Source: *Gentlemen's Quarterly*, September 1988, photograph by Neil Brown

defined and differentiated by what they are not – they are not atomic bombs. In sharp contrast to the glaringly value-laden metaphoric captions that define each image, these descriptions appear to signify a literal identification of each image. This puzzle requires that viewers recognize the metastructure of the ad page and try to deduce an association between the meaning systems depicted. But the meaning systems depicted in opposition to one another challenge the range of associations normally permissible within such a context. Whereas most ads seek to join two meaning systems to generate a new signified, there is no such signified here. We can usually figure out the new connection by following the logic of the subject–commodity relationship. What kind of sign is possible when this relationship is apparently absent, and the two meaning systems remain counterposed and without a common identity? But the atomic bomb and jeans are united in their difference by the signifier/signified, *Pepe*. This ad invites viewers to articulate a range of signifieds, but most of these will fit into a single meta-sign – i.e., the sign of difference as defined by the act of playful semiotics. Searching for a meaningful association which makes sense to the individual viewer is the pleasure/struggle of deciphering the text.

The pursuit of a differentiated commodity-sign presses this ad campaign close to pure semiotics. It also turns the notion of semiosis itself into a sign. Barthes (1972: 131) suggests that Myth rests on confusing semiological systems with factual systems. The *Pepe* ad endorses no such confusion, since the ad blatantly draws attention to itself as a semiological field in which there occurs an exchange of values. But, in turning the process of semiosis into a second-order signifier that signifies *Pepe* jeans, this ad simultaneously de-mythologizes and re-mythologizes commodity fetishism. In the long run, this may lead to deeper and deeper forms of cynicism.

TO SEIZE THE EYE!

The name of the game in advertising today is to differentiate one's sign from others. This is done by visually differentiating the look of one's ad – seizing the eye of the viewer. The style, the look, the presence of an ad campaign has become practically equivalent to the overall sign of its product. Advertisers are also motivated to produce ads which are unpredictable and whose meanings are opaque, if not impenetrable, because they *arrest* the attention of viewers. If viewers spend more time pondering the meaning of an ad, if they make more of an investment in interpreting it, then perhaps they will be more likely to recall the product name.

Do not-ads open critical space? When art invades advertising it opens a contested terrain, a space in which the hegemony of commodity discourse is momentarily disclosed and challenged. But art is also swallowed up by the commodity form – instrumentalized into another marketing ploy aimed at extending the commodification of desire.

NOTE

1 Kawakubo's radically unconventional approach to fashion has sometimes challenged western definitions of what constitutes clothing – sleeves, neckline, hem and even symmetry. Kawakubo has also pioneered the publishing of *not-fashion* catalogues that show no clothing, but offer an extraordinary vehicle for photographic art. Named *Six*, or *Sixth Sense*, to indicate a presence of mind that is unbounded, this magazine is a bundle of contradictions – for an ultra-elite audience, but grounded in a non-racist, non-western aesthetic. It is important to emphasize that *Comme des Garçons* can engage in such postmodern sensibilities because it does not operate in corporate markets governed by the rules of economies of scale.

8

LEVI'S 501s AND THE 'KNOWING WINK'

Commodity bricolage

We've sought to locate a 'deep grammar' that premises the interpretation of ads. Mapping ads as structured meaning processes has revealed the hegemony of the commodity form, while illuminating a political economy of commodity-sign production. We've tracked a predominant advertising form that reproduces a structural and narrative logic of the commodity form – channelling multiplicities of meaning and action through the univocality of commodity equivalence exchange. We now turn to *Levi's* 501 ad campaign to speak about the alienated production and consumption of commodity-signs in relation to the hegemony of the commodity form.

Despite the hegemonic significance of advertising as a means of reproducing commodity relations – and thereby, Capital – advertising is *not* a closed, or uncontested, cultural universe. Advertisements are social spaces in which commodity-sign values are constructed by joining at least two meaning systems. Viewers' interpretive participation is requisite to completing commodity-sign values. Viewers do not simply consume values, their interpretive labor actually produces and valorizes those sign values. Because viewers are constantly called upon to transact interpretively the meaning exchanges that 'drive the whole ad motor,' it is hardly surprising that viewers may become alienated interpretive laborers.

Levi's ad campaign responded to the alienated artifice of display, to commodity fetishism and its logic of equivalence exchange between commodities and self in ads. *Levi's* experimented with the very structure of advertising – its form and its system of 'reading rules.' What happens when advertisers self-consciously chat with us about the deep grammar of their ads? Shall we interpret such disclosure of ideological deception as a break in the wall of commodity hegemony? *Levi's* ads raised questions about the nature of media reality and the conditions of authentic self-identity, and seemed to sanction resistance to the frames of commodity hegemony. In fact, *Levi's* so successfully signified resistance that they turned this meaning into their sign.

173

Too often, theories of hegemony are represented as heavy-handed, conspiratorial explanations of ideological domination. Our research emphasizes, instead, the structural logic of market and commodity relations. Advertising is a system for producing a currency of signs, and though the encoding–decoding relationship is heavily overdetermined from the encoding side, it is not a mechanical process, but a dialogue which is the site for interpretive exchanges. Indeed, the very premise of *Levi's* campaign, and our analysis of it, was that previous rounds of advertising elicited readings 'against the grain.'

Hegemony is a historicized concept. In American TV advertising during the 1980s hegemony no longer comprised a single dominant ideological account nor did it depend on a closed model of subjectivity. The hegemony of capital now rests on a flexible, and extremely privatized, system of individuated meaning production. Dominant political-economic institutions and elites no longer require a *coherent* legitimating ideology. As concentrated corporate capital has found greater profits in a splintering of market niches, structuring meaning to suit this fragmentation of markets has contributed to fragmented public discourse. The *Levi's* campaign may be considered hegemonic, not because it required that spectators grasp only one meaning, but because it appropriated interpretive space within a framework that blocks off the capacity to articulate counter-hegemonic viewpoints. It obeys and sustains the logic of the commodity form.

Levi's showed how advertisers could absorb criticism of advertising by turning criticism to become a part of their meta-message. *Levi's* attempted to turn the resistance of youth to commodity culture – specifically, to the tacit ideology of pseudo-individualization piped into the background of every ad – into reaffirmation of commodity culture. To do this, *Levi's* produced *not-ad* ads. *Levi's* method was to leave interpretation of their ads open-ended, requiring viewers to supply their own interpretations. It's not the signified that is hegemonic in *Levi's* ads, but rather the act of decoding – such ads open so much interpretive space that even non-preferred counter-readings may be hegemonic. In the US (circa 1984–6) hegemonic ideologies continued to recirculate by using precisely a non-reductionist model of subjectivity.[1]

THE 'REAL'

Advertisers today compete in their denials that their products promote mass-produced consumer conformity. Advertising by the mid-1980s was suffused by concern for the 'real.' For instance, an *Esprit* print campaign listed names, ages and idiosyncratic biographical blurbs by their models. *Esprit* recruited 'real people' for its ads and consumers volunteered to be photographed. Their fold-out ad in *SELF* (March 1987) proposed: 'DON'T CONFORM – INFORM.' Across an otherwise blank page a block paragraph explained:

174

The old saying that you can't judge a book by its cover doesn't hold true for people. We can tell a lot about people by how they dress, how they cut their hair, wear jewelry or make-up. We've learned to interpret these details as signals, which we use to inform ourselves about others. Our first impressions are often guided by a person's appearance, just as others may form their judgement of us in the same way. Fashion is body language, and clothes are the vocabulary. This simple principle influences our choices every time we get dressed. The thought and care that goes into our buying and selecting process is directly linked to the message we send out – our personal style.

Folding out the pages revealed biographical photos demonstrating how real people inform through personal style. The advertisers put semiotic analysis to the purpose it ostensibly opposed – buy their mass-produced commodities in order to communicate your style. *Esprit* offered readers a choice, consume to conform or consume to inform, as if that choice lay simply with the reader.

But why would advertisers draw attention to their agenda of sign production and consumption or to how they structure processes of signification? Advertisers began posing self-reflexive questions about the nature of advertisements because self-reflexivity offers a means of positioning viewers toward a product name in a way that differs from competing brands. Shrewd marketers discern from their surveys that viewers object to 'being manipulated' by ads and don't believe much of what commercials tell them. Advertisers realize they must become more cosmopolitan in how they address alienated younger viewers sensitive to issues of authenticity and unconventionality in a world saturated by slick massification.

Because the credibility of advertising culture became suspect, a posture of self-reflexivity broke out across the field. Recall how the American Association of Advertising Agencies responded to the crisis of advertising legitimacy with its own self-reflexive print campaign debunking criticisms of advertising. The 4-A's campaign raised the question of whether 'Advertising is a Reflection of Society, or is Society a Reflection of Advertising?' in order to debunk the view that advertising has assumed a disproportionate cultural power in our society.

THE JEANS MARKET AND JEANS ADVERTISING IN THE EARLY 1980s

During the 1970s the jeans market grew 10–15 per cent each year. But basic denims sales slipped in the late 1970s and early 80s, 'squeezed by the pincers of fashion and demographics.' 'High styling – or what passes for it – dominates every kind of clothing, not just jeans.' The baby-boom generation grew up, married and moved into the work-force where they no longer wore jeans daily, and so bought jeans less often. Levi Strauss, VF Corporation's subsidiary Lee and Blue Belle Industries' Wrangler together sold 43 per cent of 500 million jeans purchased each year in the US. Confronted by a flat market, they scrambled for market share. Though designer jeans initially cut into basic denims sales, they propped up the industry as a whole until 1984, when designer sales began slumping (*Financial World*, 1984: 30). Levi Strauss, the industry leader, cut costs by closing a dozen plants and idling 3,700 workers in 1984 after closing nine plants and eliminating 2,000 employees in 1982. Inventories in May 1984 were up 16 per cent over the previous year. Earnings per share dropped from $4.61 to $1.70, second-quarter earnings plunged 85 per cent, and Standard & Poor's cut *Levi's* debt rating from AA to A (*Business Week*, 1984: 48; *Financial World*, 1984: 30).

Meanwhile, jeans advertising grew more overtly sexualized. Calvin Klein gained media notoriety for its Brooke Shields tush campaign. *Double entendres* and 'sexy' teases stole the day. Skin-hugging designer jeans grabbed market share from longtime firms like *Levi's*, Lee's and Wrangler's (*WSJ*, 13 March 1979). Jeans advertising intensified its pursuit of 'The Look.' *Jordache* print ads featuring framed images of a fetishized blue-jeaned female backside addressed viewers with 'You've Got the Look' (Figure 8.1). Designer jeans competition escalated reliance on brand names stitched on the rear, until the brand name (Lee's) could no longer compete with the name brand (Klein) in the realm of sign value. Name brands offered a more efficient commodity-sign, where the corporate name also stood for a particular status occupied by the wearer. Higher prices for *Jordache* and *Calvin Klein* jeans plus the initial marketing practice of selling them in boutiques gave *Jordache* and *Calvin Klein* a meaning associated with higher status. Higher status became, in turn, associated with the meaning of body sculpting – putting the body on display as an item of value and a measure of self-worth. 'The Look' became a resource of considerable value in the impersonal social scene of discotheques and singles bars. Advertising accelerated this self-consciousness concerning body image maintenance and performance, while endorsing a notion of the body as a machine that is a site for both identity and pleasure (Featherstone, 1983a). *Jordache* jeans advertising typified narcissistic commodity fetishism where fantasies of sexual attraction with a stranger hinged on possessing 'the look.' The 'Jordache Look' named a lifestyle commodity-sign – a look defined by tightly wrapping one's buns in styled jeans. But this advertising style soon saturated the market, making it difficult for designer jeans makers to differentiate themselves from one another.

A *Lee's* ad illustrated commodity fetishism while attempting to deny it by asking the musical question 'Is It What I Got Going Or What I Got On?'[2] Via an edited string of close-up photographic signifiers, the ad's first 25 seconds orchestrate a narrative of male and female commodity selves

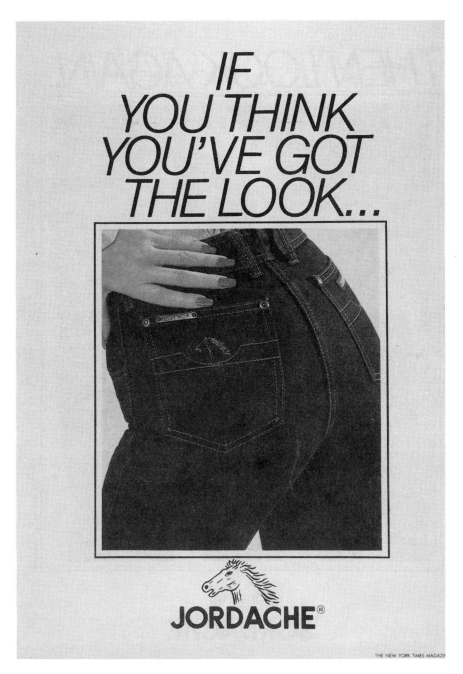

Figure 8.1 Jordache – the Look

Source: New York Times Magazine, 7 March 1982

getting dressed – *putting on the look*. This photographic style of glamour realism signifies 'real life' by encompassing apparently contradictory messages: tight-fitting *Lee* jeans are an essential part of preparing the self to be seen, but the hyperreal signification of the jeans routinizes them as objects organically located in 'everyday life.' Suddenly, however, the ad takes a sharp narrative twist. A drenching rain undoes the primping plans, and by sheer chance our soaked heroine abruptly encounters our hero at a phone booth. In the looks which pass between them, she clearly still has the look which attracts him: it must be 'What She's Got Goin'' that attracts him, since what she has on is wet and mussed up. Where do persona and desire come from – commodities or within? *Lee*'s apparent message is that individuality, of course, lies in who we are. But wait! At the ad's conclusion, *Lee's* emblematic button photographically replaces her face at center screen (Figure 8.2). Her face is literally replaced by the button as a mortise. This framing device re-reifies her jeans instead of de-reifying them.[3] This ad illustrates what is meant by *falsified meta-communication*: raising viewers' questions about the agenda of a message in order to steer the preferred response of receivers in the wrong direction (Herskovitz, 1979: 183).

Figure 8.2 Lee's (TV) – button mortise, 1985
Source: courtesy of Lee Apparel Co. Inc.

THE 501 BLUES CAMPAIGN

Levi's 1984 strategy for countering declining profits was to retreat from diversifying product lines to its basic jeanswear, and mount an advertising campaign aimed at turning its historical marketing weakness into a growth opportunity. Traditionally 'the vast majority of 501 jeans volume comes from a core of loyal users in the Western U.S.' (*Levi's* press release, 2 March 1984). In the Eastern US, however, *Levi's* name recognition was lower and the jeans were harder to find in stores. *Levi's* aimed its $36 million 1984 ad campaign at a broad audience of men, women and youth aged 12–34, although their target emphasis was the 12–24, Eastern and urban segment.

'In a shrinking or stable market, you have to go eye to eye and steal share from your competitors.' In a 'mature market it comes down to marketing' (*Marketing & Media Decisions*, 1984: 59). *Levi's* boosted its ad budget 25 per cent to $150 million for the 1984 Olympics, and hiked its advertising ratio to 5.5 per cent of total annual sales compared to *Wrangler* and *Lee* at less than 4 per cent (*Business Week*, 1984: 48). By December 1984, 'the campaign had reached 99 per cent of its target audience an average of 45 times through a combination of television, radio and magazines' (Aletto in *Patterns*, 1985: 1). *Levi's* attributed a 20 per cent sales increase and 26 per cent increase in revenues in 1984 over 1983 to the campaign. Where one year earlier retail clothiers reported basic denims as 'died out,' now 'designer jeans were out. The 501 has become a fashion statement' (*Time*, 1985: 40).[4] *Levi's* credited the ad campaign created by Foote, Cone & Belding for 'dramatically increased sales of the 501 family of products' (Ankeny in *Patterns*, 1985: 1).

To differentiate its campaign from their competitors and the image clutter, with an audience increasingly savvy and cynical about advertising in general, *Levi's* pursued a stance of apparent reflexivity along with elliptical narratives and anti-Muzak, non-jingle music. *Levi's* TV campaign during the 1984 Summer Olympics joined a musical accent on the Blues to a visually accented blue-hued street world. *Levi's* introduced characters who seemed to be non-models, just ordinary people aware of the camera. These characters connoted authenticity, appearing hiply self-aware of themselves – as consumers, and as people displaying their signs. This enabled *Levi's* to define its sign value as 'appearing unconcerned about the sign value' of one's clothing style.

The '501 Blues' campaign concentrated on connecting an audio-visual meaning of 'Blues' as a musical genre expressing solitude and alienation with the meaning of 'personal blues' as jeans. From the insistence that '501 blues shrink to fit my body' to 'I got the blues . . . ,' we encounter a dual emphasis on individuality and alienation. This duality manifests itself in a refusal to appear self-conscious about one's acts in public. Witness the anti-hero of 'Hard to please woman' (Figure 8.3) whose refusal to adhere to fashion conventions is reflected in the '502 $^1/_2$' on the door under which he sits. He won't even conform to '501s.'[5]

Despite a profound stress on self-musing individuals, these ads also include scenes of *Levi's* wearers in groups. Are 501s your ticket into being accepted by the group? Are they a means of 'fitting in' to the group? On the surface, the answer is yes. But, on closer examination the group houses individuals who relentlessly oppose conformity. Some ads imply a tight peer group, but these groups exist to permit the expression of individuality. *Levi's* group members are individuated through clothing, gesture and expression. '501'derful Blues' features four white male teens performing as an a cappella street quartet in front of a white sheet/screen. All wear *Levi's* jeans and blue-jean jackets, but each displays himself as a self-differentiated sign: one wears shades, another a round, short-brimmed hat, another a short-sleeved jacket and another has rolled-up sleeves. All wear their collars up because it reads 'cool.' Most importantly, their body movement and rhythm are not synchronized. They sing:

Figure 8.3 Levi's (TV) – 502½, 1985

Source: courtesy of Levi Strauss & Co.

Well, I was made for some body
and you could be it.
I ca-ress your body
I shrink to fit.
Keep puttin' me on
And,
I'll be true to you.
Levi's
501'derful
Blues.
My 5-0-1
Blues.
Yeahh.

In *Levi's* ads, the group is formed around a shared relationship to music and to their jeans. This, of course, is a function of the advertiser's primary agenda, connecting the meaning of *Levi's* jeans with variations on the Blues. The group affords a social space in which to share and celebrate *Levi's* as a totem of individuality. Singing about jeans in the first-person provides the glue of group life, while the lyrics describe a love relationship between a boy and his jeans. Accompanying visual imagery confirms an identity between jeans and wearer. To be sure, the boys cannot help laughing when they sing 'Keep puttin' me on, and I'll be true to you' as if they are in fact 'puttin'' you on even as they let you in on the joke.

THE KNOWING WINK

So many ads promote pseudo-individualism with the 'hey you, you wanna be a unique persona by consuming mass-produced commodity-signs' form of address, that *Levi's* campaign was constructed as a reflection on popularized critiques of consumer conformism. The stress on the self-reflective glance was joined to self-referential jokes about pseudo-individuality (e.g., '502^1/$_2$'). Precisely in this context, viewers were shown photo-realist evidence that *Levi's* unshrunk jeans actually do end up shaped to the body of the wearer. *Levi's* claimed they do not compel us to fit them, rather *Levi's* conform to our needs and shapes to become us. *Levi's* thus raised the critique of commodity fetishism as a positioning device to get viewers' attention, in order to debunk the critique for this, and only this, commodity.[6] Young viewers preferred *Levi's* to other TV ads, saying 'they look like real people' or '*Levi's* ads don't use models.' This is precisely what Foote, Cone & Belding's executive creative director, Mike Koelker, sought:

I wanted real people, but when other advertisers had tried that in the past, it came across as not real; it came across as 'pretending' to show consumers enjoying the product.

181

I wanted to say: 'If you can look at this person and fit into this role, this kind of character, if you can fit into the mood of these people, then maybe you want to give these jeans a try.'

So we picked kids on the streets of New York because they weren't conscious of doing a commercial. They didn't care. They were so cool. More often than not, we just pushed them in front of the camera and told them to do it. And the kids would say, 'Do what?' And we would say, 'Do whatever you do.' And they'd just start goofing around.

(*Patterns*, 1985: 3)

On the TV screen, *Levi's* characters connote the semiotic antithesis of 'models.' They meta-communicate that: 'We know that you're fed up with phony bullshit about owning commodities and being all you can be. We know you're fed up with mindless conformist consumerism, so . . .'

The reflexivity displayed by *Levi's* characters allows them to make several meta-statements about themselves. First, their look says 'I am streetwise and I appreciate the street because it allows me a space in which I can be self-conscious of my individuality and unfettered by others.' It also says 'I recognize I'm in a commercial, that what came before me was only a commercial, a fantasy. And you (the viewer) recognize that too. But that's okay, because I (like you) can appreciate and enjoy that.' This winking at the camera says to viewers that the characters are too hip to be snowed by the falseness of television. In 'Shades,' rather than wink, an ethnic male simply yawns in our faces, bored by the entire project. His streetwise attitude connotes the opposite of television, a world of textured reality outside television.

The self-reflexive look allows an individual to express not only an aware-ness of his context (his savvy), but also an awareness of his awareness (his self-reflexivity). Such awareness is expressed in a sophisticated look worn to suggest boredom with thinking about self in narcissistic terms and ennui with a world of shiny advertising images. *Levi's* characters give off the impression of having such secure egos that they are unconcerned with how others see them. They flat don't care! The (non)model is presented deep in thought, but viewers never know what the model thinks about.

Levi's anti-hero, the post-consumerist reflexive individual, conveys an attitude that he has detached external trappings from judgments about inner self. Of course, the very agenda of making this claim is to allow the 501 campaign to connect this image of a detached self to the object-style of *Levi's*. The self-reflexive individual looks back on the world *Levi's* has constructed and asks viewers to celebrate their own reflexive individuality by joining with him in this absence of self-consciousness. The ad cam-paign's primary hook is the identification with the metacommunication: the viewer is asked to see, and 'try on,' themselves as a potential meta-communicator.

The knowing wink enables characters to step outside the narratives and join with the viewer/spectator in a wryly speculative commentary on what we have observed. 'Hard to please woman' and 'Love ya in the morning' conclude with an anti-hero's sly gaze directly into the camera. *Levi's* anti-heroes stand between us and the action, and yet they are the action. They provide us with points of identification – as models they constitute the object of desire with which we may be made interchangeable (Williamson, 1978: 40–4, 60–7). On the other hand, they are presented as omniscient, cynical spectators who lead us in an ironic winking at the images we have just witnessed. A slyly cynical character in 'Love ya in the morning' wears his shades on the back of his head, and turning to face us, gives us a knowing look in which he shares a grin about what we have just seen (Figure 8.4). His look is heavily ambiguous, and depends on viewers to complete its meaning interpretively.[7] The pleasure of viewing comes from participating in completing the text.

'Humming' introduces a white male in his late twenties. A muscular man with dark, slicked-back, thinning hair, he appears from the waist up wearing a white undershirt. His swarthy appearance suggests an urban-ethnic, working-class background. The ad contravenes standard advertising conventions by focusing closely on him as he hums and makes faces without apparent purpose. Audiences find his unselfconscious actions humorous. Tight close-ups of his shoes shuffling on the sidewalk seem his object of consciousness; his activity has no apparent motivation, connoting instead a

Figure 8.4 Levi's (TV) – the knowing wink, 1985

Source: courtesy of Levi Strauss & Co.

reverie of self-absorption. Again, he displays a disinterest in the behavioral conventions of public space.

In 'Out on the Street' the same character encounters the camera with a look of bemused playfulness. He looks directly into the camera and his expressivity connotes ease with self and a lack of concern about what others think of his appearance. His play with the camera exhibits an awareness of it recording his appearance, and demonstrates a casual disdain, or indifference, for having his image recorded. As the ad closes and the red '501' graphic appears on screen in front of him, he good-naturedly places his palm between his face and the camera to shield his face from the camera (a gesture we recognize from the news and the world of celebrities) and then he unexpectedly steps outside the camera's frame, off the sidewalk, and then back with a grin. Playfully transgressing the camera's boundary rules initiates a self-reflexive awareness about the nature of this text *as* advertising, and a momentary refusal to participate in the society of the spectacle (Figure 8.5). The scene ostensibly exposes the cult of the image and the role of the advertiser. But instead of unmasking the ideological construction of commodity-signs, this ad fashions the self-reflexive hipster into the newest – 'most authentic' – sign yet.

Figure 8.5 Levi's (TV) – the knowing wink, 1985

Source: courtesy of Levi Strauss & Co.

'THE BLUES' AND THE POWER OF CULTURAL QUOTATION

Levi's ads are music driven. The music preceded the images, the images selected to fit the music. *Levi's* led advertisers in using rock'n'roll in a non-nostalgic way to address today's youth. Again, the primary issue concerned the question of authenticity and how to signify it. *Levi's* recognized their target audience wanted music that had not been stripped of credibility. Youth perceived the contrived, synthesized 'pop' sound that pervaded television advertising as a 'turn-off.' But they liked the *Levi's* ads because they felt 'tuned' into the music. Focus group respondents invariably described the music as 'hip' and 'cool' – 'it was good music, for a commercial.'

Music forged the connective device between popular cultural forms and the product's identity. Student viewers perceived a parallel between urban Blues and jeans as individualized art forms. *Levi's* gave free creative rein to Rhythm and Blues recording artists to bring their sound and idiom of expression to songs about *Levi's* 501 jeans.[8] *Levi's* sole directive to musicians was that songs include the phrases '*Levi's* 501 jeans,' 'shrink to fit,' and 'buttonfly.' Steered by the videotape editor, the rhythms, lyrics and phonetic sounds became structured as connecting devices that shaped *Levi's* commodity-sign. *Levi's* purposefully doubled meanings as a way of joining meaning systems together in an image. The 'Blues' as music, 'blue' as color and 'blues' as emotional state converge in *Levi's* 501s. Paradoxically, this convergence turns the 'blues' as emotional state from one of sadness and melancholy to one of energy and good times. Driven by the Blues/rock beat, a rhythm of visual body movements is keyed to the narrative action of the lyrics (e.g., 'ain't no body like my body'; or 'butt-on fly . . . ' keyed exactly to a pivoting female bottom). The music creates, along with the photographic style, an aura which seems to emanate from the life-world of *Levi's* youth.

Levi's knew youth audiences ranked the Blues below rock and country in popularity. But they gambled that it more closely conveyed the urban feeling they sought. The campaign initially drew on Blues as a musical genre, from the Mississippi Delta Blues to the urban jazz of Bobby McFerrin. 'Since then we have broadened the scope to include everything from gospel to funk to a '50s-ish a cappella number and a James Brown inspired track. But no jingles' (Neely in Levi Strauss Press Release, 1987). Other musicians included Taj Mahal, the Neville Brothers, Dan Hicks, The Nylons. Some ads intentionally retain the feeling, timbre and resonance of an 'authentic' blues sound with performances by older, non-commercial bluesmen such as Tiger Haynes (Figure 8.6).[9] But *Levi's* choice of artists more often translated the Blues in favor of youth's preference for rock'n'roll with its feelings of assertive sexuality.[10]

Figure 8.6 Levi's (TV) – Blues guitarist, 1984
Source: courtesy of Levi Strauss & Co.

Levi's chose music that articulates the physical sensuality and movement that youth associates with jeans. Editing accentuated this by cutting images to the internal rhythm (movement within frames to the music) so that characters seem more animated. And black music 'expresses the body, hence sexuality, with a directly physical beat and an intense, emotional sound – the sound and beat are felt rather than interpreted via a set of conventions' (Frith, 1981: 19). Translating the Blues to their agenda, *Levi's* stylized and softened the alienation that originally motivated the music, while drawing out an emphasis on the phenomenology of the body.

PLEASURE IN THE TEXT

Lyrics connect the salient visual images and the 501 jeans as object. *Levi's* lyrics positioned both the audience and the product, cuing viewers about how to decode the images and how to think about the jeans. After the ads play on the screen, the lyrics are the aftertaste of the ads. The *Levi's* 501 lyrics, however, constantly change the position of the audience, the characters and the product. The product meaning constantly shifts from emotional state, to body awareness, to a relationship with another, to a

186

sense of identity.[11] Juxtaposing personal pronouns in the lyrics allows an equivalence to be established between the jeans and a range of social relations. Unlike most ads, this equivalence is not static, but shifts and interweaves, thus maximizing space for audience decoding. Along with the ads' ambiguity and ellipsis, this postmodern appellation structure of shifting referents in the lyrics makes interpretation of the ads a potentially playful act.[12] *Levi's* discovered that not all images need to be decoded; neither must there always be closure in order to establish the commodity-sign. In the final scene of their 1984 wrap-up ad, the anti-hero of 'Hard to please woman' leans against a wall. When he walks away there appears a crude dark shadow painted on the wall where he stood. The meaning? Does it matter?

Return for a moment to the '501'derful Blues' ad discussed above. Why do the boys laugh? Again, we delve into the polysemic character of ads and the pleasure of deciphering them. Focus group members consistently decoded the *Levi's* ads in ways that produced a community of shared discourse. Yet the ads also invite young viewers to interpret actively and try to make sense of unresolved contradictions and gaps in the texts. The *Levi's* ads encourage a playful viewing stance. Some teenagers record the *Levi's* ads, show them to friends, study them and create meanings out of them: they treat the ads as mini-cinema. One ad closed with a scene of a young man trying to push a jukebox up the street; the jukebox starts to tip over and the boy strains to keep it from falling as the ad ends. The desire for completion is a powerful one and *Levi's* received countless letters wondering if the jukebox fell. Return now to our question, 'why do they laugh?' An obvious possibility is that this lyric is patently silly. Wouldn't you laugh if you were singing about your jeans as a true love? If their pattern was consistent, *Levi's* chose a (mis)take which had the guys breaking up in laughter during the song.

Yet, the lyrics constantly shift the position of the viewer, the characters and the product, and, like many ads, the lyrics deliberately play on double meanings. Perhaps a single meaning does not reside here. What kinds of latent, non-preferred meanings are available here? Listen to 'keep puttin' me on, and I'll be true to you' when heard as a command from the advertiser to viewer. Taken this way, the lyric could refer to brand loyalty. Now repeat the line as it elicits laughter. Thus far we have only pointed out the shifting meaning of the subject, but suppose the verb's meaning is also doubled. In daily linguistic use, 'puttin' me on' means to kid or deceive (a relationship which does not normally produce loyalty). Are they laughing about this being a 'put-on'? Interpreted this way, their laughter might be construed as a joke about advertising – and its relation to pseudo-individuality.

Far-fetched you think? A similar word play forms the pivot for another jeans advertising campaign. This time the relationship between advertiser and viewer is drawn out as a method of denying falsified communication. In *Elle* (May 1987), a jeans ad appeared for a brand named *hype*. Above the two-page image of the model lying on her hip is the text: 'hype (hīp) v. to put on.' The gambit of a dictionary definition provides an easy route to making an 'ironic' connection between the jeans name and the image, while the double (actually triple) meaning calls attention to the viewer's awareness of the possibility of falsification in advertising. Once again, apparent reflexivity about deception is turned to form another connective device.

Levi's music and shifting lyrics pose the 501s as enabling wearers to deal with a harsh and unfriendly urban life-space by accepting it, celebrating it or transcending it. The 1987 *Levi's* campaign literally transformed urban 'warning' signs into stylized signifiers of transcendence. And although the external world is connoted by signs of alienation (the Blues, the street, boredom, the 'warning' signs), this is offset by human contact (touching, glancing, singing together, teasing and playfulness). Reflexivity provides the opening for viewers to enter this world.

IMPERFECTION AND ERRANT BEHAVIOR

A recurring signifier in *Levi's* campaign is the accident – e.g., the jukebox tipping over; a leg cast; spilling a pail of water. Tripping, losing one's hat or glasses, and missing a ball become expressions not of clumsiness but individuality. 'Other people edit their mistakes, we make our mistakes our ads' (Christon, 1987). What come across as imperfection were serendipitous accidents during filming. In a world of images saturated by technical perfection, the unplanned moment stands out visually. Imperfection affirms the campaign for true individuality. There need be no simple identity between model and consumer. As a young focus-group member put it: 'they show that even a total goofball can be hip wearing a pair of *Levi's*.'

Second, in a bureaucratically rationalized world organized around bourgeois norms of self-control, spontaneity falls in the interstices of socialized space. Errant behavior signifies this unsocialized space (Goffman, 1959: 54). *Levi's* symbolically celebrates the individual's awkwardness. Individuality equals the distance or space between everyday life and the models in the *Jordache* designer jeans ad. *Levi's* claims to occupy that space.

Third, *Levi's* distances itself from the premise that commodities can solve all your problems. If you are crippled they will not help you walk. But scenes including wheelchairs and broken legs suggest that even individuals with physically encumbered bodies (and, those with psychologically inhibited middle-class bodies) can engage in playful, joyful relationships in which others recognize and appreciate one's personhood. In keeping with their overall theme of greater realism and candor, these ads do not proclaim the self as perfect. *Levi's* campaign was predicated on its opposition to conventional ads which depict a self that is inaccessible. One of the architects of *Levi's* campaign viewed the encoding problematic in these terms:

> Commercials are an important part of our culture. They shape or define reality for a lot of Americans. I think people in advertising have a real responsibility. They should be very careful how they show the world. If we show everybody as beautiful, then people who aren't beautiful feel inadequate and unpopular and lack of success is impossible for them.
>
> In these advertisements, we didn't show all beautiful people. We showed plump people, skinny people and handicapped people. We got close to real life. The ads have had an upward effect on sales. I think we left viewers with a good feeling about *Levi's*.
>
> (*Patterns*, 1985: 3)

Imperfection in *Levi's* campaign connotes an accessible, socially scaled-down level of 'cool.' The ads show real people trying to be cool, but not fully succeeding, which makes them seem all the cooler.

In one form of errant behavior 'the performer may act in such a way as to give the impression that s/he is . . . too little concerned with the interaction' (Goffman, 1959: 54). The stylistically differentiated urban male who throws a ball against the wall, fails to catch it and merely shrugs, exemplifies this behavior. His stance and glance suggest a nonchalance which signals a refusal to participate fully in doing facework, and his act of missing the ball actually demonstrates a 'cool' that is beyond ordinary cool. Likewise, his exaggerated yawn signifies disinterest and disrespect. In our daily performance of facework, 'a certain bureaucratization of the spirit is expected so that we can be relied upon to give a perfectly homogeneous performance at every appointed time' (Goffman, 1959: 56). *Levi's* characters deny the necessity for such self-regulation and the self-consciousness that goes with it, even as they simultaneously heighten concern about the self.

PHOTOGRAPHIC HYPERREALISM

Levi's use of hyperrealism refers to a technique, not necessarily to what is depicted. *Levi's* employed dramatic lighting and severe color schemes along with a grainy photographic style to convey a sense of 'grittyness' that seems less processed. Viewers see greater realism in 1) characters who appear unique and real ('They are not models that we cannot identify strongly with. The people portrayed are us'); 2) jeans worn faded, torn, cut up; 3) the street setting as opposed to a studio or out in nature. The street implies freedom – a world where constraining rules of work, school and home are absent.

In relation to the street itself, *Levi's* images are incomplete – they've been purged of poverty, street people, violence, petty crime and cops. Relationships in *Levi's* 'active urban environment' are peer oriented with no references to school, home or work. *Levi's* romanticizes poverty – giving it authenticity by cleaning it up and *colorizing* it. In fact, this ad is only 'real' in relation to what has previously been seen on television. Relative to the street, *Levi's* account is not hyperreal, but stylized. The hyperreal is a fiction, its reality differentiated only from previous mass-mediated concepts of reality. We see here a pervasive referential circularity which builds on a closed system of discourse.

Levi's 'blueing' of the street and the entire ghetto environment, captured young viewers' imaginations. Blues was the sign *Levi's* staked out for itself, and *Levi's* photographic technique reinforced the connection between 'Blues' as musical expression and emotional state and 'blues' as bodily/personal expression. The blue hue also connoted an absence of the splashy color photography which pervades the selling of clothes and most consumer-goods (for some youth, slick color photography has come to symbolize the art of advertising manipulation).

Levi's gave the ads a documentary look by shooting street scenes with a 1000 mm. lens from as far as two blocks away.

> The way we achieved the natural look was to use a telescopic lens that enabled us to be as far as two blocks away from the kids. The camera crew was completely removed from the kids, so they were not conscious of us.
>
> (Koelker in *Patterns*, 1985: 3)

The telephoto lens also threw the background out of focus, emphasizing the movement and gestures of characters. When the background is in focus, it is flat and has no movement in it. Flattened mural-like scenes supply the signifiers of street life (e.g., graffiti-littered walls, storefronts) and also animate the characters who perform in front of these street canvases. While traditional cinematic realism is signified by equivalence between character and background, *Levi's* opted for the psychological realism of a narrow depth of field which directs audience attention to the characters and their clothing: making the characters seem sharp and animated – they 'seem more alive.'

Corporate advertisers in the 1980s adopted photographic style as the decisive ground of competition. The struggle to differentiate each product name in consumers' minds in a world saturated by images now turns on deviating from conventional photographic techniques. Competition now revolves around methods of photography and what the method itself says to viewers. The chief message is 'notice me' and this is achieved by playing on elements of a realist code. Ads for *Bell Systems* use a jumpy, jerky close-up camera style with no cuts or edits to give the impression of home-movie style. The technique catches our eye because it makes what is seen not immediately identifiable as an ad, and it seems to deny the usual ad fictions at work in the codes of commercial photography. The home-movie, grainy quality of sepia-tinted black and white images has less polish to it, and thereby is allowed to connote authenticity, a harder, realer everydayness.[13]

Levi's emphasized non-professional actors, open scripts, long lenses and grainy film in order to connote realism. Bringing out the grain to connote realism has since spread to campaigns for *Miller's* ('It's Real'), *Honda*, *Wrangler* and *Sun Country*, to mention but a few. This choice of photographic style creates a rupture in the meaning of style relative to the ads which surround it. Photographic style is not simply a neutral conduit carrying the ad's message, but becomes the signified itself.

RACE AND CLASS RELATIONS

Rounding out their 1986 campaign, *Levi's* produced a collage of the characters who appeared in the campaign. Using a gospel-influenced musical anthem, the one-minute ad entitled 'Celebration' begins and ends – with close-up portraits of a mature black woman's face – as a celebration of the spirit of black and ethnic working-class people. A two-storey mural-type painting on a white sheet could, at a glance, easily be confused with the mural style of socialist realism. Throughout, the campaign emphasizes a 'one-world' ethos which shows youth transcending the boundaries of race. The conventions of race, class and gender appear subordinated in these ads to 'your' expression of individuality and to recurring representations of interracial male–female relationships. The ad summarized the campaign's effort to romanticize the experience of being black. Blacks who appear on screen seem 'connected' and 'in tune' with their total social space. *Levi's* sells the ghetto – a space which transcends social convention, restraint and repressiveness. Throughout the campaign, we could easily substitute Lou Reed's 'I wanna be black. I don't wanna be a fucked-up middle-class college student any more,' for the Rhythm and Blues backgrounds used in the ads. Jack Kerouac popularized, or gave voice to, the desire to escape the boundaries of middle classness and its constant self-consciousness in *On the Road*:

> At lilac evening I walked with every muscle aching among the lights of 27th and Welton in the Denver colored section, wishing I were a Negro, feeling that the best the white world had offered was not enough ecstasy for me, not enough life, joy, kicks, darkness, music, not enough night .... I wished I were a Denver Mexican, or even a poor overworked Jap, anything but what I was so drearily, a 'white man' disillusioned.
>
> (Kerouac, 1955:148)

191

Few advertising campaigns are set in lower-class urban environments. Where Kerouac romanticized the ghetto, *Levi's* glamorized it to 'dramatize the passions of youth: Love and Music . . . . White people can be accepted as hip if they share the concerns not of black people, but of the all-important youth market' (McWilliams, 1985: 51).

Editing of scenes repeatedly sequenced a relationship between blacks as 'role models' and individuated white hipsters. In 'Elevator' we see an expressively impassive, visually cool, white youth who plays his chest with drum sticks – using his body as his musical instrument. His image immediately follows a scene of four black males walking together on the street, one of them carrying a pair of drumsticks. Moving from black group solidarity to the solitary white sequences a pattern of cultural appropriation and adaptation in which 'wearing *Levi's* can permit you to interpret black hipness and express it in your own way.' In one interracial scene in 'Celebration' a black youth appears to teach a white youth how to dance in harmony without inhibition.

'Coolness' is the predominant motif in these ads. 'Street cool' has to do with conceptions about acting in public spaces and how blacks accomplish this. Black males seem to move without inhibition to the rhythm of the street. They signify soul, movement, expressiveness, the body unencumbered by tight, stiff middle classness. Juxtaposed against these scenes are white males whose coolness takes the form of ironic detachment. They appear cool by being distant, psychologically removed from reality.

> In our society, anxious self-scrutiny (not to be confused with critical self-examination) not only serves to regulate information signalled to others and to interpret signals received; it also establishes an ironic distance from the deadly routine of daily life.
>
> (Lasch, 1979b: 171)

Historically, US advertising has played on this sense of deadly routine by offering an alternative vision of 'rich experience' through the consumption of commodities. 'They promise not cynical detachment but a piece of the action, a part in the drama instead of cynical spectatorship' (Lasch, 1979b: 173). *Levi's*, however, offers a piece of the action through cynically detached spectatorship.

GENDER DIFFERENCE

Levi's ads seem to put aside race, class and gender conventions. Yet gender representation does not substantially deviate from conventional definitions. Males predominate in *Levi's* street-world. *Levi's* ads are male narratives in which women receive validation through the male voice or the male eye. Of twenty-six commercials, only two feature a female singer, and lyrics express a 'sexual point of view that is overwhelmingly male but aching to snare a female' (McWilliams, 1985: 51): e.g., 'Got me a hard-to-please woman'; 'I've been crazy for you girl since we were terrible twos'; 'She has a thing about *Levi's* 501 jeans. The way they curve every curve I've had the nerve to notice.'

Female independence and individuality are defined in relation to males, even if negatively. In 'Rainy Day' a male stands in a doorway during a steady rain watching a girlfriend walk away. His eyes and face reveal sorrow and regret as she leaves him. The lyrics reek of the 'tortured romanticism of white youth,'

> Watchin' you walk away, nothin' left to say
> wearin' your 501 Blues on a rainy day.
> I must admit they shrink to fit
> so much better than you and I,
> bye bye
> *Levi's* buttonfly 501 Blues and you.

Her leaving represents a form of power, but her power is defined in terms of a patriarchal paradigm and through his eyes. What makes him so 'blue' is that their differences have gotten in the way of his being able to possess that great rear end of hers again.

Women do not express their personalities in these ads. They appear rather as jean-wrapped tushes or as companions to males. Infrequently, the campaign showed women engaged in playful and/or expressive acts. But even in playful expressivity, women appear in states of 'licensed withdrawal' (Goffman, 1976). As gender traits, licensed withdrawal is the female corollary to the male trait of reflexivity. Women are not shown engaging in knowing winks. Only five women make eye contact with the camera in twenty-six ads (two other women acknowledge the camera's presence as members of otherwise all-male groups). And, only one black and one 'Italian' matron in the 'Celebration' ad are shown in tight close-ups actually fixing the camera with their gaze.

Women were less likely to appear in groups than males: only one female group is shown (four young black girls jumping rope). Where males are concerned the group affords a social bonding space. Male aggressiveness is a common motif – a menacing gang approaches stretched across the screen; rolled up sleeves; gang graffiti. Women, however, appear alone (depicted for an absent male gaze) or in the presence of males. Or, as John Berger summed it up in *Ways of Seeing*, 'Men act, women appear.' While *Levi's* seems to speak the language of liberation, patriarchal codes still dominate.

LEVI'S AND THE ART OF CORPORATE BRICOLAGE

A recurrent imagistic prop in the *Levi's* street scenes is the white sheet/ screen. In '501'derful Blues' the screen functions as a street stage and provides an omnipresent statement about our awareness of the camera. The sheet 'speaks about' the staged-ness of the ad. The screen refers back to the presence of the camera, and about presentation of self in a world of cameras. The camera's perspective becomes a metaphor for self as seen by others. Like devices of mirrors and photo booths in other ads, the screen permits a dialogue (with viewers) about the relationship between viewer and model (cf. Williamson, 1978: 60ff).

Levi's campaign put the sheet/screen to multiple uses: using it literally to wrap and bind the group together; as a portrait backdrop; as a street stage; and as a canvas for a larger than life mural. As a screen, the sheet silhouettes the dancing expressivity and fluidity of jeans wearers while also concealing their individual identities. Each usage suggests a form of street art. Presenting their ads as a reflexive art form, *Levi's* mixes artistic performances with everyday life. Their stage is usually the street – aka the blue urban meta-space of *Levi's*. Males are seen performing as street artists (there is one female exception) who perform mime, do magic tricks, create illusions and juggle. They focus attention on objects such as sticks, balls, cards, a toy helicopter, a robot and camera, or display themselves with dogs, geese, pigeons. They perform as street musicians, from a cappella quartets to playing the body as an instrument (drumming the chest). They dance uninhibited jigs on the street and improvisational routines on the sidewalk. They turn dribbling a basketball into a dance form. The whole world is a stage on *Levi's* street where self-identity is also represented as an art object. Self appears as an extension of gesture, clothing/*Levi's*, profane objects and animals (Figure 8.7).

Each 'art form' might be considered as bricolage. Hebdige (1979: 103–4) observed that youth culture confronts commodity culture by transforming the use and meaning of objects (e.g., punks turn narcissism into the threat of violence by honing their combs into sharpened weapons). *Levi's* pursuit of counter-bricolage stemmed from their understanding of the perils of 'phoniness.' *Levi's* sought to capture youth and youth culture photographically as they are in *Levi's* jeans. Signs of bricolage are everywhere – from the used object/commodity collages arranged in street thrift-shops, to males who pose as art objects (e.g., with a fluorescent light on a couch).

Levi's campaign success has been in direct correspondence to their finesse as *corporate counter-bricoleurs*. The campaign's emphasis on bricolage grows directly from its non-traditional approach to casting and composing the ads. The casting process aimed at locating elements of authenticity rather than pre-choosing images. *Levi's* looked for 'natural' characters who would seem at ease when filmed. Casting interviews aimed at getting to know the job applicants (actors), rather than have them read lines. *Levi's* did more than simply locate 'natural' characters, they also looked for stylistic quirks. For example, the scene of a 'James Dean'-looking male fondling a white goose while lying on his back on the sidewalk emerged

Figure 8.7 Levi's (TV) – graffiti, 1985
Source: courtesy of Levi Strauss & Co.

from the casting interview. The casting director asked interviewees to bring some object (or animal) that revealed something of their persona, and this guy brought his goose. Similarly, there were no structured written scripts, no story-boarding. There was an idea, not a script (Christon, 1987).

This emphasis on serendipity was duplicated in the filming process, which transformed the bricoleur's nuance into a subtle focal point of the ads (Christon, 1987). The corporate bricoleur's task is to join together two otherwise disparate meaning systems in a new image-style. *Levi's* producers tried to tap into the product's actual culture of use. One powerful image of the 1985 campaign featured a gang of young urban males aggressively striding toward the camera in their well-worn jeans with red bandannas tied around a pants leg or the sleeve of a denim jacket. Here we see how hegemony operates, still rooted in the commodity form's capacity to re-absorb resistance and opposition. The corporate bricoleur creates a new commodity-sign by joining the image of the quirk, or the tied bandanna/ resistance, to the meaning of *Levi's*. Elements of opposition are thus re-assimilated when passed through the reading conventions of the adver-tising form: so viewers may read back, 'wearing *Levi's* might enable me proudly to express my quirk or my defiance.'

The commercials present themselves as a form of collage. The interplay between their form and content allows space for the audience to recognize this and position themselves inside or outside the ad. It says you can be an artist, and, in a culture which values expressive individualism, the artist becomes an ego ideal. The ads extol street art as a form of individuated celebration and represent the antithesis of institutional art. The street artist appears inventive, non-conformist and unrepressed.

MIMESIS AND REALISM

Levi's advertising success spawned imitators. *Budweiser* and *Sprite* soon attempted to take on the spirit and feel of the *Levi's* campaign through photographic techniques (e.g., *Sprite*) or using Rhythm and Blues music and a glimpse of reflexivity (e.g., *Budweiser*). But such imitation carries costs for advertisers. Attentive viewers see through these second-generation ads. They are less believable because each recent rip-off involves characters getting too much out of life – they are too zany and uninhibited (Sprite) or not alienated enough (Bud). Though each attempts to re-articulate a vision of authenticity – 'he's a genuine Bud man' – the act of commodification remains too visible and too glossy in photographic terms. *Budweiser* celebrates the male who transcends 'trends' by 'pledg(ing) allegiance to the king of beers,' and *Sprite* equates non-conformist subjectivity with ingestion of their product, 'we love the Sprite in you!'

Levi's immediate competitors also jumped on the bandwagon. *Chic* used an earthy rendering of the song 'I Feel Like a Natural Woman' with a grainy, gritty photographic style that moves from black and white to color. *Wrangler's* 'American Hero' ads draw heavily on the realist code of heavy grain, but in slow motion. *IOU* moved its act from the highway to sepia-tinted inner-city streets as has *Jordache*. Designed to play off similar realist encoding strategies, the *IOU* ads highlight the uninhibited expressivity of youth by keying on a gestured image now popular in many ads – young women aggressively pushing off/away a male. *Le Tigre* addressed questions of individuality and conformity with a series of 'non-professional' dancers/you(s). Their next campaign ventured further into exploiting techniques of flashy reflexivity by inviting viewers into a rest-room to watch the models dressing for the ads.

Meanwhile, *Swanson's*, *Safeway* and *Burger King* have jacked up the realism level in their depiction of working-class people. Have working-class consumers become pissed at the sanitized, middle-class fantasy versions of themselves? In a world of segmented consumer markets, some marketers now figure that it may be better not to address working-class audiences visually in fantasy terms, but in terms of how they actually look. Imagewise, the 'working class' has become popular with Madison Avenue. But greater denotative realism in TV ads does not necessarily produce an absence of ideology.

WHITHER COMMODITY HEGEMONY?

Hegemony refers to 'a whole body of practices and expectations . . . our shaping perceptions for ourselves and the world . . . . It thus constitutes a sense of reality for most people in society' (Williams, 1977: 110). Hegemony

> defines within its terms the mental horizon, the universe, of possible meanings, of a whole sector of relations in a society or culture; and carries with it the stamp of legitimacy – it appears coterminous with what is 'natural', 'inevitable', 'taken for granted' about the social order.
>
> (Hall, 1980: 137)

The concept of hegemony links the tacit frames of signification to the class politics of discourse. Hegemony is not the result of mechanically imposed ideas, but derives from processes of 'framing all competing definitions of reality within its range' (Hall, 1977: 133). Hegemonic ideology refers to tacitly privileged *ways of framing or seeing* the world around us (Berger, 1972). Such ways of seeing are predicated on taken-for-granted cultural codes and rules of discourse. Gramsci located this process in the practices and language of daily life. Elaborate philosophical systems were not necessary to reproduce or justify the dominance of a ruling class; rather, everyday language replicated and transmitted a

> 'spontaneous philosophy' which is proper to everybody. This philosophy is contained in: 1) language itself, which is a totality of determined notions and concepts and not just words grammatically devoid of content; 2) 'common sense' and 'good sense'; 3) popular religion and, therefore, also in the entire system of beliefs, superstitions, opinions, ways of seeing things and acting, which are collectively bundled together under the name of 'folklore.'
>
> (Gramsci, 1971: 323)

As cultural and political processes, hegemonic ideologies tend to be partially resisted and contested, while, at the same time, pliable and able to encapsulate oppositional discourses. In the *Levi's* ads we can see the dialectical relations of resistance and consent played out. *Levi's* ads illustrate how hegemonic ideology and cultural practice get stretched and resisted; and how advertisers and marketers have learned to turn that resistance into new positioning devices, and thus extend – and dialectically evolve – hegemonic definitions. The *Levi's* TV ads are an exemplar of corporate *counter-bricolage* where advertisers institutionalize the act of bricolage. If bricolage – the consumer's version of pastiche – had any critical function, it is negated when the sign of *Levi's* or *Converse* or *Reebok* can turn any woman or man into a bricoleur. To position themselves outside the mainstream media clutter, a daring advertiser *puts on* the pose of the bricoleur as a means of identifying themselves with the bricoleur's form of authentic individuality. But, as we all know, this blows it for the bricoleur, because now there are mass-produced bricolage looks. The bricoleur's playfulness is instrumentalized to create a new surface for commodification.

Critics charge that hegemony theory presumes a privileged interpretation of texts and ideologies based on a reductionist model of human subjectivity and a closed model of meaning production. Do arguments about hegemony commit an objectivist fallacy that there is one correct interpretation of cultural texts (Gottdiener, 1985)? Why must a theory of hegemony presume closed texts that viewers decode in a single way? True, we have argued that commodity culture cultivates preferred readings, but this does not mean that hegemony depends on a single unified reading of social and cultural texts. We think the *Levi's* campaign demonstrates precisely the opposite – the motor of hegemonic ideology now lies in the very openness of the ads as texts. In the *Levi's* ads, this openness (elliptical, ambiguous texts) is essential to drawing the viewer into the ads' space where they participate in the construction of ideology. What kind of hegemony could this reproduce? Interpretation is wide open except for the closed circuit between the commodity name (*Levi's*) and the overall interpretive *sign* of the text, which may vary. But, a plurality of significations is not the same as 'pluralism.'

Hegemonic relations in contemporary capitalist society no longer rest on a monolithic normative formation. The semiotic logic of commodity culture chops and dices meaning systems into pastiched signifying chains which have temporally briefer and briefer half-lives before they fade out of sight. Any meaning system, normative or otherwise, is grist for the signifier mill. Baudrillard maintains that into this 'gigantic black hole . . . bourgeois myths are swallowed up and made truly meaningless' (Frith and Horne, 1987: 11; see Baudrillard, 1983a). Commodity-sign production devours bourgeois myths just like any other meaning system, and reduces them to signs so that hegemonic signifieds are turned into decontextualized commodity signifiers. The unified coherence of bourgeois ideology – its transcendental signified – is negated by this process of sign production, and replaced by the over-determined 'ambiguity' discussed earlier. The internal logic of a political economy of commodity-signs undermines the reproduction of bourgeois hegemony. But this does not mean the end of capitalist hegemony. Rather than a singularity of interpretation, hegemony now rests on atomized, subjectivized interpretations which block the formation of shared public discourse.

Ad campaigns such as *Levi's* recognize that today no shared moral grounding exists as a basis for securing consent and legitimacy. *A disjuncture now exists between hegemony and legitimacy in the 1980s.* Legitimation crises have become a near-permanent institutional feature of US society, but these crises have not imperiled the rule of corporate capital. Legitimation claims have lost credibility, exhausted by overuse by the corporate mass media and the Presidency so that, when heard or seen, they merely excite cynical skepticism or boredom. In the absence of tenable legitimation claims, the hegemony of the knowing wink encourages us to be savvy but private interpreters of the world – it fractures our discourse, blocking the capacity for public discursive exchanges. Interpretation is treated as a private act that may be converted into discrete units of sales or opinion polls. Frames work by steering inquiry away from the structural hegemony of interests (economic, social, political) which prevail today in the United States.

Foote, Cone & Belding recognized that megadoses of advertising had eroded the credibility of achieving authenticity through consumption. *Levi's* gambled that their target audience had grown contemptuous of the ideal of commodified perfection, and were ready to buy the appearance of the non-imitative in commodity form. If their public no longer bought into the hegemonic practice of perpetually pursuing commodified perfection, *Levi's* was prepared to offer back the signified/signifier of resistance to commodification in commodity form. So they stretched the parameters of acceptable images in advertising (e.g., interracial couples, physically disabled, street gangs, disdain for the camera) and used realist codes to signify liberation. Now 501 jeans signify wearers able to transcend social roles confined by alienated institutional structures and constrained by cultural norms governing race, gender and class. *Levi's* seems to articulate the lives of individual subjects as an alternative to an artificial, absent, world of consumer conformity. Freed from self-consciousness and dandyism, 501-people are capable of expressing authentic individuality. They are free to express their alienation.

Levi's likewise scrapped the 'jingle,' introduced music with a bite and used blurred, ambiguous narratives to signify *difference* from decades of ads built around overdetermined signifying processes. Viewers reacted to openness by filling in and completing narratives and actions. Further, the ads build on inferences of reflexivity about the relationship between viewer and advertising – the mode of appellation. These appeals to reflexivity become a stance calculated to pique the interest of alienated, bored decoders/consumers. This reflexivity serves as a method of encouraging (enticing) the viewer to participate (rather than withdraw from) in the decoding process. The twist in all this is that *Levi's* encourages youth to participate in the reproduction of both the commodity form and commodity-sign by identifying with images of non-participation.

When considered as meta-messages, the *Levi's* campaign is about the dual subject of deception and authenticity. Flashy photographic reflexivity joined with music that stands on its own (i.e., that does not prostitute itself for the product) beckons skeptical viewers to enter the space of the ad. It is a positioning device that invites the viewer into the ad by saying, 'hey, you. You're no sap, you recognize the world of advertising for what it is. So, come on in, you might belong in our world.' The question of interpretive space becomes essential (Williamson, 1978). How do viewers position themselves in the ad? Do they identify with the non-models who have themselves been positioned as occupying a marginal space between ad and real life? The open structure of the text provides more space for interpretation and provides some minimalist guarantee of the promise that both commodity and advertisement provide: *freedom of choice*. Where a previous generation of TV ads closed off interpretive space in order to guarantee the completion of commodity-signs, *Levi's* widened the space because they recognized that closure was disrupting the circuit of commodity-sign production and reproduction. Young viewers appreciated *Levi's* ads because they permit a real freedom to construct personalized meanings. The *Levi's* ads are predicated on denying that meanings in the ads – or the relationship between viewers and ads – are preconstituted. And yet, 'this openness is, of all the masks, the most impenetrable' (Haug, 1986: 60). The *Levi's* campaign demonstrates that, though appeals to self-reflexivity do contain a kernel of liberatory potential, when they remain enmeshed within the framework of commodity form and advertising form they do not realize the journey toward self-consciousness, but rather comprise an abstract negation: turning the real into the ideal.

NOTES

1 Thanks to Dean Christon at *Levi's* for providing information, documents and video tapes about the ad campaign's production.
2 *Calvin Klein* ads joined the navel-gazing with a more cynical inflection, 'Is there a real me, or am I just what you see?' These ads tackled questions of ontology and identity with a 'postmodern' twist – perhaps a stable identity consists of no depth and no substance, but all surface.
3 Another *Lee's* ad confirms the campaign's agenda to ratify the commodified 'look' when we see the same muscular male model applying his tight-fitting jeans as he peers into his mirrored appearance. This affords him a chance, and the viewer through him, to 'check out' his 'look.' Once out in public, he encounters the young woman who gives him 'the look,' confirming that what he/we saw in the mirror was 'real' and that 'it worked.'
4 *Time* reported the resurgence of basic denim was aided by Bruce Springsteen wearing a pair of faded *Levi's* on his 'Born in the USA' album cover. Christon (1987) notes, however, the article stemmed from a reporter's interest in finding a novel Springsteen story-angle, and exaggerated Springsteen's influence on 501 sales, although it subsequently became part of a self-fulfilling phenomenon.
5 *Levi's* consistently joined their denial of the centrality of consumerism and commodities to the theme of authentic individuality throughout the campaign. Print ads in *Rolling Stone* (using scenes from the TV campaign) point to characters involved in their lives and not the advertiser's agenda. The ads explicitly deny the characters' status as models. Perhaps they are merely subjects captured by a candid camera. One ad shows a young woman gesturing and talking

to her male companion, who just happens to be carrying a sausage-shaped bull-dog in his arms. The text below reads:

> Surely, she is not telling him about our jeans.
> It's also likely she's not saying that Levi's 501 jeans are made of a special denim that shrinks in the wash to fit only you. Your waist, your hips, you.
> In fact, she's probably forgotten that while button-fly 501 jeans used to be made just for men, they're now also cut especially for a woman's figure. For a fit so personal, it's like having them custom tailored.
> But she is wearing 501 jeans. And it does look like she's about to have a very special day.
> And that's good enough for us.

6 Does *Levi's* actually stand alone here? Individuality, in *Levi's* ads, is expressed by an ensemble of meaning-laden objects and signifiers defined as style. Rather than deny consumerism, the ads confirm it at a higher level.

7 Using ambiguity and ellipsis as advertising strategies is high-risk, but can also bear huge dividends. If viewers do not try imaginatively to resolve the ambiguity or fill in the ellipsis, then the ad flops. The up side is equally obvious: viewers are much more likely to make a cognitive investment in a product sign if they have actively 'worked through' the puzzle.

8 'We let the artists be themselves. It's not unlike the instruction we give people appearing in the ads, which is "just be yourself and we'll film." We tell the musicians to do what they do, not what they think we want them to do' (Steve Neely, executive producer).

9 Student focus groups consistently named the 'Blues Brothers' ad featuring two rural black Blues players as the 'most authentic.'

10 Prior to his celebrity status, Bruce Willis appeared in 1984 *Levi's* 501 ads, bopping to the beat. Willis, as a personality, symbolizes a style that emphasizes irreverent media-reflexivity and white appropriation of black hipness. Willis appears in ads as an aficionado of black musicians. In a recent *Seagram's* ad, Willis dresses 'black' in a Run DMC hat while performing the white 'Seagram's Blues.'

11 Specified more closely, the meanings of jeans in the lyrics can be categorized as: 1) an emotional state, 2) an emotional generator, 3) an empowerer in a relationship, 4) a human subject, 5) a substitute for a relationship, 6) an extension of one's body, 7) an identity.

12 Focus group members described the ads as playful because they found decoding the ad was fun and enjoyable.

13 In the late 1980s, TV advertisers hustled to out-home movie one another. If seamless editing promotes the impression of a fantasy world which is too perfect, then, advertisers reason that jump-cuts and amateur home video will signify the opposite.

9

THE POSTMODERNISM THAT FAILED

Postmodernism became the hip and trendy cultural catchword of the late 1980s. There is even a 'Postmodern Hour' on MTV. And why not, in a world where *images* supplant what they represent, 'simulations' confront us at nearly every turn until we seem to live in a world of materialized *déjà vu*. Postmodern aesthetics marks a cynical, incredulous stance toward this world along with a nihilistic facework strategy of indifference regarding the promise of individual difference.

There is a shallow consensus that 'the postmodern' encompasses a loss of unified meaning, a loss of certainty – the price of too much individuation, too much social construction of reality and too much commodity hyperbole. Television often registers as the heart and soul of postmodernism because of its relentless scrambling of signifieds and signifiers, mixing and matching meanings. Routinely bombarded by signifiers and signifieds detached from referent systems, spectators react by assuming stances of ironic detachment. Blank, but knowing, indifference thus affects a defensive posture *vis-à-vis* processes of media 'manipulation.'

Postmodernism is partially a product of the history of commodity culture. Advertising dedicated to generating sign values is routinely grounded in a language disorder, the continuous rerouting of signifiers and signifieds. Postmodern *schizophrenia* is the result of undoing the ties that bind signifiers with signifieds, so they can enter into the exchange process necessary for assembling commodity-signs. When abstracted to their logical extremes, advertising's rudimentary processes of engineering meaning exchanges – *juxtaposition* and *superimposition* – become the hallmarks of postmodern signification practices. Postmodern aesthetics are an outgrowth of cultural contradictions generated by the society of the spectacle, where the commodity form has re-absorbed and incorporated ideological opposition.

Has not this society, glutted with aestheticism, already integrated former romanticisms, surrealism, existentialism and even Marxism to a point? It has indeed, through trade, in the form of commodities! That which yesterday was reviled today becomes cultural consumer-goods; consumption thus engulfs what was intended to *give meaning and direction.*

(Lefebvre, 1971: 95)

Postmodern aesthetics represent both the extreme commodification of images and an auto-critique of that process, now packaged for sign consumption.

This chapter probes advertising's connection to postmodernism via a *Reebok* sneaker ad that was part of a failed advertising campaign. The *Reebok* campaign hitched postmodern aesthetic codes to the commodity form in the context of a commodity-sign war with *Nike*. This ad highlights a postmodern aesthetic characterized by

pastiche; blankness; a sense of exhaustion; a mixture of levels, forms, styles; a relish for copies and repetition; a knowingness that dissolves commitment into irony; acute self-consciousness about the formal, constructed nature of the work; pleasure in the play of surfaces; a rejection of history.

(Gitlin, 1989: 100)

On the surface, this choice of texts joins in a primary agenda of postmodernism – namely the blurring of boundaries between High Culture and Mass/Commodity Culture. At the intersection of art and commerce, advertisements are packed with the relations and contradictions between aesthetics and economics, signs and commodities, spectators and cultural producers – all within an arena governed by the logic of corporate capital. The *Reebok* campaign appropriated a postmodern cultural field to devise another dimension of interpretive space for viewing subjects, thereby intimating liberation and autonomy. But can interpretive openness and polysemy negate hegemonic ideologies, or in commodity form are they abstract fetishes worn to chase away the spirits of conformism? Postmodernism admittedly blurs the boundaries between high and mass culture, but such blurring challenges neither capitalist nor commodity hegemony:

'postmodern art' derives, on the contrary, from a concerted and systematic *reinforcement* of the category of bourgeois high culture, which is, in the 1980s, as wholly parasitic on capitalist commercial culture as it is on the high bourgeois tradition.

(Britton, 1988: 16)

Reebok's postmodern ad turns cultural critique into a commodity signifier of 'the end of desire.' In advertising, postmodernism manifests itself as a later

203

stage of commodity culture in which hegemonic contests are displaced to metacommunicative forms.

THE IMMEDIATE CONTEXT: THE FIELD OF TELEVISION CONSUMER-GOODS ADS

Television commercials in the 1980s embodied more capital, artistic labor and creative energy than most programming, because the competitive structure of commodity culture pressures advertisers continuously to position their brand images against competitors. Indeed, the value of a product *is* its position: its value *is* its visual sign. Advertising culture in the 1980s was also conditioned by the constant tendency of media costs to rise; more cynical viewers; and a remote control technology which lets viewers 'drive' through the channels and 'zap' away ads. Advertisers thus continuously searched for innovative aesthetic structures and salient signifiers to capture viewer attention and hold their interest.

Technological advances changed the look of TV ads in the late 1960s, and slicker color and graphics pushed commodity aesthetics in pursuit of *picture perfect*. By the 1980s, the conventions of *commodity perfectibility* had been exhausted as a means of generating product differentiation, and the sheer surfeit and banality of images generated consumer 'indifference.' Numerous styles surfaced to combat viewer skepticism about ads. *Levi's* pioneered a *realist* trend that eliminated jingles and replaced perfect models with non-professional, mistake-prone 'people like us.' Realism of character and setting provided space for viewers to celebrate their own individuality without the anxiety of comparing themselves to the 'unattainable' perfection of models. Despite this interpretive space, *Levi's* steered viewers toward the proposition that individuality might best be expressed while wearing 'personalized shrink to fit' 501 buttonfly jeans. Individuality and commodity were now linked at a deeper level. Viewers could position themselves against conformity (the model image) by buying a mass-produced but personally named commodity. Despite the semiotic twists and turns, a preferred interpretation still rested on pseudo-individuality and the commodity self.

By 1988, the advertising landscape had become cluttered by 'realist' images and styles. Imitators used every realist technical device: black and white photography, grainy images, non-continuity editing, jerky camera movements, back regions and hypersignified close-ups. Amid this climate of realist clutter, *Reebok* and Chiat/Day released the *Reeboks Let UBU* campaign in June 1988.[1] This $20 million campaign broke with realism *and* professed to relocate individuality in postmodern aesthetic codes. The campaign aired during TV primetime and late night programming, while print ads surfaced in fashion and lifestyle magazines.[2] The campaign lasted only into the Fall, its death officially announced in February 1989. *Reebok*'s market research showed *Reebok* was less a *badge brand* indicating status (e.g., *BMW*) than a marker of 'individual' preference and use. Across the demographic board – from youth to ethnics to grandparents – consumers reported wearing *Reebok* shoes. Researchers found men and women wearing *Reebok* shoes with formal attire for social occasions. *Reebok*'s advertising strategy 'played on the personal uniqueness aspect' and the 'diversity of ways the shoes can be used.' They positioned their shoe as a *lifestyle* product targeted at 'style-conscious adults' between the ages of 18 and 34. It was positioned against *Nike*'s performance-oriented 'Just Do It' campaign featuring Michael Jordan and Bo Jackson.[3]

The *Reebok* campaign initially drew critical acclaim. Trade journals called it 'something that didn't look like advertising,' 'the new school of advertising for the media-savvy consumer,' 'clever fashion advertising that involves marketing's most cherished brand-image stratagems, while cauterizing our nerve endings like a hot knife through clutter.' The only negative response came from sporting-goods retailers who deemed the campaign too fashion-oriented for performance-oriented customers. *Reebok*'s next (1989) campaign – 'Physics of the Physiques' – stressed performance-oriented, stylized bodyshaping.[4] That campaign subsequently gave way to the high-tech performance campaign of 'Pump It Up.' Still, *Reeboks Let UBU* moved consumer advertising toward an aesthetic that relies on video abstraction, non-linear editing and 'layered execution that benefits from multiple viewings.' It presumed media-literate viewers familiar with styles learned from MTV.

> It's stark and conceptual. It's self-conscious. It's inspired by video art, photography and the theater, rather than film. It's not linear and it doesn't use rock'n'roll. It's advertising's new abstraction.
>
> (Davidson, 1988: 1)

REEBOK'S COMMERCIAL TEXT

The first TV campaign spot shown was a 30-second ad that got the most play during the campaign. Because the color coding is unusual and images are framed off-center, the *Reebok* ad's twenty-four photographic scenes connote an absurdist, surreal aura. Scenes shot from below distort the sense of vertical space and perspective, while the soundtrack consists of oddly detached, carefully phrased maxims by what sounds like a 1940s radio voiceover. The musical score composed by Oingo-Boingo and Todd Rundgren is *intentional kitsch*, and sounds vaguely like gypsy music. The quotes have been abstracted from Ralph Waldo Emerson's essay on 'Self-Reliance' written in 1841, but are *not* identified as such. Between each epigram is a meaningful pause.

Who so would be a man, must be a non-conformist.

Consistency is the hobgoblin of little minds.

To be great is to be misunderstood.

There is a time in every man's education when he arrives at the conclusion that envy is ignorance.

Insist on yourself, never imitate.

To believe that what is true for you in your private heart is true for all men – that is genius.

Mapping the ad:

Sc.1) Two elderly male–female couples dressed in red and white square-dancing garb stand on a stage set in a living room with an artificial potted tree at right and a picture on the wall above it. On the left is a sign with the letters U B U, above two flower pots. The couples wear red sneakers. They step forward and bow as if completing a performance; two hold trophies under their arms. This is sequenced to the narrator voiceover, 'Who so would be a man, must be a non- conformist' (see Figure 9.1).

Figure 9.1 Reebok UBU (TV) – squaredancers, 1988

Source: © Reebok

Sc.2) A hyper-magnified close-up of the typed letter *U* is white on black and off-center on the screen. The typeface is so magnified that its edges appear as pock-marked surfaces.

Sc.3) A second *U* appears, this time black on white. Do the letters represent connective tissue, an abbreviation, or a reference point from which to decipher the apparently aberrant coding?

Sc.4) Keyed to 'Consistency is . . . ' is a middle-aged man mechanically hitting a paddleball on a string – mind and body appear disassociated. His white shirt and black tie connote a professional civil servant or bureaucrat. In profile from the waist up, he occupies the right side of the screen, set against a 'True Stories' blue sky. Like the ensuing scene of American Punk-Gothic, this is framed off-center horizontally and vertically. A disproportionate amount of background above the subject, and not enough ground, creates an absence of perspective; the images are flat, with no reference points to locate the subjects spatially.

Sc.5) Black *B* cut off across the bottom of the screen.

Sc.6) White *B* enlarged even more and cut off at both top and bottom. This corresponds to the words 'is the hobgoblin of little minds.'

Sc.7) This phrase flows over into an image of two punks (female and male) carrying a bucket of sloshing milk between them. A cow in the background matches an image of a cow on her t-shirt. The blonde female wears black-checked pants and the male wears a leather jacket, tacky plaid-checked pants and a black spiked mohican haircut. Shot from a low angle, their bodies extend beyond the sides of the frame. The voiceover continues 'To be great . . . ' (see Figure 9.2).

Sc.8) Two apparently elderly women wearing identical red hats, white Miss Marple suits and red hightop sneakers with white socks pose in front of a modernist architectural monument – the stylized 1950s Diner. The women step forward, smile and in unison do a two-step dance. This is matched to the phrase ' . . . is to be misunderstood.'

Sc.9) Cut to their legs and red feet. The *Reebok* name is barely visible on the shoes and socks (on first viewing few viewers could read this). Later we realize their red-shoed expressions of personality are *Reeboks*.

Sc.10) A black *U.B.U* appears at center screen. The period is absent after the last *U.*

Sc.11) Behind a line of trees on the horizon (against an overly-blue sky) human figures are running in silhouette. Copied from Woody Allen's *Love and Death,* this scene connotes an absurdist cinematic

Figure 9.2 Reebok UBU (TV) – rural punks, 1988
Source: © Reebok

aesthetic. Allen adapted the scene from Ingmar Bergman's *The Seventh Seal* which foregrounded the black and white silhouette of Death with scythe. Death disappears in *Reebok*'s version, replaced by vividly colored absurdist hide-and-seek silliness.

Sc.12) A black woman wears a blue and white paisley ankle-length dress and white sneakers. She smiles, turns to the camera, and curls a barbell with her right arm, revealing a muscular biceps. A camera tilt makes her appear to stand straight while the grassy ground and trees about her slope; behind her a large tree trunk divides, and then is cut off by the frame. This creates an imbalance in the frame, keyed to the narration, 'There is a time in every man's education . . . ' Note the obvious gender mismatch between the visual image and the spoken words.

Sc.13,14,15) Three consecutive shots begin with a large white *U* on black and a large white *B* on black (cut off at the bottom) followed by a black *U* on white (cut off on the bottom and to the left). These images flash by as the narrator presses forward ' . . . when he arrives at the con . . . '

Sc.16) An androgynous youth wearing a ballerina outfit and white sneakers vacuums a pink oriental rug on a suburban front lawn while practicing a plié. Shot from below with a wide-angle lens, a blue sky dominates the background. The narration continues ' . . . [con]clusion that envy is ignorance' (see Figure 9.3).

Sc.17,18) A *U.B.U.* white on black, then a *U.B.U.* reversed to dark on white.

Sc.19) Three young boys dressed in white shorts and hawaiian green print shirts all look alike as they swing on white tires past a rose bush. They swing through a bright streak of light, turning their heads toward the camera in mechanical unison. Their lack of expressivity makes them seem programmed, but the narrator contradicts this – 'Insist on yourself . . .'

Sc.20,21,22) Three shots in rapid succession: an enlarged white on black *U.* (the period extends outside the frame on the right), followed by a large black on white *B* and another large black on white *U.* The voiceover continues ' . . . never imitate.'

Figure 9.3 Reebok UBU (TV) – suburban ballet, 1988

Source: © Reebok

Sc.23) A bride in white walks towards us and stops to pose (beneath her gown are red shoes). A groom in a gray tuxedo pops into place next to her; then a minister pops into the scene, and a beekeeper in a white protective suit and mask carrying a smoker; finally, the middle-aged man in long shorts playing with the paddleball wanders in. All wear sneakers. They pose in front of a white rural church structure before an un-manned camera on a tripod. The nature-like setting is given an artificial twist as four mechanical geese waddle through and exit the frame. Jump cuts make the subjects appear as if by magic, popping into the scene out of thin air. Luminescent lighting gives the scene an eerie feel. The narrator declares, 'To believe that what is true for you in your private heart is true for all men [pause] . . .'

Sc.24) A black screen, then the screen reads,

> '*Reeboks*
> Let U.B.U.'

as the voiceover concludes, ' . . . that is genius.'

DECONSTRUCTING SURFACES

Non-adness

The *Reebok* campaign built on how advertisers *normally position the spectator*. The *Reebok* ads present an advertising strategy to disguise the fact that an ad is an ad. *Not-ad* ads tend to encode a self-reflexive awareness of their own ad-ness. The *meta-ad* contains within itself a tacit commentary on the conventional structure of ads and how ads position spectators to execute the preferred interpretive procedures of abstraction, equivalence and reification. *Advertising Age* observed the disguised nature of the *Reebok* ad.

> Still, a lot of people don't get it. They look at director David Bailey's execution of art director Martin Weiss' vision and feel they are being MTVed to no purpose. They say the message doesn't register. They complain that they had to pay close attention to the commercials before they ever realized *Reebok* was the sponsor! Um, doesn't that make these, ipso facto, extraordinarily effective commercials? I kind of thought it was a rare achievement to get TV viewers scrutinizing anything without multiple cubic yards of cleavage.
>
> (Garfield, 1988)

Designed *to deny its adness*, the ad keeps viewers dangling in terms of its agenda. Music, narration, calligraphy, *mise-en-scène* and editing overlay the commercial nature of the ad with an innovative aesthetic structure that

210

encourages viewers to see an artistic text. The U.B.U calligraphy appears in an obtuse form: off-centered fragments of oversized typed letters give each calligraphic element an aesthetic as well as a discursive function. Likewise, the color, angle of shot and framing of each image violate realist coding. While the product appears in some shots, the only direct view of *Reebok* sneakers occurs in scene No. 9 when two matrons do a two-step dance. Only when the tagline '*Reeboks* Let U.B.U.' appears in the final shot can the puzzle be solved – this was an ad for *Reebok*. This last shot is underscored by the narration 'that is genius' – connoting that *Reebok* creates possibilities for individual style, and that you the viewer are a genius if you figured out you were watching a *Reebok* ad.

Ambiguity/rupturing the conventional

Since 'everything is now fake,' the postmodern text celebrates itself as a fictional artifact. It does not attempt to hide its constructed nature, but luxuriates in its arbitrariness. The postmodern text flaunts its own contrived arbitrariness by exaggerating the unconventional use of codes through devices such as juxtaposition, interpolation, superimposition, mis-attribution and intertextual integration. The *Reebok* ad appears to create a 'heterotopia,' linking together the incongruous and packing each frame with contradictions, non-conventional elements and film code violations. Scenes draw on culturally contradictory signifiers: punks in the countryside with a milk-pail or an androgynous ballerina vacuuming the lawn of a suburban home. The ordinary is transformed into the improbable or the bizarre. Color is either oversaturated or inappropriate. Skies are too blue; grass is too green; and the boys are too white and antiseptic. Heavy-handed color tinting calls attention to the constructed nature of each image, raising ontological questions. Whose world is this? Unbalanced frames violate realist conventions – characters are weighted too much to one side, or not centered vertically, e.g., too much headroom. The contrast with conventional framing rules contributes to a style that Chiat/Day's Bill Hamilton dubbed, 'American Gothic on its ear.'

Many ads now use non-narrative, kaleidoscopic montages of images to target different lifestyles, but maintain continuity by relying on realist conventions, music and voiceover narration. But here the codes governing the relationship between image, music, voiceover and titles are disjointed. With twenty-four shots in this 30-second ad, viewers do not have time to make sense of every shot. The diegetic structure is no help because the characters seem completely extraneous to one another, and the worlds they inhabit appear unrelated and outside historical time and space, in a world of artifice. And the music and narration offer no help to viewers who attempt to find *the* meaning of the ad text. Why the radio announcer's voice? Hungarian folk music? Emerson quotes? Instead of supplying answers to a puzzling, contradictory visual text, they add more layers of disparity.

The ad mismatches signifiers and signifieds, defying our expectation that voiceovers (like captions in print ads) will name visuals. Viewers soon recognize that each spoken concept is the *reverse* of the visual signified to which it is keyed, or a 'clever' conceptual joke. Narration and image are mismatched to draw attention to the mismatch itself. The narrator says 'there is a time in every man's education' but we see a black female weightlifter. 'Insist on yourself' corresponds to identical triplets in identical clothes with identical blank stares.

Reebok's ambiguity represents *difference* – its meaning is defined by that which sets it apart from other meanings. This is not, however, the radical ambiguity which Derrida identifies, but ambiguity generated by intentional discontinuity and suspension of conventional reading rules. Ambiguity has been turned into a signifier. Though ambiguity masquerades as inter-pretive openness, it is turned to a *mere* second-order signifier of difference (cf. Barthes, 1972). In the *Reebok* ad, *ambiguity is over-determined* – a function of market imperatives to seek commodity difference.

The death of affect

Conventional ads attempt to enhance brand recognition by associating a positive feeling with recognition. Devices such as identification with char-acter, music, narrator intonation, humor and emotional appeal aim at heightening affect and correlating it with a product. The *Reebok* ad cele-brates anti-affect. It appellates viewers as stonefaced, disinterested and disengaged. The narrator's voice is radio-flattened as it delivers third-person quotes. The inappropriateness of the music is dissociative rather than associative, and characters display masks of blank indifference. Mechanical gestures, disruption by titles and the 'freakish' nature of characters exalt anti-affective fascination. Here we find desire gone numb. Who you are has nothing to do with how you feel. The commodity-sign simply functions to separate you from other sign users. Wearing blankness as a sign metacommunicates that wearers see through the sham of com-modity culture.

Ads customarily position viewers to occupy what Berger calls the surveyed–surveyor relationship, thinking of self as 'an object of vision: a sight' – mentally trying on this or that look. *Reebok* takes an ambivalent stance on the position of viewers *vis-à-vis* the commodity-self as an object of visual desire. *Reebok* still locates personal identity as a function of the freedom of visual appearance, but *Reebok*'s blank subjects seem mutely to abstain from participation in the normalizing conventions of commodity-sign surveillance, while the voiceover disparages the envy–desire dialectic as 'ignorance.' No character in the ad seems concerned about how they are surveyed by others; the young rural punks at the center of the ad refuse even to acknowledge the surveyor's gaze.

Reebok embraces 'poor taste' as a sign for anti-style that might beckon skeptical viewers to enter the space of the ad. The U.B.U. ad links alienation from the mode of appellation to the artifice of style. *Reebok* flatters viewers, bummed out by endless reruns of formulaic commodity narratives, with images of commodity ennui, while offering them a field of ambiguous pastiche to decipher. *Reebok* thus heralds a new super-individuated subject who wears artifice as a sign indicating personal freedom. Artifice worn with blank affect offers a mask which insulates the individual wearer from the industrialization of culture.

Strategies for interpretation

Williamson (1978) shows how ads require that spectators produce the meaning. Devices such as absence of the product, puns and puzzles, calligraphy and contradictory language are used to create space and a feeling of interpretive freedom. Williamson shows, however, that these devices direct spectators to the preferred answer that is *already* in the ad. The freedom of interpretation which the text promises is an illusion.

Whether it is the breakdown of the grand narratives of Western Civilization or the not so grand narratives of consumer culture, postmodernism celebrates the participatory role of the spectator in deconstruction. No longer is there a single authoritative interpretation to a text but a multiplicity of interpretations which lead to a supposed cultural pluralism. Indeterminacy and ambiguity in postmodern texts elicit participation because ambiguity impels viewers to fill in interpretive gaps.

Does the *Reebok* ad extend the participatory role of spectators? The ad mimics the hermeneutic structure outlined by Williamson, creating a puzzle by the noted absence of the product, disconnected imagery and fragmented calligraphy. Unconventional, eccentric and obtuse images and encoding practices further complicate the puzzle. As a string of signifiers, the ad demands self-conscious interrogation. And yet, it supplies a solution to its puzzle in the tagline. Viewers have four options.[5] Traditional viewers socialized to expect realist conventions simply refuse to play the interpretive game. The imagery and structure are too far outside this viewer's coding boundaries, and require too much work for the satisfaction that interpretation might provide. A modernist viewer demands a clear meaning. *Reebok* has created a puzzle-like structure, so the pleasure comes from piecing it together and finding the 'correct' solution. Subsequent viewings may be used to find and verify meanings, posit relationships between images, attach signifieds to the signifiers. However, the *Reebok* ad is a postmodernist text in that its meaning does not lie within the text. It entices viewers with a puzzle-like structure, but the pieces don't fit. To escape the labyrinth, a third strategy does not ask 'what does this mean?' but rather 'where does it come from?' Instead of finding a signified, one recognizes similarly stylized arrangements of signifiers. Here, signifiers take on a life of their own – their significance eclipses their signifieds. While intertextual allusion does not focus meaning, it creates a sense of interpretive potency based on media literacy. A fourth strategy makes no attempt to find meaning. This viewer simply enjoys the 'weird' or fantastic nature of the imagery. Fleeting fascination replaces a quest for meaning as this viewer accepts the surface and its contradictions without experiencing a need for coherence. 'The pleasure-seeking bricoleur replaces the truth-and-justice seeking rational subject of the Enlightenment' (Hebdige, 1988: 166). This relationship to texts is conditioned by having experienced a continuous flow of disjointed, fragmented imagery such as is offered by heavy ad or MTV viewing.

> What characterizes the postmodern video is its refusal to take a clear position *vis-à-vis* its images, its habit of hedging . . . a clear signified . . . each element of a text is undercut by others: narrative is undercut by pastiche; signifying is undercut by images that do not line up in a coherent chain; the text is flattened out, creating a two-dimensional effect and the refusal of a clear position for the spectator within the filmic world. This leaves him/her decentered, perhaps confused, perhaps fixated on one particular image or image-series, but most likely unsatisfied.
>
> (Kaplan, 1987: 63)

Ironically, the indeterminacy and contradiction of a postmodern ad elicits greater participation when encountered by a modernist viewer who seeks coherence and completion.

PASTICHE AND SCHIZOPHRENIA

The *Reebok* ad *is* pure pastiche. Pastiche designates a cultural form built on copying, scavenging and recombining particles of cultural texts regardless of context. Pastiche is the visual representation composed of decontextualized and fetishized signifiers. This cultural form is conditioned by a language disorder – a breakdown of the relationship between signifiers and signifieds – that Jacques Lacan conceptualizes as schizophrenia.

> The schizophrenic experience is an experience of isolated, disconnected, discontinuous material signifiers which fail to link up in a coherent sequence.
>
> (Jameson, 1983: 119)

Without the context of sentences or narrative and without a guiding syntax or codes, time implodes into a perpetual present. Without time there is no

214

identity, 'no persistence of the "I" and the "me".' Television presents just such a perpetual present in its technical capacity for stringing together images as signifiers in any order regardless of the historical context of any given image. Ads sequence images to permit the goal of transferring their meaning – their value – to a named commodity. All images thus become instrumentalized, their importance reduced to *their capacity to signify a meaning which is transferable*. The consequence is a heightened awareness of each isolated signifier and 'a change in the *mode of narration*' (Berger, 1974: 40). Stories which unfold sequentially become rarer 'because we are too aware of what is continually traversing the storyline laterally.' 'Simultaneity and extension' push aside 'sequence' in the mode of narration – we now live in the world of *the segue*. Pastiche as a schizophrenic textual form abstracts from different socio-historical moments and brings disparate elements together into a collaged present.

Reebok's pastiche is a bit more convoluted yet, since it raises ostensibly self-reflexive questions about the agenda of the ad message (see Herskovitz, 1979). Pastiche is simultaneously turned into a metaphor for individuality, even as it metacommunicates indifference to 'instant style' or 'the look' (the currency of individual appearance and persona in a consumer society). Most TV consumer ads position viewers to complete a relationship between floating signifiers and signifieds. TV ads instrumentally splinter signifieds and signifiers into a universe of pastiche, and *Reebok*'s use of pastiche as textual strategy to deny this positioning is, itself, cynical.

Reebok tries to install itself as the totem of bricoleurs. *Reebok*'s use of pastiche constitutes a recognition that advertising has turned the human body and its surrounding landscapes into visual zones of consumption which may be filled by any meaning system reduced to a visual seme. As an apparently random and arbitrary approach to presenting signifiers, pastiche registers as a denial of the power of Style-makers and Designers. But this reassertion of amateurishness reconfirms, at another level, the fetishism of the discrete image and its power over us. When self is presented as an eclectic amalgam of random signifiers, each body part offers an axis on which to differentiate the self visually. The number of combinations and permutations of signifiers becomes immense. Jameson claims 'the disappearance of the individual subject, along with its formal consequences, the increasing unavailability of personal style, engender . . . pastiche,' but paradoxically, the extreme fetishism of this cut-up style may set the stage for a rampant pluralism of commodity personalities. We take no solace from this kind of commodity pluralism, because it contributes to the privatized commodity hegemony we have been tracking. Pastiche as commodity pluralism favors privatized, fractured discourses over shared public discourse. Pastiche demands neither specific nor in-depth knowledge of a text or genre, but draws only from the surface of other texts. Its allusions become digression – tangential and oblique. Simulated surfaces and fleeting moments of pastiche reverberate a sense of continuous *déjà vu.* Since the text is a collage of signifiers, deconstruction is less an unraveling procedure than an expansionary one. Viewers must locate associations to create significance and the *Reebok* text confirms an ever expanding allusory labyrinth. Pastiche

> celebrate(s) the accretion of texts and meanings, the proliferation of sources and readings rather than the isolation, and the deconstruction of the single text or utterance.
>
> (Hebdige, 1988: 191)

Pastiche – plundering culture for signifiers

Readers of *The Medium is the Massage* will recognize how much of *Reebok*'s pastiche is lifted – plagiarized – from McLuhan's book, starting with the 'American Gothic' image adjacent to a discussion of the 'shock of recognition,' including the 'Dance of Death' imagery from Ingmar Bergman's *Seventh Seal,* and playing with magnified print. Plundering 'high culture' for signifiers extends into the Theater of the Absurd where Alfred Jarry's *UBU Roi* satirized the repressive orderliness of bourgeois culture. The ad also carries hints of Diane Arbus's photographic style (her 'fascination' with 'freaks') and Richard Hamilton's 1950s photographic influence (the suburban weightlifter). Of course, *Reebok* only appropriates the surface of Jarry's surrealism and, as in every instance noted here, pastiche *elides* critique.

Grant Wood's painting 'American Gothic' is an icon known for its simultaneous symbolism and parody of American individualism. Its absurdist quality hovers between the real and the surreal, a sense of the 'off-real' that makes it difficult to place. But whereas 'American Gothic' captured a repressed strait-laced midwestern personality, *Reebok*'s 'Gothic on its Ear' represents an anything-goes leisure ethic. American Gothic 'off-realness' appears in postmodern films like David Byrne's (1986) *True Stories* which used exaggerated characterization, oversaturated color, distorted framing and pastiche to explore individuality and the American social landscape. Like Wood's 'American Gothic,' Byrne's caricatures poke fun at small-town people, while also treasuring their capacity for peculiarity in the face of cynical cosmopolitan sophistication. Drawn from tabloid stories, Byrne's caricatures are mimicked by *Reebok* – as idiosyncratic mixtures of eclectic signifiers found in commodity culture but personalized through use. Byrne uses obvious rear-screen projection to flatten perspective and to hail surface and artifice as he drives and narrates. His postmodern agenda mocks the conventions and illusions of television by visually exposing them. Byrne's blank parody also disrupts the usual relationship between spectators and the visual textual message. When *Reebok*

216

appropriates this blank narrative strategy, spectators' relationship to the text is momentarily dislocated, since most ads invite viewers to desire (identify with) the voice of cynical sophistication.

True Stories toured a commodity culture shaped by mega-corporations and shopping malls where standardization and hyper-individuality exist simultaneously. At the mall, commodity pluralism is 'the cultural dominant' predetermining the boundaries of individuality while the logic of Capital presses those boundaries to hyper-individualist absurdity in order to expand markets. Byrne remarks that we are all constantly 'inventing' our 'systems of beliefs' as his characters try to find selves in the cultural chaos of administered corporate life. The paradox finds expression in ironic ambiguity at 'The Celebration of Specialness,' when a character resolves his personal crisis by singing 'no freedom, no justice, but love.' Byrne recognizes the entrapment but empathizes with desires for uniqueness, recognition and belonging. When *Reebok* abstracts Byrne's film images and inserts them into its advertising format, the contradiction between commodity culture and individuality is disguised by varying the ad's appellation structure and by giving primacy to the visual aesthetic style that marked *True Stories* from standard film fare. This illustrates how a political economy of sign value transforms the 'specific ambivalent content of a cultural expression . . . it is first abstracted as a general equivalent style . . . and then circulated as so many commodity signs' (Foster, 1986: 86).

A CRISIS OF INDIVIDUALITY AND THE CORPORATE OVERSOUL

Postmodernists reject the notion of a stable, unified, coherent self and corresponding theories of depth psychology, insisting that there is nothing other than *surfaces* and disjointed fragments. Nietzsche's warning that the 'subject' is 'a fiction' has been inflated into postmodern 'protest(s) at the coercive unification implied by the notion of a self-conscious, self-identical subject' (Dews, 1986: 31). The autonomous (unified and stable) ego may have been the bourgeois corollary to the ethic of possessive individualism during the heyday of modernity. This was the seductively idealized ego that stared back at subjects from the advertising mirror for decades. But the mirror has transformed this self from one anchored in depth to one floating in appearances. In a society where the transcendental signified has withered away, and signifiers erratically bounce across time and space, the 'schizophrenic fragmentation of experience and loss of identity' becomes a central social modality. If 'death of God' declarations heralded the rise of modernism and the decline of *gemeinschaft* relations, then does the 'death of the subject' signal the postmodern era? Capitalist society has already encountered the 'death of the social,' claims Baudrillard (1983b), and the *Reebok* ad seems to echo his message.

217

Unconventional in design and mode of signification, the *Reebok* ad aimed to convince viewers that *Reebok* endorses an anti-style position. But the ad's structure defined *Reebok* itself as the *field* in which questions of individual style and appearance are played out. *Reebok* was positioned as a non-conformist lifestyle addressed to *wanna be* non-conformists. Violations of realist aesthetic codes are made to stand for individuality: just as the ad consists of aesthetic code violations, viewers are asked to consider that wearing the *sign* of *Reebok* sneakers will allow parallel violations of appearance codes and enable unique self-construction. *Reebok*'s press releases stressed individuality and diversity in their target audiences.

Reebok does not represent one lifestyle, but many lifestyles.

Reebok is not a 'badge brand' like Rolex or BMW.

Reebok has become a phenomenon because people use the brand in many ways, allowing each to express their own individuality.

People want to interpret *Reebok* into their own active, individual style.

Reebok's campaign invited viewers to draw an analogy between *Reebok*'s disregard for conventions and their personal disregard for the opinion of others. *Reebok* presented itself as anti-totemic, by celebrating the enchantment of freakish, carnivalesque, anti-rationalist selves as if they articulate a dimension of individuality outside of the social. Unlike conventional ads which associate commodities with signs of individuality, *Reebok* disassociates those signs from status, sexuality, esteem, acceptance or desirability. These traits necessitate affect, concern and a sense that the social exists. *Reebok* offers a commodity soul that is flat – images are cold and distant and there are no avenues for identification, empathy or any emotional connection between the viewer and the ad's characters. Individuality is signified as an ensemble of eclectic signifiers in which signifier disparity equals non-conformity. *Reebok* positions itself as the sign of this ensemble.

Reebok offers a re-tread version of the bourgeois self, but flattened of affect and depth. This self is defined as a function of sign consumption. Individuality is measured by the appropriation of contradictory signifiers worn in an ambiguous ensemble. An idealist, romantic construction that floats outside the material reality of social production, the authentic self unfolds in relation to itself, a solipsistic self whose reality is narcissism. Self-construction apparently takes place in a world without reference points – no nature, no time, no history, no society. Indeed, if narcissism is the 'tendency to measure the world as a mirror of self' (Sennett, 1977: 177), then *Reebok*'s scenic backgrounds may be read as signs indicating the idiosyncratic personalities of the foregrounded subjects. The flattened background maps the blankness of their subjectivity.

218

Quoting Emerson further embellishes this conflation of the self-contained soul and the outside world. A 'transcendentalist' essayist and poet dedicated to the 'divine sufficiency of the individual,' Emerson's writing has been a bulwark of the mythological system of the self-sufficient and uncompromising integrity of the autonomous individual. When Emerson wrote, there was still enough social, economic and political space for white males to carve out this grandiose victory of self over society. Emerson's transcendentalism rejected the authoritative God of Protestantism as well as a need for others. 'By thus transcending society itself, they abstracted man into a set of principles which they ultimately presented as moral absolutes' (Williams, 1966: 42). Though this search for individual freedom has often been quoted to justify laissez-faire philosophies, its romantic and anti-rationalist vision could not be reconciled with the realities of an ever-expanding market economy.

There is a similarity between *Reebok*'s message about *meta-style* and Emerson's notion of the *Over-soul*. Emerson claimed each person shared in the Over-soul, or God, 'whose influence in this world was rather less than even the Hidden Hand that guided the system of Adam Smith' (Williams, 1966: 242). *Reebok* has phrased it otherwise, but latently identifies itself as our corporate *over-sole*. *Reebok* endorses unusual expressions of individuality, but ends by suggesting that *Reebok* is the hidden hand, or rather foot, that permits the articulation of uniquely individuated meaningful styles.

Reebok presents a romantic view of the individual unencumbered by the social, but still reasserts itself as the *named* product through which a self can realize its essential being. *Reebok* appellates the viewer, but waits until the last moment to do it. The commercial pseudo-individuality denied by the narrator is the solution to the rebus. The hegemonic construction of self central to the logic of advertising is not escaped by stylistic unconventionality and appeals to non-identity.[6]

The relationship between appellation protocol and non-identity is critical. The viewer's relationship to the *Reebok* mirror is never straightforward: are viewers asked to read themselves into these images? Instead of appellating viewers at the start of the ad, viewers are hailed at the conclusion when *U.B.U.* appears on screen as a complete concept. At ad's end we grasp the hypermagnified letters as a disguised commodity appellation structure:

*Reebok*s
Let U.B.U.

Reebok is the commodity-sign. 'Let' designates the logic of reification. *U* appellates the viewer. The *B* designates self-identity and the second *U* completes the circuit of desire/commodity self à la discussion of 'already-ness' (Williamson, 1978).

219

Desire eclipses self

Reebok brought 'postmodernism' to the television screen by reducing it to an *aesthetic style*. This image of aesthetic sensibility represents one response to internal contradictions between commodity culture and bourgeois/modernist culture.

On *Reebok*'s feet, postmodernism is no more able to avoid being re-absorbed by the commodity form of culture than any other cultural protest or moment of deviance. The postmodern problematic identifies a crisis of representation which we conceptualize as a *crisis of privatized subjectivity (individualism) in relation to a political economy of sign value*. What happens when individuals are repeatedly directed toward commodified images in their search for authenticity? In the model of the commodity self, the negation of authenticity takes place when the named commodity (the means of self-satisfaction) displaces or pushes aside the ego – it de-centers the self since fetishized self-identity becomes lodged in its many subdivided object-parts. Where the ideal bourgeois character structure once defined the self-made man, today's experienced consumer cannot help but recognize the ideal consumer self makes itself not just once, but repeatedly – the ideal ego is not sturdy or fixed, but plastic.

Enshrined in the possessive individualism of Hobbes and Locke, the self-sufficient ego was free to appropriate, to own, to alienate the world around it. The bourgeois ego-ideal also tapped into a belief in the self as an expressive totality:

> the middle classes embarked upon a strenuous campaign to promote an aesthetic which served both to endorse their real preferences and to advance a character ideal which made appreciation of beauty a matter of genuine emotional sensitivity and responsiveness. Correspondingly, they advocated an interpretation of taste which presented it as a quasi-charismatic quality of near-spiritual dimensions. This was naturally not to the liking of the aristocracy, who could detect the vulgar tone of 'enthusiasm' which inspired this formulation.
>
> (Campbell, 1987: 159)

Self-expression as the hallmark of individual freedom emphasized the aesthetic cultivation of the senses while Enlightenment Reason emphasized the individual as master and maker of his world. Capitalism and Science, however, united through the course of the nineteenth century to undo the conditions that would permit the necessary social space for autonomy to occur. Wage labor and the commodification of daily life along with the application of instrumental rationality to the labor process led to social separation in daily life (privatism) and deskilling of work – thus undermining the capacity for achieving freedom defined as self-articulation through one's production activity.

An initial crisis of individualism around 1900 coincided with the transformation from competitive to corporate (Fordist) capitalism and an intensifying urban experience. At the same time that bourgeois intellectuals began to experience their first collective crisis of individualism, early corporate capitalists enlisted the *terrain of the self* in their search for new markets. As the middle class modernized, gave up their localized bonds and moved to industrial urban environs they experienced a sense of separation from nature (a 'loss of reality') and doubt about self-identity. Rationalized workplaces and bureaucratic organizations diminished their occupational autonomy. While repressive religious ideologies declined, the medical profession and a corresponding belief in the truth of science emerged to promise a new method of privatized salvation. Having lost much of their Protestant faith in hard work as the source of individual identity and morality, they became susceptible to advertisements that promised to harness scientific expertise to the search for self-realization. Advertising as a 'therapeutic ethos . . . originated in the thickets of the troubled self' (Lears, 1983: 37). Advertising offered to restore psychic health, an organic link to nature, a sense of wholeness and self-identity by means of personal commodity consumption. Parallel to the deskilling of labor, advertising relocated individuality and autonomy in commodity consumption. Advertising constituted a new language of social life anchored by 'parables' and 'narratives' that were 'guideposts to a modern logic of living' (Marchand, 1985).

A new middle class arose after World War II, no longer self-employed, but university educated with salaried jobs in state and corporate bureaucracies (Mills, 1951). As traditional ethnic enclaves and social bonds were spatially and experientially eclipsed, the forces of education, bureaucratic regulation of the workplace, suburban privatism and the mass media (especially television) became more salient in people's lives. The new middle class no longer controlled the means of production, but were bound instead as a class by their consumption and education. The media unabashedly presented a commodity solution to every need or itch, and the media world-view of consumerism and anti-communism seemed uncontested.

By 1950, the apparent plenty of commodity culture and the new medium of television inaugurated a 'hegemonic' stage of advertising characterized by Wilson (1988) as follows:

1) 'Everyone is assumed to be a consumer first and foremost. Consumers' needs are replaced by consumers' desires. The consumer role has become second nature . . . '
2) '"A commodity aesthetic" becomes autonomous and then dominant.'
3) 'The "code" which connects [image, good and consumer] is written in meta-language. We consume the "sign" of the commodity,

not the commodity itself; moving from the consumption of signs to consuming signs of consumption.'

4) 'We "buy into" not a commodity but a world of commodities, a world in which time and space are structured by commodities.'

5) 'Consumption is a prerequisite for the performance of roles.'

No sooner had commodity culture become hegemonic than it began to breed its own criticism. Critics perceived 'overconformity' and a paradox of individuals freed from traditional bonds and constraints, but too privatized to realize freedom in action, except as 'choices' from among the models of consumer behavior offered by the culture industries. Rock'n'roll reacted against the repressive alienation of this cultural dominant, even as its expressions of resistance were re-absorbed via the commodity form. Anti-heroes such as James Dean signified a struggle to articulate depth and not surface, while the beat movement resisted the crass materialist assumptions of consumerism. As traditional norms (ethnic and Protestant) continued to erode, and consumer alienation grew, the self and its construction became politicized. But the therapeutic ethos and the quest for self-realization went awry and the Self emerged from the 1960s neither free nor autonomous but empty and uncertain, and filled with rage. Bureaucratic dependency, celebrity culture, advertising and the breakdown of paternal parental authority bred a narcissistic personality that used commodity culture to validate self to both self and others. The 1970s, popularly dubbed the 'me' decade, took the notion of a self constructed via the accumulation of commodity traits to new plateaux. Driven by competition, commodity culture continued to differentiate itself internally. Spiraling specialization of commodities and signs had its correlate in a fragmentation of the self (Lasch, 1979b). Each self is encouraged to navigate through the flood of signifieds and signifiers and attempt to construct a unified whole self which can be represented as an image, *the look*. A significant sociocultural break came with the Punk subculture of the mid-1970s which conducted a 'semiotic guerilla warfare,' turning 'narcissism into an offensive weapon' and transforming conventional commodity paraphernalia into '"empty" fetishes, objects to be desired, fondled and valued in their own right' (Hebdige, 1979: 104–5). By the early 1980s, the cultural contradictions of advertising had become obvious as the relationship between consuming commodity-signs and individuality was pressed to its limit. A new crisis of believability unfolded – who could take seriously the claim that an authentic self is available via consumption of commodity aesthetics? But who could distance themselves from this socialized desire to be special, to stand out?

Some 1980s advertisers attempted to circumvent this crisis tendency by denying that they colonize the self – taking the surface of a postmodernist critique and converting it into an aesthetic style. Postmodernism offers a critique of a decentered subject or, in more extreme formulations, the death of the subject and the demise of the social. The critique recognizes how the subject has been eclipsed by commodities and commodity-signs. Exactly how authentic is the self when defined by a collection of commodity-signs? This is the critique of plastic man! Chiat/Day has appropriated this critique of the collapse of subjectivity and fused it to a critique of the representational form driven by the logic of commodity-signs. Their *Reebok* ads turn blankness and the lack of engagement to deny any formal equivalency of the self and commodity-sign. Viewers are asked to appreciate this lack of equivalency as decentered on screen – decentered in relation to themselves. We interpret this as a metanarrative about the commodification of *desire* – the blank affect is a posture which denies the centrality of desire.

Modern advertising aims at reproducing the commodity form by colonizing the domain of Desire. Advertisers have belabored the desire for recognition – to be recognized and acknowledged by Other. Unlike early critical theorists, we perceive this desire for Self-constitution and Identity to be a contested terrain. Cynicism and blank indifference are defenses prompted by the endless circuit of sign-value production in advertising, and become disruptive of the sign-valorization process. At the same time, the death of affect and blank indifference are turned into signs directed at stemming a broader crisis of sign completion.

The distance between early modernists and contemporary consumers is encapsulated in the semiotic opposition between 'enthusiasm' and 'indifference.' The early middle class aimed to express a sense of self in terms of 'taste' and 'style.' Aesthetic preferences were taken to be signs of character, providing a measure of personal identity. A century later, this world-view had evolved into a self-contradictory knot for the Victorian bourgeoisie who behaved as if every choice of objects could be read as a 'personality omen' revealing an inner self. Joined with their residual puritan ideology of personal shame and ascetic self-denial, the result was 'a contradictory, tense attempt to read others for signs of their private lives while at the same time one attempted to shield oneself from being read by anyone' (Sennett, 1977: 174–5). Today, the *Reebok* ad may be read as both an extension and a sublation of this cultural dialectic, now driven by the pursuit of pleasure. The logic of commodity consumption directs us to identify ourselves by the signs we accumulate and display – we read one another as sign constellations as we 'engage in market transactions of self-revelation . . . the semiotics of 20th century personality are only the consequences of 19th century terms, taken to an extreme' (Sennett, 1977: 183). The *Reebok* ad is yet another promotion for self-revelation of one's personality *as* an ensemble of signs; but isn't it also about shielding oneself from being read behind a veil of dispassionate blankness – a calculated denial that the surface has anything to do with a deep self?

These crises of subjectivity and representation are simultaneously a crisis of the commodity form – or, to be historically more specific, they are intertwined with a crisis of a political economy of commodity-sign values.

THE WIDER CONTEXT: CONTRADICTIONS OF A POLITICAL ECONOMY OF SIGN VALUES

Advertising is an institutional process in *a political economy of commodity-sign value.* A more focused analysis of the cultural implications of ads is possible if we rethink advertising and commodity-signs in the context of the historical development of capitalist political economy and class relations. Where commodity form and advertising form converge lies the sphere of commodity-signs.

From the vantage point of political economy, development of a regime of sign values can be traced to multiple historical forces in the early twentieth century: 1) crises of overproduction and underconsumption (Ewen, 1976); 2) barriers in the velocity of commodity circulation between production and consumption (Haug, 1986: 23; O'Connor, 1987: 81); 3) temporary saturation of investment capital in primary goods production led to increased investment in leisure and consumer-goods industries (Sklar, 1969); 4) the bourgeoisie's struggle to maintain hegemony over a public sphere of discourse (Brenkman, 1979); 5) bourgeois norms of deferred gratification became an obstacle to expanding consumer-goods markets.

These forces spurred an institutionalized political economy of sign value, but once the circuit of marketing and advertising gained some history, the political economy of sign value took on its own internal dynamic. Modern advertisers face a never-ending imperative of enhancing the value of products by linking those products to a symbolic value, while differentiating their images from others. Over time, success in this endeavor intensified the competition to come up with effective commodity-sign values. Just as a political economy of sign value arose historically because of contradictions in the political economy of the commodity form, a political economy of commodity-signs is subject to its own internal contradictions (see Marx, 1967). Corporate advertising (1900–25) initially responded to a structural crisis of commodity realization. Corporate advertising developed as a means of reducing circulation time between production and the realization of a commodity sale. But solving the problem of circulation time and the realization of commodity value has generated alienated readers and viewers and contributed to a new crisis of valuation. After roughly seventy-five years, the unrelenting reduction in circulation time has propagated contradictions in the reproduction of sign value.

'Intensified commodity circulation' stimulates 'fragmentation and "destabilization" of the categories of needing' and prompts 'a growing indifference to the qualities of needs or wants.' Attempts to constantly expand consumer markets have proliferated and fragmented needs. Because marketers are under constant pressure to revolutionize needs and the means to their satisfaction, there follows a 'destabilizing' of categories of needing. When there are so many needs constantly being divided, subdivided and redefined, consumers become less able to attend fully to the satisfaction of any given need: 'the individual must become increasingly *indifferent* to the fine shadings and nuances of both wants and the objects which s/he pursues in the search for satisfaction.' Confronted with an endless procession of objects and their signs, consumers grow 'indifferent' to the specific qualities of those objects, and their lack of attachment to them 'is merely the other side of the developing shallowness and triviality in our articulation of the needs themselves' (Leiss, 1976: 88–90).[7]

Proliferating commodity brand names have prompted a corresponding proliferation of commodity-signs. Competition within the sphere of commodity-sign production and consumption leads to a tendency for the rate of circulation of sign values to accelerate. Intensified commodity-sign circulation has also sparked a crisis of credibility linked to a crisis of representation, along with a self-conscious relativizing of value. Competition for market share accelerates the circulation of commodity-signs until the swirl of signifier and signified becomes dizzying and fusion of signifier and signified occurs. When we are no longer able to differentiate signifier from signified there is no fixity of meaning. 'The devaluation of meaning in postmodern signification is simultaneously the de-differentiation of signifier and signified' (Lash, 1988: 391). Williamson (1978) detailed how advertisements aim to create 'a currency on the level of signs' by steering the transfer and exchange of meanings. This process necessarily converts signifieds into signifiers in order to reproduce a commodity-sign currency, but the repeated transfer and exchange undermines the reproduction of the commodity-sign currency system when signifier and signified become fused. Driven by the motor of exchange value, a crisis of realist representation can be traced to the pervasive and continuous process of mixing and remixing signifiers and signifieds detached from referent systems.

Advertisers face the task of establishing and maintaining a differentiated position in the sign field of mass culture, while the growth of corporate markets demands a continuous expansion of the commercial sign field. In practical marketing terms, product and sign recall gets problematic when too many finely differentiated signs compete within the same space. Neither Desire nor Meaning is exhaustible per se. But just because Desire and Meaning are potentially infinite does not mean their continuous appropriation for purposes of expanding the field of exchange values is without social-psychological consequence. Ceaseless competition within the field of commodity-sign value leads to a diminishing half-life of sign values, ad campaigns and attention spans. Routinized glamour also reinforces this tendency for the rate of sign value to decline – saturate a currency and you devalue it. Of no less consequence in a mature political economy of sign value, the constant symbolic construction and reconstruction of value draws attention to the very category of value – value becomes relativized and the authority of the value production process becomes transparent. Whereas the ideological justice of nineteenth-century capitalism rested on premises of equivalence exchange and the universal absolute of exchange value as a category, today's consumer world is a contest in which advertisers and marketers seek to undermine the sign-exchange value of their competitors while enhancing (via differentiation) the value of their own products. Under these circumstances, the category of value has exhausted its truth claims. Ads like *Reebok* acknowledge that sign value is plastic and transitory, based on artifice and superficiality.

Finally, an accelerated rate of circulation alienates viewers, like a speed- up in the assembly line of commodity-signs. The relationship between ads as vehicles for structurally reproducing commodity-sign values and the social construction of alienated interpretive labor can be specified as follows.

(1) Ads structure meanings so that they become *a means of producing commodity-sign value.* To produce sign values, advertisers colonize the sphere of cultural life in their search for meanings which will *add value* to their product or service. The raw materials (the meanings) for commodity-sign production come from the cultural life-world. The competition to extract and revalorize those meaning systems eventually reaches the point where it exhausts the referent world of everyday life. Then advertising begins to cannibalize itself, feeding on the recycling and recombining of previous advertising styles and signs, in the quest for new twists on old meanings. Hence it becomes increasingly self-referential or intertextual (see Lefebvre, 1971).

(2) Viewers are able to interpret most ads because they know the rules which govern the movement and connection of meanings in ads. Ads ideologically reproduce the logic of commodity relations – not necessarily because of the content of this or that ad, but because of the *structure or form* of ads, and the interpretive rules which the structure carries. Ads' ideological force comes through their format rules which viewers must execute performatively in order to interpret the ads. Viewers' interpretive participation is absolutely necessary to the *completion* of commodity-signs (Williamson, 1978). Consumers *produce value,* they don't just consume it. Because viewers are integral participants in the valorization of sign values, the production of surplus meanings invariably transcends the functional agendas of advertisers. In particular, *desire* is a volatile and disruptive force. Attempts to colonize desire as a means of expanding the domain of commodity value are, indeed, risky business.

226

(3) To compete efficiently within a political economy of sign values, advertisers have continuously rationalized their production methods – e.g.,
innovations in market research, lifestyle categories such as VALS, focus
groups and product positioning. Because of their sales agenda, ads
tend to be systematically over-structured to elicit preferred meanings.

(4) Efficiently over-structured encoding practices and formats turn popular cultural meanings into the raw materials for producing new commodity values. This not only requires abstracting that which is
meaningfully valuable to us from the real social relations of daily life, it
also entails *positioning the spectator-reader vis-à-vis* a mode of address
(Williamson, 1978). Over time, spectator-readers have developed patterns of resistance to ads, particularly to the process of being *positioned*
by ads to complete the formulaic exchange of meanings.

(5) Advertisers in the 1980s have recognized viewer resistance and attempted
to incorporate images of resistance in new rounds of advertising. Ad
saturation and clutter combined with viewer skepticism have inaugurated
the so-called postmodern era in advertising. Postmodern ads show us
ourselves as too media hip to be taken in by ads. During the 1970s,
advertisers rationalized and over-structured advertisements in order to
produce competitive sign values, but, since 1984, a new stage of advertising
has developed in response to viewer alienation. Advertisers incorporated
criticism of advertising into their ads by adopting postures of reflexive
self-awareness about the project of advertising itself.

There is an obvious contradiction between viewer participation in the construction of meanings and the death of the subject used as a positioning theme
in the *Reebok* ad. Advertisers recognize the need for savvy subjects to complete
their own meanings and seek new strategies to engage subjects at that level. But
this participation is over-determined and formulaic – it forces viewers to cope
with absences in terms of coding rules and sequences. Can appeasing cynicism
and trying to take on the stance of nihilistic ennui stem the crisis of sign-
completion (what Marx called a crisis of valuation)?

These abstract crisis tendencies of sign value have material parallels in
the marketplace. Mass markets have splintered into an array of niche and
specialty markets. Market fragmentation, proliferating commodity brands
and the displacement of a mass national viewing audience by cable television are forcing changes on the advertising industry. Total ad spending
rose from $43.3 billion in 1978 to $118.1 billion in 1988, growth rates
dropped from 15.7 to 7.7 per cent and profits slipped from 20 to 10 per
cent industry-wide.

Agencies are being lashed by several separate but allied trends. Slow
population growth has compelled companies to try to raise market
share by stealing customers from their rivals, which they are doing by

cutting prices and by creating products with slight differences to appeal to specific audiences.

(Rothenberg, 1989: 1, 23)

To compete with foreign producers on price, US manufacturers went high tech and sought cheaper labor forces abroad. This led to 'producing more goods, flooding the market with wares, many of them barely distinguishable.' Whereas new products fueled the advertising industry's growth during the 1960s and 1970s, now brand proliferation has overwhelmed advertising's ability to differentiate brand images (sign values).

PRODUCTION BACKGROUNDED

The truth of postmodernism is that production has been pushed to the inner recesses of our collective consciousness, while consumption and desire have become the overwhelming presence in our lives. Unfortunately, like the positivist paradigm which it claims to undo, postmodernism grasps only its own moment of truth – it grasps the surface. Despite its imaginative grasp of the texture and feel of the culture of appearances, postmodern social theory grasps the historical significance of those appearances only weakly because it dispenses with the study of negations and glosses over the relations of capitalist production (see Kellner, 1988; Debord, 1977). The culture industry generates a heterogeneity of meaningful styles that is more apparent than real, structured institutionally on a narrow axis of social action – the practices of commodification. Postmodern theories frequently appear *ungrounded* because they leave out production relations and class relations.[8] Flitting from one cultural text to another, theoretical postmodernism *abstracts* the culture of appearances from the self-contradictory relations of advanced corporate capitalism.

Postmodernism dwells on what Baudrillard terms 'the triumph of signifying culture.' Postmodern cultural analysis celebrates *texts* and wages intellectual battles over their deconstruction. Shopping malls, hotels, wrestling matches, America itself, all become treated as inscribed texts to be read as a 'hyperspace' of signs and simulacra. But while postmodernism locates the social centrality of sign production and a new phenomenology of simulacra, it fails to go beyond the 'texts' into the relations and practices that condition and inscribe the texts. Postmodernism ignores the uneven class relations which premise the society of the spectacle. It ignores the other side – namely de-industrialization. Fascinated by the glossy surface of the simulacrum, Baudrillard declares the 'end of political-economy, the end of production.' Kellner summarizes Baudrillard's view:

Modernity is the era of the bourgeoisie, of the primacy of industrial production, where . . . the imperatives of production determined social life. With the technological revolution, however, reproduction

228

replaces production as the centre of social life, and then models, codes, simulacra, spectacles, and the 'hyperrealism of simulation' replace the use-values of commodities, the imperatives of production, class struggles or differences.

(Kellner, 1987: 131)

But the 'hyperrealism of simulation' does not replace commodity production and class struggle; it is, rather, a product of their mutually contradictory articulations. Jameson hypothesizes that 'postmodernism expresses the inner truth of that newly emergent social order of late capitalism' (1983: 15). He addresses a correspondence between the 'cultural logic of postmodernism' and the 'mode of production' of multinational corporate capitalism, but then fails to specify this relationship beyond noting 'that aesthetic production today has become integrated into commodity production generally' (1984: 56). *Commodity aesthetics* is motivated by, and helps reproduce, the political and market hegemony of corporate capital.

What is the relationship between the *Reebok* ad as a postmodern cultural text and the structural relations of corporate capitalist development? Behind every text there endures a real world of production relations, however distant geographically. Resources and Labor must still be brought together and exploited to create an object. The commodity-object is then transported, distributed, marketed, advertised, sold, used and disposed. Commodity chains weave through and across national, cultural lifestyle, race, class and gender boundaries. These chains of relations are structured not by signs, but by relations of producing and enforcing commodity values. By the time *UBU* enters the commodity chain, the commodity's actual origins have disappeared from view.

Reebok sought to gain a competitive market advantage in the fast shoe industry by changing their methods of producing and distributing products.

> A worldwide product sourcing effort begun in 1986 has been highly successful. Since then, suppliers in several new countries have demonstrated the ability to meet *Reebok*'s stringent quality specifications. Those suppliers have accommodated the Company's growth needs and now account for a substantial percentage of production, thereby diversifying our sourcing and reducing our exposure to swings in various international currency values.

(*Reebok*, 1989: 13)

Diversified product sourcing means *Reebok* products are produced by independent manufacturers outside the United States. All manufacturing is performed in accordance with detailed specifications furnished by *Reebok*'s operating units, subject to quality control standards, with a right to reject products that do not meet specifications (*Reebok*, 1988).

229

In 1988, the Company continued efforts to increase the diversity of its production sources. Currently the Company sources its footwear primarily in South Korea and Taiwan, with these two countries accounting in 1988 for 61% and 20%, respectively, of the Company's total footwear production.

A wholly-owned subsidiary of Pentland Industries plc (a principal shareholder of the Company) provides assistance to *Reebok* . . . in their production efforts in Korea, Taiwan, and other countries in the Far East, inspecting finished goods prior to shipment by the manufacturer, facilitating the shipment of goods from foreign ports, and arranging for the issuance of letters of credit, which are the means used to pay manufacturers for finished products.

The Company's manufacturing operations are subject to the usual risks of doing business abroad, such as export duties, quotas, foreign currency fluctuations, labor unrest and political instability.

(Salomon Brothers, 1989: 8–9)

Reebok's relationship to the manufacturing process is typical of the footwear and fashion industry. The production process is farmed out – raw materials are brought together for Third World production while an intermediary buffers *Reebok* from producers. In this story of *de-industrialization, Reebok* seeks cheaper, more docile, labor pools in Southeast Asia. Yet, postmodern theorists show no more interest in discussing this underside of commodity production than does *Reebok.*

Since we are talking about commodities and the relations which link them, let's take a quick jaunt over to the mall retailer where *Reebok* running shoes, basketball shoes and cross-trainers range in price from $54.95 to $99.95. Who purchases these exchange and sign values, and what kind of labor do they perform to get the money? Teens work primarily in service and retail industries (McDonald's is the largest youth employer) at unskilled, low-income jobs with irregular hours and no benefits. Much of this labor is motivated by a desire to have consumer goods and sign values.

> As more teenagers developed expensive tastes and a hunger for luxury goods, they found it necessary to go to work; and as more youngsters entered the labor force and began earning money that they could spend as they wished, more money was spent on developing and expanding the youth market.
>
> (Greenberger and Steinberg, 1986: 30)

At minimum wage, a pair of *Reeboks* is equivalent to 20 to 30 hours of expended labor. Extensive teenage employment for purposes of elevated luxury consumer spending subverts educational achievement, contributes to stress and increased substance abuse, and 'the *coup de grâce* – teenage employment, instead of fostering respect for work, often leads to increased cynicism about the pleasures of productive labor' (Greenberger and Steinberg, 1986: 6). A political economy of sign values has thus become linked with part-time youth employment in a cycle of reproduction that undermines a motivating ideal of the modernist era – unalienated productive labor as a means toward self-perfectibility.

Postmodernism celebrates and laments a world that has become superficial and flat when seen through the frame of the TV screen. The culture of the image is, indeed, all surface; unfortunately, postmodernist critiques are as flat and one-sided as the world of simulations they refer to. In a world of free-floating signifiers that advertising celebrates and post-structuralism criticizes, the critiques become as free-floating as the celebration. As postmodernism makes its way into mass culture, it becomes little more than a fetishized fascination with the image, the edit and the jump cut. Cynical fascination replaces critique and self-reflexive consciousness materializes as a new form of consumer fetishism.

Postmodernism fails not because of its readings of social texts, but because of its inability to go beyond the text into the world of production. Even in the stylized shopping malls identified as sites of 'postmodern hyperspace,' the society of the spectacle is subsidized by paying substandard wages to an urban service proletariat. Postmodern theorists so intently foreground the simulations that they miss the exploitation and inequality which make possible a public space devoted to glorifying, and reproducing, sign values.

NOTES

1 Chiat/Day was 'coming off the poorly received "Built for the Human Race" Nissan campaign' (Warner, 1988: 1) based on ultra-realist signifying practices. The leap from there to 'UBU' demonstrates that market forces dictate commitment to cultural styles.

2 TV ads appeared on primetime and late night programming such as *Night Tracks, Cosby, L.A. Law, Cheers, Miami Vice, Thirty Something, The Tonight Show*, and *Letterman*. Ads appeared in fashion, entertainment and lifestyle magazines such as *People, Rolling Stone, GQ, Elle, Esquire, Seventeen, Glamour, Sassy* and *New York Woman*.

3 *Nike*'s 'Just Do It' campaign won. *Reebok*, the brand-name phenomenon of the 1980s, had 1987 sales of $1.79 billion compared to $1.20 billion for *Nike*. 'In athletic footwear alone, *Reebok* had 26.7 per cent of the market, and *Nike* had 23.3 percent.' But in 1988 *Reebok* posted a 20 per cent earnings decline, and *Nike* edged ahead in the footwear market, while surging ahead in the wider sports apparel markets. See *New York Times*, 1989: C1.

4 The 'Physics of the Physiques' campaign combined glamour and realism in the name of performance. *Glamour realism* reverted to rapid-fire editing of fetishized body signifiers along with a narrative based on how viewers are appellated *vis-à-vis* the model. The message that mastery over your body equals performance and is a means to gaining style/appearance/identity presents an inverted Protestant ethic – discipline and performance in non-work activity produces desire and muscular pleasure in self.

5 Gitlin (1989) distinguishes premodernist (realist), modernist and post-modernist texts. The premodernist text 'aspires to unity of vision and cherishes continuity.' The modernist work also seeks unity, but continuity is disrupted. Postmodernist texts abandon the quest for unity.
6 Though the ad claims to circumvent the usual ad fictions about reconciling subject and object, the advertising form itself requires the subject–object split or its motor force is negated.
7 Leiss also identifies 'an increasing environmental risk' due to intensified commodity circulation.
8 See Mike Davis's (1988) critique of Jameson on the relationship between multinational capitalism and architecture. Where Jameson elided the relationships that went into the making of his text, the St Bonaventura Hotel, Davis *materializes* the relationship between 'postmodern' architecture and the corporate political economy of late capitalism.

REFERENCES

Abrams, Bill (1982) 'Why Revlon's Charlie seems to be ready to settle down.' *Wall Street Journal,* December 23: 9.

Achen, Sven T. (1981) *Symbols Around Us.* New York: Van Nostrand Reinhold.

Adorno, Theodor (1941) 'On popular music.' *Studies in Philosophy and Social Science,* 9: 117–48.

Advertising Age, March 7, 1988: 30–1, S-7.

'ARF's Object: Out to improve advertising's image.' (1983) *Broadcasting,* March 14: 158.

Arlen, Michael (1980) *Thirty Seconds.* New York: Penguin.

Atlas, James (1984) 'Beyond demographics.' *Atlantic Monthly,* 254 (October): 49–58.

Balbus, Isaac (1977) 'Commodity form and legal form: an essay on relative autonomy.' *Law and Society Review,* 11: 571–88.

Barnouw, Erik (1978) *The Sponsor.* New York: Oxford University Press.

Barthes, Roland (1972) *Mythologies.* New York: Hill & Wang.

—— (1977) *Image – Music – Text.* New York: Hill & Wang.

Bateson, Gregory (1972) *Steps to an Ecology of the Mind.* New York: Ballantine.

Baudrillard, Jean (1981) *For a Critique of the Political Economy of the Sign* (trans. Charles Levin). St Louis: Telos Press.

—— (1983a) *Simulations.* New York: Semiotext(e).

—— (1983b) *In the Shadow of the Silent Majorities . . . Or the End of the Social.* New York: Semiotext(e).

Benjamin, Walter (1969) 'The work of art in the age of mechanical reproduction,' in Hannah Arendt (ed.) *Illuminations.* New York: Schocken Books, pp. 217–52.

Berger, John (1972) *Ways of Seeing.* New York: Penguin.

—— (1974) *The Look of Things.* New York: Viking.

Berger, John and Mohr, Jean (1982) *Another Way of Telling.* New York: Pantheon.

Bernstein, Peter W. (1979) 'Psychographics is still an issue on Madison Avenue,' in John W. Wright (ed.) *The Commercial Connection.* New York: Delta, pp. 135–40.

Best, Steve (1986) 'The commodification of reality and the reality of commodification.' *Chicago Literary Review,* September 26: 14–15, 17.

Birnbaum, Jeffrey (1979) 'The squeeze is on: snug designer jeans capture a market.' *Wall Street Journal,* March 13: 1.

Bluestone, Barry and Harrison, Bennett (1982) *The Deindustrialization of America.* New York: Basic Books.

Boiko, Karen (1977) 'Jontue: Revlon does it.' *Product Marketing,* March: 26–30.

Bologh, Roslyn (1979) *Dialectical Phenomenology: Marx's Method*. Boston: Routledge & Kegan Paul.

Boorstin, Daniel (1961) *The Image: A Guide to Pseudo-Events in America*. New York: Atheneum.

Braverman, Harry (1974) *Labour & Monthly Capital*. New York: Monthly Review Press.

Brenkman, John (1979) 'Mass media from collective experience to the culture of privatization.' *Social Text*, 1: 94–109.

Britton, Andrew (1988) 'The myth of postmodernism: the bourgeois intelligentsia in the age of Reagan.' *CineAction!*, Summer: 3–17.

Buck-Morss, Susan (1977) *The Origin of Negative Dialectics*. New York: Free Press.

Busacca, Richard and Ryan, Mary P. (1982) 'Beyond the family crisis.' *Democracy*, 2, 4(Fall): 79–91.

Byrne, David (1986) *True Stories*. New York: Penguin.

Campbell, Colin (1987) *The Romantic Ethic and the Spirit of Modern Consumerism*. Oxford: Basil Blackwell.

Carton, Barbara (1988) 'Reebok opens $20 million drive.' *Boston Globe*, June 17.

'C-E's O'Connor Critiques Ad Biz "Client"' (1980) *Advertising Age*, November 10: 475.

Christon, Dean (1987) Interview with Director of Product Publicity, Levi Strauss & Co., 1 July.

'Consumer Magazine Ad Linage' (1987) *Advertising Age*, November 16: 81–2.

Cook, Louise (1983) 'Lessons of the recession may stick, analyst says.' *Lexington Herald Leader*, May 21: D-8.

'Cosmetics: Kiss and Sell' (1978) *Time*, December 11: 86–96.

Cott, Nancy (1987) *The Grounding of Modern Feminism*. New Haven: Yale University Press.

Cox, Meg (1981) 'McDonald's ad account won by Leo Burnett.' *Wall Street Journal*, October 12: 44.

Czitrom, Daniel J. (1982) *Mass Media and the American Mind*. Chapel Hill: University of North Carolina Press.

D'Amico, Robert (1978) 'Desire and the commodity form.' *Telos*, 35: 88–123.

Davidson, C. (1988) 'Reebok et al.: ad-stract art!' *Adweek*, June 20: 1,4.

Davis, Mike (1978) '"Fordism" in crisis.' *Review*, 2: 207–69.

—— (1988) 'Urban renaissance and the spirit of postmodernism,' in E. Ann Kaplan (ed.) *Postmodernism and its Discontents*. London: Verso, pp. 79–87.

Debord, Guy (1977) *Society of the Spectacle*. Detroit: Black & Red Press.

'Despite Less Blatant Sexism, Ads Still Insult Most Women' (1985) *Wall Street Journal*, August 1: 19.

Dews, Peter (1986) 'Adorno, post-structuralism and the critique of identity.' *New Left Review*, 157: 28–44.

Douglas, Susan (1988) 'Flex appeal, buns of steel and the body in question.' *In These Times*, September 7–13: 19.

'Ears on Politics and Economics at CTFA Meeting' (1980) *Product Marketing*, April: 1, 27, 40.

Ellenthal, Ira (1979) 'Vogue: 'the ultimate authority.' *Product Marketing*, March: 19.

Ellis-Simms, Pam (1984) 'Ailing Levi's stitches together a new strategy.' *Marketing & Media Decisions*, 19 (August): 58ff.

Ennis, F. Beavin (1982) 'Positioning revisited.' *Advertising Age*, March 15: M-43,46.

Enzensberger, Hans M. (1974) *The Consciousness Industry*. New York: Seabury Press.

Ewen, Stuart (1976) *Captains of Consciousness*. New York: McGraw-Hill.

Featherstone, Mike (1983a) 'The body in consumer culture.' *Theory, Culture & Society*, 1(2): 18–33.

—— (1983b) 'Consumer culture: an introduction.' *Theory, Culture & Society*, 1(3): 4–9.

—— (1987) 'Lifestyle and consumer culture.' *Theory, Culture & Society*, 4: 55–70.

Fish, Stanley (1982) *Is There a Text in this Class? The Authority of Interpretive Communities.* Cambridge: Harvard University Press.

Fiske, John and Hartley, John (1978) *Reading Television.* London: Methuen.

Foster, Hal (1986) 'Signs taken for wonder.' *Art in America*, June: 86.

Frith, Simon (1981) *Sound Effects: Youth, Leisure, and the Politics of Rock'n'Roll.* New York: Pantheon.

Frith, Simon and Horne, Howard (1987) *Art into Pop.* London: Methuen.

Fromm, Erich (1955) *The Sane Society.* New York: Fawcett.

Garfield, Bob (1988) '"U.B.U." Takes shots at non-conformity.' *Advertising Age*, October 3: 70.

Gendron, Bernard (1986) 'Theodor Adorno meets the Cadillacs,' in Tania Modleski (ed.) *Studies in Entertainment.* Bloomington: Indiana University Press, pp. 18–36.

Gitlin, Todd (1980) *The Whole World is Watching.* Berkeley: University of California Press.

—— (1981a) 'Review essay.' *Theory and Society*, 10: 139–59.

—— (1981b) 'The new video technology: pluralism or banality?' *Democracy*, 4: 60–76.

—— (1989) 'Postmodernism: roots and politics.' *Dissent*, Winter: 100–8.

Goffman, Erving (1959) *The Presentation of Self in Everyday Life.* New York: Anchor Books.

—— (1976) *Gender Advertisements.* New York: Harper.

Goldman, Robert and Dickens, David (1983) 'The selling of rural America.' *Rural Sociology*, 48, 4: 585–606.

Goldman, Robert and Wilson, John (1977) 'The rationalization of leisure.' *Politics and Society*, 7: 157–88.

Goode, W.J. (1970) *World Revolution and Family Patterns.* New York: Free Press.

Gottdiener, Mark (1985) 'Hegemony and mass culture: a semiotic approach.' *American Journal of Sociology* 90, 5: 979–1001.

Gouldner, Alvin (1982) *The Dialectic of Ideology and Technology.* New York: Oxford University Press.

Gramsci, Antonio (1971) *Selections from the Prison Notebooks.* New York: International Publishers.

Greenberger, E. and Steinberg, L. (1986) *When Teenagers Work: The Psychological and Social Costs of Adolescent Employment.* New York: Basic Books.

Habermas, Jürgen (1970) *Toward a Rational Society.* Boston: Beacon Press.

Hall, Stuart (1972) 'The determinations of news photographs,' in S. Cohen and J. Young (eds) *The Manufacture of News.* Beverly Hills: Sage.

—— (1977) 'Culture, the media, and the "ideological effect,"' in James Curran *et al.* (eds) *Mass Communication and Society.* London: Arnold, pp. 315–48.

—— (1980) 'Encoding/decoding,' in Stuart Hall *et al.* (eds) *Culture Media and Language.* London: Hutchinson, pp. 128–38.

Haug, Wolfgang F. (1986) *Critique of Commodity Aesthetics: Appearance, Sexuality and Advertising in Capitalist Society.* Minneapolis: University of Minnesota Press.

Hebdige, Dick (1979) *Subculture: The Meaning of Style.* New York: Methuen.

—— (1988) *Hiding in the Light.* London: Routledge.

Henkoff, Ronald (1979) 'Ads for advertisers: how advertisers see their audiences,' in John W. Wright (ed.) *The Commercial Connection*, New York: Delta, pp. 192–8.

Herskovitz, Richard (1979) 'The Shell answer man and the spectator.' *Social Text*, 1 (Winter): 182–5.

Hodge, Robert and Kress, Gunther (1988) *Social Semiotics.* Ithaca: Cornell University Press.

Hohendahl, Peter (1979) 'Cultural theory, public sphere and culture: Jürgen Habermas and his critics.' *New German Critique,* 16: 89–118.

Horkheimer, Max (1947) *Eclipse of Reason.* New York: Oxford University Press.

Horkheimer, Max and Adorno, Theodor (1972) *Dialectic of Enlightenment.* New York: Herder & Herder.

Houghton, Jay C. (1987) 'Semiotics on the assembly line.' *Advertising Age,* March 16: 18.

Hyde, Jack (1981) 'Following the scent.' *Sky,* December: 68–75.

Jakobson, Roman (1961) 'Linguistics and poetics,' in Thomas A. Sebeok (ed.) *Style in Language.* Cambridge: MIT Press.

Jameson, Fredric (1983) 'Postmodernism and consumer society,' in Hal Foster (ed.) *The Anti-Aesthetic Essays on Postmodern Culture.* Port Townsend, WA: Bay Press, pp. 111–25.

—— (1984) 'Postmodernism, or the cultural logic of late capitalism.' *New Left Review,* 146: 53–92.

'The Jeans Industry: Fashioning a New Look' (1984) *Financial World,* September 19–October 2: 30–1.

Kaplan, E. Ann (1987) *Rocking Around The Clock: MTV, Postmodernism & Consumer Culture.* London: Methuen.

Kellner, Douglas (1979) 'TV, ideology, and emancipatory popular culture.' *Socialist Review,* 45 (May–June): 13–54.

—— (1983) 'Critical theory, commodities and the consumer society.' *Theory, Culture & Society,* 1(3): 66–83.

—— (1987) 'Baudrillard, semiurgy and death.' *Theory, Culture & Society,* 4: 125–46.

—— (1988) 'Postmodernism as social theory: some challenges and problems.' *Theory, Culture & Society,* 5: 239–70.

Kerouac, Jack (1955) *On the Road.* New York: Signet.

'A Kick in the Pants for Levi's' (1984) *Business Week,* June 11: 47–8.

Kline, Steven and Leiss, William (1978) 'Advertising, needs, and "Commodity Fetishism."' *Canadian Journal of Political & Social Theory,* 2: 5–30.

Koten, John (1984) 'Coca-Cola turns to Pavlov.' *Wall Street Journal,* January 19: 31.

Kovel, Joel (1978) 'Rationalization and the family.' *Telos,* 37 (Fall): 5–21.

—— (1981) 'Desire and the family.' *The Age of Desire.* New York: Pantheon.

Kroeber-Riel, Werner and Barton, Beate (1980) 'Scanning ads – effects of position and arousal potential of ad elements,' in James H. Leigh and Claude R. Martin, Jr. (eds) *Current Issues and Research in Advertising 1980.* Ann Arbor: University of Michigan, pp. 147–64.

Kuhn, Annette (1985) *The Power of the Image: Essays on Representation & Sexuality.* London: Routledge & Kegan Paul.

Lakoff, Robin T. and Scherr, Raquel L. (1984) *Face Value: The Politics of Beauty.* Boston: Routledge & Kegan Paul.

Landis, Dylan (1981) 'Disengaging the engaged.' *Advertising Age,* March 2: S-2, 4.

Lasch, Christopher (1979a) *Haven in a Heartless World.* New York: Harper.

—— (1979b) *The Culture of Narcissism.* New York: Warner Books.

Lash, Scott (1988) 'Discourse or figure? Postmodernism as a regime of signification.' *Theory, Culture & Society,* 5: 331–6.

Lauerman, Connie (1980) 'Does your perfume make you feel like a star?' *Lexington Herald* Leader, December, 18: B-1.

'Lawsuits Filed over Polo Symbol' (1984) *Lexington Herald Leader,* February 24: A2.

Lears, T.J. Jackson (1983) 'From salvation to self-realization,' in Richard Fox and

Jackson Lears (eds) *The Culture of Consumption: Critical Essays in American History, 1880–1980.* New York: Pantheon, pp. 3–38.

Lebowitz, Glenn (1979) '"Liberated woman" replaces "sex" as emphasis for fragrance ads.' *Product Marketing,* October: 10.

Lefebvre, Henri (1969) *The Sociology of Marx.* New York: Vintage.

—— (1971) *Everyday Life in the Modern World.* New York: Harper.

Leiss, William (1976) *The Limits of Satisfaction.* Toronto: University of Toronto Press.

Levi Strauss Press Release (1987) 'Music celebrities happy to sing the blues,' July.

Lukács, Georg (1971) *History and Class Consciousness.* Cambridge: MIT Press.

McGill, Douglas (1989) 'Nike is bounding past Reebok.' *New York Times,* July 11: C1,3.

McLuhan, Marshall (1967) *The Medium is the Massage.* New York: Bantam.

McWilliams, Michael (1985) 'Levi's highlights low-life setting.' *Advertising Age,* October 21: 51.

Madison Social Text Group (1979) 'The new right and media.' *Social Text,* 1: 169–80.

Marchand, Roland (1985) *Advertising and the American Dream: Making Way for Modernity, 1920–1940.* Berkeley: University of California Press.

Marcuse, Herbert (1960) *Reason and Revolution.* Boston: Beacon Press.

—— (1964) *One-Dimensional Man.* Boston: Beacon Press.

Marshall, Christy (1980) 'PRIZM adds zip to consumer research.' *Advertising Age,* November 10: 22.

Marx, Karl (1967) *Capital.* Volumes 1 & 2. New York: International Publishers.

—— (1973) *The Grundrisse.* Baltimore: Penguin Books.

Mayer, Martin (1958) *Madison Avenue, U.S.A.* New York: Harper.

'Men's Scents on Trial: What Sells Them Best?' (1979) *Product Marketing,* April: 48.

Miller, Mark Crispin (1988) *Boxed In: The Culture of TV.* Evanston: Northwestern University Press.

Mills, C. Wright (1951) *White Collar.* New York: Oxford University Press.

—— (1967) 'Situated actions and vocabularies of motive,' in I.L. Horowitz (ed.) *Power, Politics and People.* New York: Oxford.

Moog, Carol (1989) *Are They Selling Her Lips?* New York: William Morrow.

Morris, William (ed.) (1976) *American Heritage Dictionary of the English Language.* Boston: Houghton Mifflin.

Mowen, John C. (1980) 'On product endorser effectiveness: a balance model approach,' in James H. Leigh and Claude R. Martin (eds) *Current Issues and Research in Advertising 1980.* Ann Arbor: University of Michigan, pp. 41–57.

Murray, Sir James A.H. (ed.) (1962) *A New English Dictionary on Historical Principles.* Oxford: Oxford University Press.

Nichols, Bill (1979) 'Sanger Harris profits from fantasies.' *Advertising Age,* February 26: S-2, 4.

O'Connor, James (1987) *The Meaning of Crisis.* New York: Basil Blackwell.

Ogilvy, David (1983) 'Ogilvy on advertising.' *Advertising Age,* August 1: M-4, M-5, M-48, M-52.

'Panting for Bruce's Jeans' (1985) *Time,* September 2: 40.

Papson, Steve (1990) 'The IBM tramp,' *Jump Cut,* 35 (April): 66–72.

Parker, Richard and Churchill, Lindsey (1986) 'Positioning by opening the consumer's mind.' *International Journal of Advertising,* 5: 1–13.

Pashukanis, Evgenii (1978) *Law and Marxism: A General Theory.* London: Ink Links.

Patterns (1985) 'Big ad campaign comes up winners: a business success, an artistic triumph.' January, 2, 1: 1, 3.

Plummer, Joseph T. (1979) 'Life-style patterns,' in John W. Wright (ed.) *The Commercial Connection.* New York: Delta, pp. 125–34.

Rapp, Rayna (1988) 'Is the legacy of second wave feminism postfeminism?' *Socialist Review,* January–March 98: 31–7.

Reebok (1988) *Press Release Package.*

Reebok International Ltd. (1989) *1988 Annual Report.* Canton, MA.

Reebok, *Form 10-K* filed with the Security and Exchange Commission, Washington, DC, for Fiscal Year ending 31 December 1988. Commission file number 1-9340.

Rose, Gillian (1978) *The Melancholy Science: An Introduction to the Thought of Theodor W. Adorno.* New York: Columbia University Press.

Rothenberg, Randall (1989) 'Change in consumer markets hurting advertising industry.' *New York Times,* October 3: A1, D23.

Salomon Brothers (1989) 'Reebok International LTD. – from athletics to fashion and back again' (Stock Research), May 19.

Schudson, Michael (1981) 'Criticizing the critics of advertising: towards a sociological view of marketing.' *Media, Culture and Society,* 3: 3–12.

Schwartz, Tony (1979) 'Hard sell, soft sell, deep sell,' in John W. Wright (ed.) *The Commercial Connection.* New York: Delta, pp. 320–30.

Seeman, Debbie (1981) 'Made-to-odor times are in for changes.' *Advertising Age,* March 2: S-16, 18.

Sennett, Richard (1977) 'Destructive gemeinschaft,' in Norman Birnbaum (ed.) *Beyond the Crisis.* New York: Oxford University Press, pp. 171–97.

—— (1978) *The Fall of Public Man.* New York: Vintage.

Sennett, Richard and Cobb, Jonathon (1972) *The Hidden Injuries of Class.* New York: Vintage.

Sklar, Martin (1969) 'On the proletarian revolution and the end of political-economic society.' *Radical America,* 3: 1–41.

Sloan, Pat (1980) 'Scoundrel is Revlon's latest.' *Advertising Age,* September 1: 1, 59.

Smith, Joan (1981) *Social Issues and the Social Order.* Cambridge: Winthrop.

Smythe, Dallas (1977) 'Communications: blindspot of western Marxism.' *Canadian Journal of Political & Social Theory,* 1, 3: 1–27.

'Spots Put Free Spirits into Reeboks' (1988) *New York Times,* June 17.

Stacey, Judith (1987) 'Sexism by a subtler name?' *Socialist Review,* September–October 96: 7–28.

Tarule, R. (1979) 'The mortise and tenon timber frame: tradition and technology,' in Paul Kebabian and William Lipke (eds) *Tool and Technologies: America's Wooden Age.* Burlington: University of Vermont.

Warner, J. (1988) 'Reebok premieres U.B.U. campaign.' *Adweek,* June 20: 1,6.

Wernick, Andrew (1984) 'Sign and commodity: aspects of the cultural dynamic of advanced capitalism.' *Canadian Journal of Political & Social Theory,* 8: 17–34.

White, Arthur (1978) 'Business: embattled on two fronts.' *Public Relations Journal,* 34, 1 (January): 16–18.

Williams, Raymond (1977) *Marxism and Literature.* New York: Oxford University Press.

Williams, William A. (1966) *The Contours of American History.* Chicago: Quadrangle.

Williamson, Judith (1978) *Decoding Advertisements: Ideology and Meaning in Advertising.* London: Marion Boyars.

—— (1986) 'Woman is an island: femininity and colonization,' in Tania Modleski (ed.) *Studies in Entertainment.* Bloomington: Indiana University Press, pp. 99–118.

Wilson, John (1988) 'Stages of advertising.' Unpublished paper.

Winship, Janice (1980) 'Sexuality for sale,' in Stuart Hall *et al.* (eds) *Culture, Media and Language.* London: Hutchinson, pp. 217–23.

REFERENCES

—— (1987) *Inside Women's Magazines*. New York: Pandora.

'Working Women: Beauty Products Aid Confidence' (1980) *Product Marketing*, Winter: S-56.

Wren-Lewis, Justin (1983) 'The encoding/decoding model: criticisms and re-developments for research on decoding.' *Media, Culture and Society*, 5: 179–97.

Wuthnow, Robert (1982) 'The moral crisis in American capitalism.' *Harvard Business Review*, March–April: 76–84.

NAME INDEX

SUBJECT INDEX